CW00933195

Biopolitics, Militarism, and Development

DISLOCATIONS

General Editors: August Carbonella, *Memorial University of Newfoundland,* Don Kalb, *University of Utrecht & Central European University,* Linda Green, *University of Arizona*

The immense dislocations and suffering caused by neoliberal globalization, the retreat of the welfare state in the last decades of the twentieth century, and the heightened military imperialism at the turn of the twenty-first century have raised urgent questions about the temporal and spatial dimensions of power. Through stimulating critical perspectives and new and cross-disciplinary frameworks that reflect recent innovations in the social and human sciences, this series provides a forum for politically engaged and theoretically imaginative responses to these important issues of late modernity.

BIOPOLITICS, MILITARISM, AND DEVELOPMENT

Eritrea in the Twenty-First Century

Edited by
David O'Kane &
Tricia Redeker Hepner

Berghahn Books
NEW YORK • OXFORD

First published in 2009 by

Berghahn Books

www.berghahnbooks.com

© 2009, 2011 David O'Kane and Tricia Redeker Hepner
First paperback edition published in 2011

All rights reserved.
Except for the quotation of short passages
for the purposes of criticism and review, no part of this book
may be reproduced in any form or by any means, electronic or
mechanical, including photocopying, recording, or any information
storage and retrieval system now known or to be invented,
without written permission of the publisher.

Library of Congress Cataloging-in-Publication Data

Biopolitics, militarism, and development : Eritrea in the twenty-first century /
edited by David O'Kane & Tricia Redeker Hepner.
    p. cm. — (Dislocations ; v. 6)
    Includes bibliographical references and index.
    ISBN 978-1-84545-567-5 (hbk) -- ISBN 978-0-85745-289-4 (pbk)
    1. Eritrea—Politics and government—21st century.   2. Nation-building—
Eritrea—History—21st century.   3. Biopolitics—Eritrea—History—21st
century.   4. Economic development—Eritrea—History—21st century.
I. O'Kane, David.   II. Redeker Hepner, Tricia M.
JQ3583.A58.B56 2009
963.507'2—dc22

                                                              2008052539

British Library Cataloguing in Publication Data

A catalogue record for this book is available from the British Library

Printed in the United States on acid-free paper

ISBN 978-1-84545-567-5 hardback
ISBN 978-0-85745-289-4 (paperback)

CONTENTS

ABBREVIATIONS

AMCE	Automotive Manufacturing Company of Ethiopia
ASEAN	Association of South East Asian Nations
BBC	British Broadcasting Corporation
BMA	British Military Administration
CCM	Chama Cha Mapinduzi
EDF	Eritrean Defense Force
ELF	Eritrean Liberation Front
EMDHR	Eritrean Movement for Democratic and Human Rights
EPLA	Eritrean People's Liberation Army
EPLF	Eritrean People's Liberation Front
EPRDF	Ethiopian People's Revolutionary Democratic Front
EPZ	Economic Processing Zones
IFI	International Financial Institutions
IGAD	Intergovernmental Authority on Development
FDI	Foreign Direct Investment
FLN	Front Liberation National
FRELIMO	Front for the Liberation of Mozambique
ILO	International Labor Organization
IMF	International Monetary Fund
ISI	Import Substitution Industrialization
JWs	Jehovah's Witnesses
KMT	Kuomintang

MNC	Multinational Corporation
MT	Modernization Theory
NEP	New Economic Policy
NGO	Non-governmental Organization
NHCC	National Holidays Coordinating Committee
NIEO	New International Economic Order
NUEW	National Union of Eritrean Women
NUEYS	National Union of Eritrean Youth and Students
OAU	Organization of African Unity
ODA	Official Development Assistance
POE	Party Owned Enterprise
PFDJ	People's Front for Democracy and Justice
UoA	University of Asmara
UNDP	United Nations Development Program
UNHCR	United Nations High Commissioner for Refugees
UNICEF	United Nations Children's Fund
UNMEE	United Nations Mission in Ethiopia and Eritrea
WTO	World Trade Organization
ZANU-PF	Zimbabwe African National Union – Patriotic Front

INTRODUCTION
Biopolitics, Militarism, and Development in Contemporary Eritrea

℮⁓

Tricia Redeker Hepner
and
David O'Kane

In the Horn of Africa, along the coast of the Red Sea, lies the troubled and turbulent country of Eritrea. Although still unfamiliar in many circles and increasingly controversial in others, Eritrea is perhaps best known for waging a three-decade liberation war against Ethiopia (1961–1991) that culminated in its independence in 1993. More recently, the country has appeared on the world stage due to both an intractable border conflict with Ethiopia and its deteriorating relations with the United States and other Western powers. Far from a terra incognita, Eritrea's legacy of armed conflict, its intensive nation-building efforts, and the contemporary politi-cal-economic crises unfolding there today are of great significance beyond the nation's (disputed) borders. For the patterns at work in Eritrea—docu-mented in the rich ethnographic studies that comprise this book—are not limited to those parts of the world which share its status as poor, margin-alized, or chronically unstable within the global political economy. Rather, they extend to all those regions and historical moments where structural forces and the power of states have penetrated, often violently, the most intimate spaces of human life and consciousness in the name of develop-ment, national security, and sovereignty.

Like many countries around the world, Eritrea's origins lie in the cru-cible of anticolonial revolutionary transformation. Its trajectory since that time has been shaped simultaneously by the internal dynamism of its so-ciopolitical configuration and the challenges of building a new country in the age of globalization. Three decades of dramatic upheaval produced an independent state as well as a ruling nationalist ideology and a revolutionary movement that emphasized, above all else, popular and obedient mobilization for development and defense. In the forging of a new society amidst the prolonged destruction of warfare, mass mobilization for both development and defense formed crucial, interrelated components of nationalist ideology and political praxis. Eritrea was a country defined by its government's fierce military ethic and singular focus on retaining sovereignty, a nation that, in the words of Information Minister Ali Abdu, would kneel down for two reasons only: to pray or to shoot a gun.[1] Certainly these dynamics were highlighted following the outbreak of the border war with Ethiopia in 1998, which claimed an estimated 100,000 lives and marked a crucial turning point in the history of Eritrea and the wider Horn of Africa.

Eight years after the end of that war in 2000, new problems have beset the citizens of free Eritrea. In addition to widespread poverty, the ever-present threat from regional neighbors, and potential intervention by the United States—for whom the Horn has become another front in the "War on Terror"—the Eritrean people also contend with a government that has transformed itself from liberators to oppressors. This metamorphosis should not have been surprising, however. The Eritrean nationalist movement, like many others in twentieth-century history, liberated the country through authoritarian and militaristic methods. These methods persisted into the seven years of optimism that followed independence in 1993. If the border war with Ethiopia had been avoided, then Eritrea might perhaps have experienced a gradual transition to at least some form of democratic rule, and the habits of repression inherited from the struggle of 1961–1991 might have been broken. Instead, under conditions of national emergency, those habits have flourished and thrived, condemning the Eritrean people to a fate defined increasingly by forced conscription, unending military and national service, economic impoverishment, and political crisis. Their revolution, like so many others, is a revolution betrayed.

A central, defining feature of contemporary revolutions like Eritrea's is that they were not only modern, but *modernist*. That is, strong elements within the revolutionary forces aspired to the rationalization of society in the name of progress. It is this rationalization—usually conceived as the indispensable solution to problems of poverty and "backwardness" in the so-called periphery of the world economy—that provides an impetus for both the making of the Eritrean revolution and its ultimate betrayal. As Scott's seminal work *Seeing Like a State* (1998) demonstrated, the pursuit of modernization by an elite leadership has often produced perversions of governance and power. Similarly, the various facets of contemporary Eritrean politics and social life explored in this book highlight, how, in both war and peace, the Eritrean state's "modes of seeing" have lead inexorably to biopolitical strategies for managing the populations under its control. That is, the state apparatus intervenes in the lives, bodies, and consciousness of its people in a way that is consistent with other modernist revolutions of the recent past, and indeed, with newer processes associated with neoliberal globalization in the twenty-first century. Eritrea therefore exemplifies features of modernity that have not disappeared in the post–Cold War world, but on the contrary, have intensified in perhaps unanticipated ways.

In what follows, we provide a critical framework for simultaneously rethinking Eritrea's revolution and nation-building process; its relationship to the international system of nation-states and the changing global political economy; and the considerable tension emerging between the single-party regime and the populations it administers. This tension is produced in no small part, we argue, due to the perils of postcolonial nation-state building in a global system characterized by paradoxes of inequality and opportunity, and the considerable failures of neoliberal development discourses and policies in Africa and beyond. Moreover, to better comprehend the crisis now overtaking Eritrea, we attempt here, like Scott, to "see like a state." Why has the single-party regime adopted the particular policies and orientations it has, and to what effect? What elements of these policies and orientations emerge from specifically Eritrean experiences, and which emerge as a result of wider political-economic forces acting on all poor, postcolonial societies? If the substantive chapters of this volume address these questions from the perspective of everyday Eritrean people and society, we address them here in the introduction at the level of the state, as it interfaces with both world historical trends and the global system. Both perspectives are crucial to understanding Eritrea in the twenty-first century.

Some Fates of Optimism in Eritrea and Elsewhere

A decade ago, Eritrea's relevance seemed to be that of a newly independent country charting a course away from a past characterized by destruction and oppression towards a future bright with the promises of democratization and development (see Ruth Iyob 1997, for example).[2] Such a notion was underpinned by political-economic trends and discourses unfolding globally after 1989. In the last decade of the twentieth century, it was generally assumed that the fall of the Soviet Union meant that history had come to an end (e.g., Fukuyama 1992) and that the global triumph of capitalism and neoliberal ideologies was not only assured, but destined to lead to peace and development. The prevalent belief was that all nations would adopt liberal capitalist forms of economic and political organization, inevitably leading to respect for human rights and an end to absolute poverty. Among those on both the right and the left, moreover, the celebrated rise of "civil society" in Eastern Europe and the potential for democratization seemed to herald a genuinely new era following decades of totalitarian rule (e.g., Arato and Cohen 1990).

Today, in the first decade of the twenty-first century, these hopes have largely been unmet. Nor should this have been surprising, especially to those aware of the negative impacts of structural adjustment policies across much of Africa in the 1980s. The wave of democratization that swept across Africa in the early 1990s, overturning one-party rule in country after country, has been followed by a period of stagnation and the continuation of colonial legacies and neoliberal strictures, which have in turn precipitated further sociopolitical and economic crises of staggering proportions. Across much of the former Soviet world, liberalism has yielded to authoritarianism; in the People's Republic of China the restoration (and acceleration) of capitalism has not, so far, corresponded with political reform or opening. Even in the "democratic" North/West, the years since 11 September 2001 have witnessed a relaxation of restraints on the power of the state, including its ability to imprison without charge or trial. As for those parts of the world where the majority of humanity lives, and especially in Africa, post–Cold War "development" has resulted in neither poverty reduction nor "good governance," but rather in the intensification of political and economic instabilities (Ferguson 2006).

Rather than ushering in an era of unfettered freedom and prosperity, the age of globalization and the expansion of neoliberal pressures have been accompanied by the subjection of societies and individuals to distinctive forms of governance and power. As states compete in the global capitalist system—some for markets and others for basic survival—and, as state functions are increasingly parceled out to multilateral agencies and corporations that replace or undermine previous modes of "sovereignty," human lives and nation-states alike are reshaped in unpredictable and often violent ways. Indeed, some scholars have talked about "apparent states," or those countries whose domestic economies and political institutions have been so impacted by foreign and transnational interests that the state now appears little more than a shell, merely dressed in persuasive symbols and rituals of sovereignty and independence (Glick Schiller and Fouron 2001; see also Ferguson 2006). Hansen and Stepputat (2005) thus argue that sovereignty and territory have become decoupled in the last decades of the twentieth century and suggest that more ethnographic attention be devoted to understanding this process and "what sovereign power really means" today (2005: 5).

These approaches contrast with the vision of sovereign power in earlier centuries, wherein states often (if not invariably) arrogated to themselves the right to decide not only matters of national policy but who should live and who should die, effectively maintaining and exercising a monopoly on violence (Agamben 1998; Norris 2000; Hansen and Stepputat 2005). With the expansion of modernity as a social force in the nineteenth century and its acceleration after World War II, however, the ways in which power could be exercised over human life have proliferated in proportion to technological developments, advancing market forces, and deepening inequalities. For example, the eugenics movement, which was by no means confined to fascist regimes, attempted to reconstitute populations in a biological sense (Dickinson 2004), while rapid-growth economies crafted bodies and minds into hyperproductive work forces (Ong 1988). Modernist states also aspired to control the life cycle of individuals and to shape the very aspirations that individuals possessed (e.g., Harrington 2005). This was done through the control of national education systems, for example, which disseminated new national identities and sought to bind people to their states affectively (Althusser 1971; Hobsbawm 1990). It was also accompanied by cultural, political, and economic strategies that simultaneously fostered xenophobia and encouraged the penetration of military structures and metaphors into civilian and other private spheres (Ben-Eliezer 1997; Enloe 1988, 2000; Green 1995; Handelman 2004).

Two motives driving political elites in such circumstances were the procurement of the means of national defense (or of national aggrandizement through military action), and the need to "catch up" with those states in the core of the world economy that had gone through processes of economic development in earlier centuries; examples include Turkey under Mustafa Kemal, Japan for much of the period after 1870, and the East Asian tiger economies after the Second World War (Hann 2006: 115; Harris 1987; Moore 1966; Nairn 1977). Protecting and nurturing the sovereign state therefore depended upon molding bodies that were both docile and fierce, capable of (re)producing the nation and defending it simultaneously. In this way, modernist states carried out strategies that were distinctively *biopolitical*. That is, not only did they exercise power over "their" populations (at home and in colonial settings) for purposes of national development, military defense, and a competitive edge in the evolving global system; they exercised power of a particular kind: power over life itself, or *biopower*.

Throughout this book, we collectively explore the nexus between biopolitical strategies of state power, development, and militarism in Eritrea within the context of anticolonial revolutionary change and the dynamic but deeply inequitable global environment in which Africa — like all other world regions—has long been enmeshed. Led by an avowedly stubborn and truculent government, Eritrea exemplifies a "natural experiment" of sorts: pursuing high modernist agendas in a postmodern world, the single-party state has for the past fifteen years—since "the end of history," as it were—sought to forge a model for national development that rejects most neoliberal strategies as imperialist in nature and morally corrupting to the collective values forged in revolutionary nationalist struggle. At the same time, it exploits trends and mechanisms associated with globalization in order to achieve its own nationalist ends (Hepner 2005, 2008, 2009; Bernal 2004, 2006). Among those ends are an intense focus on the idea and practice of "self-reliant development" and maintaining the putative integrity of cultural and political boundaries at all costs.

While the notion of self-reliant development has deep roots in the Eritrean colonial and revolutionary past, as examined below, it has also been transposed to the contemporary encounter with global capitalism and neoliberalism. Representative of enduring nationalist visions of independence and liberation, self-reliant development indicates at once a commitment to the sovereign state form while also depending upon the transnational political and economic participation of Eritreans in diaspora and a highly selective engagement with foreign markets, investors, and technologies. But beneath the shadow of the state's aspirations, and the forcefulness with which it pursues them, everyday Eritreans pursue aspirations of their own, many of which are at considerable odds with those of the state. The skepticism with which rural Eritrean communities perceive the government's proposed nationalization of the land is one example of the disjuncture between state and society in Eritrea. The risks that Eritrea's young people are willing to take as they defy the state's programs of militarization and compulsory labor to emigrate illegally, is another.

Disjunctures: Global and National

The clear disjunctures between state and society in Eritrea support Ferguson's view (2006) that globalization and neoliberalism in Africa are profoundly complex when examined from the vantage point of lived social reality, confounding conventional approaches to understanding these interrelated phenomena. Contrary to the (neoliberal) charge that African societies have largely rejected globalization or have been clearly marginalized by it, Ferguson views Africa as intimately interconnected with global forces in ways that cannot be predicted nor recognized by analyzing the political-economic transformations taking place in Asia or Eastern Europe, for example. Subjected to stringent structural adjustment policies and the proliferation of nongovernmental organizations and nonstate actors by whom many state roles have been supplanted, African countries are hardly peripheral to global pressures. At the same time, globalization has been extremely uneven and discontinuous throughout the continent, such that the oft-cited concept of "global flows" seems meaningless. Ferguson instead characterizes globalization and neoliberalism in Africa as nodal, partial, ad hoc, and perhaps only comprehensible when viewed in lived social contexts (Ferguson 2006). It is both Africa's legacy as apart from the North/West and Other to it (see also Mbembe 2001), and the discontinuous, unequal character of global dissemination, that make Africa an "inconvenient" case for analyses of globalization (Ferguson 2006).

Countries like Eritrea, which still fail to appear on many world maps, let alone mental maps, perhaps seem even more marginal. If Africa is an inconvenient case for understanding globalization processes, the Horn of Africa is perhaps the continent's most inconvenient example. (To wit, neither Ferguson nor anyone else addressing globalization in Africa focuses on that region). There is a distinct irony at work here. Despite Eritrea's apparent strangerhood in the global system of nation-states, the country has long been the sine qua non of superpower intervention and mischief, a "pawn in world politics," as it were (Okbazghi Yohannes 1991). Most recently, journalist Michela Wrong (2005) has written achingly about Eritrea's history as irreparably scarred by the machinations of foreign governments from Italy and Great Britain, to the USSR, Ethiopia, and the United States, who used Eritrean territory and people for waging proxy wars, staging international espionage, and extracting resources. Yet even amid recent developments around the War on Terror, Eritrea remains seemingly distanced from the fray, still intensely preoccupied with its recent nationalist revolution and state-building project over and above international currents.

Entrenching this sense of isolation and otherness today is the fact that Eritrea's single-party regime seeks to control the form and manner in which globalization impacts the state and society at all levels. Articulated in the modernist language of sovereignty and revolutionary nationalism, the party-state rejects neoliberal interventions and North/Western-dominated global forces at the same time that it seeks to govern its large diasporic population by transnational means (Hepner and Conrad 2005; Hepner 2008), constructs one of the largest and most sophisticated armies in Africa, intervenes into regional matters of global concern (e.g., Somalia and Darfur), and grows ever closer diplomatically and economically to China. Thus, Eritrea was not ever, and is not today, globally or regionally isolated. Rather, it has constantly responded to interrelated pressures at all times, contending always with forces and interests so much larger than itself, albeit engaging selectively with foreign powers and often rejecting norms of international diplomacy.

If the relationship of Eritrea to the wider neoliberal and globalizing world is neither straightforward nor easily understood, then "sovereignty" in Eritrea is likewise no simple matter, and cannot be reduced to glib explanations regarding the fetishization or failure of the nation-state form. The Eritrean state's current obsession with sovereignty may indeed be about authoring a collective destiny vis-à-vis a hostile "outside" through control of national policies, markets, and borders. But it also reveals a conceptualization equally concerned with "the ability and the will to employ overwhelming violence and to decide on life and death" (Hansen and Stepputat 2005: 1). In an increasingly closed political environment in which visas or clearance are routinely denied to researchers, where no free press and few if any foreign journalists may operate, in which virtually all foreign nongovernmental organizations have been expelled and multilateral aid is often rebuffed, and where democratic political reforms have been delayed indefinitely but glossy reports on successful state-run development projects are broadcast daily over the internet, the Eritrean government seems determined to pursue a model of development that runs contrary to trends induced and legitimated by the powerful North/West. It also remains acutely concerned with the intentions of its erstwhile occupier, Ethiopia. Harboring an intense xenophobia amid an urbane cosmopolitanism that any visitor to the capital city of Asmara finds both disorienting and intoxicating, the state looks towards protectionism and militarism as dominant strategies for development and defense. This includes defending national territory not only from regional foes like Ethiopia, but also from the political-economic and cultural exigencies of neoliberal globalization emanating from the North/West. Witness, for example, the precision (and paranoia) with which President Isayas Afeworki expresses the government's views on the latter:

> NGOs … are obstructing the establishment of effective and competent governments and governmental institutions in Africa, especially in the states that won their independence recently like us. … They bring employees and the unemployed and the retired officials from outside and employ them while the citizens of the concerned country find no opportunity for work with the exception of the few who stick to those organizations for realizing personal interests and benefits at the expense of the country's public interest. … In many instances we find that the super powers are using these NGOs as tools in weaker states in order to practice any activities easily, and thus intervene in the political affairs which do not concern them, and thus become tools for covering up the agendas of foreign organizations and political forces. … The NGOs are employing those who could be its tools from among our citizens. Thus they work in defense of

them, and cover up what these organizations are causing and inflicting of damage in order that they preserve their jobs in these NGOs. They also forge tricks and plans for deceiving the people. ... We reject the work in the field of relief aid and employing it as a cover up as well as using religious names, which have got their weight and exploiting this in the field of spying, espionage, sabotage and terrorist acts.[3]

Coping with such regional and global besiegement, however, requires internal discipline and patience, similar to that which helped free Eritrea from Ethiopian rule. It also entails punishment for resistance and transgression within the national ranks, thus making the state's pursuit of sovereignty a key factor in the emergent rift between itself and the citizenry. The Eritrean state is today considered by many rights groups and foreign governments to be one of the worst violators of human rights in the world. New refugees flee the country almost daily (Assefaw Bariagaber 2006a). Many of them are young people who have escaped from the military, which provides not only a low-paid pool of labor for state-run development projects (Gaim Kibreab 2006), but also a cover for the "re-education" of youth whose aspirations, beliefs, or opinions have strayed beyond (or "betrayed") the nation as conceived in the regime's ideological paradigm. In response to charges of human rights abuses, however, the government has argued that such claims merely exemplify the kind of imperialist hypocrisy to which it will neither bend nor subscribe, despite the fact that the country is party to numerous human rights conventions.[4]

In contemporary Eritrea, we therefore witness a striking interrelationship between state-sanctioned modes of discipline and the effort to engage with the regional and global environments in ways that are antithetical to trends observed elsewhere. Biopolitical control over minds and bodies and the militarization of society emerge from the revolutionary past and orient the nation-state towards the future, providing a blueprint for sociopolitical, cultural, and economic development articulated by political elites as a nationalist alternative to ongoing foreign domination. At the same time as the Eritrean state undertakes this revolution from above, however, everyday people respond to the state's project. Whether rural or urban, local or diasporic, the people of Eritrea are not only the foundation of the state's sovereignty, and the source of its legitimacy. They are also the bearers of the minds and bodies that the state uses as raw material for its project of social reconstruction and economic development. As the state pursues one mode of (dis)integration with the outside world, however, many citizens harbor alternative views and strategies. Understanding the logic of state-society relationships, and how these play out on the ground, is vital to recognizing Eritrea's orientation as differentiated and complex, even as official policies and pronouncements signal the state's antipathy towards the global environment in which it the country is situated, for better or for worse.

From Modernist Revolution to Postmodern Statehood

Eritrea's relationship to the twenty-first century world is the product of a specific historical trajectory that began in the late 1800s. From the late nineteenth to the early twenty-first centuries, the country passed through several forms and periods of foreign rule that finally culminated in its long-awaited independence. From Italian colonialism, British occupation, and an ill-fated federation with Ethiopia, to sovereign statehood in 1993 following three decades of war, the true liberation of Eritrea may still remain elusive fourteen years later.

When the Italians first laid claim to the Red Sea region in 1889, they brought together within one territory a central highland region that was a geographical and cultural extension of the Ethiopian highlands, a lowland region to the west with close ties to neighboring regions in the Sudan, a long "dogleg" that stretches eastward through miles of desert to the port of Assab, and in the north-west of the country a remote plateau area, which many decades after the Italian conquest became the stronghold of the Eritrean liberation forces. The people of the central highlands were peasants and largely (though not exclusively) Orthodox Christian. The lowlands to the west, like the northern plateau, were home to Muslim pastoralist groups. So too were the eastern desert regions towards Assab.

During the period of Italian rule, the 3.5 million people of these lands, despite their diverse sociocultural backgrounds and political interests, began groping towards a common identity. This was largely the result of the brutality of Italian colonial policies, informed as they were by fascism and segregation, as well as the introduction of infrastructure that made Eritrea one of the most advanced industrial economies in colonial Africa. Italian colonialism was followed by a ten-year interlude under the British Military Administration (1941–1952), which fostered the growth of new and "modern" sociopolitical institutions in the towns especially, such as trade unions and political parties, even as it cynically dismantled and sold off most of Eritrea's industrial resources (see Wrong 2005; Tekeste Negash 1984).

After Eritrea was federated to Ethiopia in 1952, and placed under the ultimate control of the imperial monarchy of Haile Selassie, this groping towards nationhood became a desperate search for freedom. Under the terms of the federation, a profoundly transformed Eritrea had been promised internal autonomy and self-government, but these rapidly eroded under pressures exerted from both within the country and without (Tekeste Negash 1997). Partly in response to intensifying violence perpetrated by Ethiopian forces, and partly due to the perception of colluding highland Christian-Imperial hegemony, armed rebellion broke out in 1961 among Muslim, lowland pastoralist groups, launching a war that would last for thirty years. Amidst this war and the subsequent social revolution that took place within it, the Eritrean nation as we know it today arose, steeped in sacrifice, displacement, isolation, and loss. By 1989 it was possible to argue that the extremity of suffering in the liberation war against Ethiopia had forged a genuinely new identity (Cliffe 1989). Also key to this process was the conscious development of nationalism by emergent political elites as a unifying force, albeit one that was neither straightforward nor easily achieved.

The Eritrean Liberation Front (ELF), which led the struggle in the 1960s, based its strategy on the methods used in Algeria by the National Liberation Front (FLN) . Eritrea was divided into several zones, for which different branches of the ELF were responsible, thus dividing the front itself according to regional, religious, and ethnic differences (Ruth Iyob 1995; Pool 2001). By the end of the decade, refugees were streaming across the border into Sudan as a result of Haile Selassie's brutal counterinsurgency (Assefaw Bariagaber 2006c; Gaim Kibreab 1985; Murtaza 1998). Within the ranks of the ELF, moreover, discontent was growing among the younger members of the front in particular. These were often (though not always) Christian highlanders who were dissatisfied with the leadership's strategy and apprehensive about its vision for Eritrea's future alignment with the Arab world. The sectarianism so often attributed to ELF in the literature was reflected and reinforced by the front's own administrative and military structure (Connell 1997; Pool 2001). For disaffected members, the liberation struggle required a different approach altogether, one which would remake Eritrean identity by synthesizing, homogenizing, and neutralizing all other loyalties into a common commitment to the front-as-nation (Pool 2001; Hepner 2003; Tekle Woldemikael 1993).

The late 1960s thus brought a split in the ranks of the ELF that led to the birth of the Eritrean People's Liberation Front (EPLF) in 1970, which subsequently developed a state-like structure through which it ruled, de facto, large portions of the embattled region. As the Eritrean rebel forces fought the Ethiopian army, backed by the Soviet Union and Cuba, they also fought amongst themselves. The brutal civil war waged between the EPLF and its progenitor, the ELF, left lasting impacts on Eritrean society and consciousness. Not only was the civil war the source of some of the largest refugee flows out of the region (and thus the contemporary diaspora), but it resulted in feelings of political and personal betrayal whose depths can hardly be told. In no small part, it is the legacy of strife among Eritreans themselves that informs the government's current intolerance of dissidence and necessitates both its transnational strategies for control over the diaspora as well as its rejection of discourses about democracy and rights. Seen to emerge largely from neoliberal or North/Western sensibilities and interests, these discourses also represent modes of intervention through which the historic and ever-reconstituting opposition would destabilize the ruling regime via transnational movements and transcultural identities (see Hepner and Conrad 2005; Hepner 2008, 2009).[5]

Following independence, the EPLF was reconfigured "from guerrillas to government" (Pool 2001) and became the current single-party regime, the People's Front for Democracy and Justice (PFDJ). Throughout the 1970s and most of the 1980s, the EPLF was (at least in theory) a Marxist-Leninist organization of the kind common throughout the lands of the old colonial empires. After the Ethiopian revolution of 1974 it found itself faced with a dilemma, however: the military junta known as the Derg, which now ruled the former empire of Haile Selassie, soon became aligned with the Soviet Union, which served as its international patron. In addition to precipitating a series of Soviet-backed campaigns intended to reconquer and pacify Eritrea, this shift left the nationalists with no clear political niche in the Cold War environment. Adopting a purely "toolbox approach," the EPLF selected from an array of left-wing revolutionary ideologies to forge its own (Papstein 1992). Waging a lonely anticolonial struggle where the colonial was not readily identified as such, transgressive to the logic of the Cold War by its positioning against the Soviet-backed Ethiopian Derg regime, aligned with secular Arab nationalism and yet waging its own civil war against Islamic sectarianism, the Eritrean People's Liberation Front, and by extension the whole nationalist struggle in Eritrea, resisted facile categorization. The EPLF itself fostered Eritrea and its own organization as both isolated and inscrutable, insisting on pragmatism as its main ideological thrust, and turning inward to foster a strategy for national liberation that was predicated on popular mobilization and strict military discipline.

By building state-like institutions and implementing policies that placed the guerrilla army in direct administrative contact with the largely rural masses of Eritrean people, the EPLF forged the foundations of biopolitical strategies for development and the militarization of society. Through, for example, the teaching of new agricultural techniques, the administration of underground medical services, the carrying out of land reform, the abolition of child betrothal and female genital cutting, and through the induction of ever-increasing numbers of young people into the highly disciplined and ascetic world of the fighters, the EPLF crafted in the course of war both the elements of the future state and the strategies through which nationalism and self-reliant development would take place. As Connell observed with some alacrity:

> The EPLF accomplished extraordinary things with meager resources. Despite the continuing absence of sustained external support, the Front steadily improved its military capacity, while simultaneously building basic infrastructure (construction, transportation, communications), promoting economic development (agriculture, animal husbandry, commerce and trade), delivering social services (education, health, emergency relief), and campaigning to alter fundamental power relations within rural society (land reform, marriage reform, restructuring of village administration). A dynamism was evident that was difficult to explain (Connell 2001: 346).

This dynamism was made possible largely by the strict disciplinary practices of the front. Pool has viewed these as firmly rooted in the Maoist model, in which the EPLF's secretary general and current President, Issayas Afeworki, himself was trained in the 1960s in China:

> Establishing clear lines of internal organization and discipline within the front were symbiotic with a rigorous programme of political education to root the EPLF's version of Eritrean history and society firmly in the minds of members. In conjunction with this stress on internal organization were the political and military imperatives of expanding the EPLF's structures into broader Eritrean society. The organizational outreach of the EPLF resembled that of the Chinese communist guerrilla practice of constructing a 'frame of steel' so that when the frame moved so did the people (Pool 2001: 105).

While much is made of the fact that Eritrea, at the time of independence in 1993, had been relatively "sealed off" from the rest of the world for over three decades, we must temper this view by acknowledging not only the swirl of foreign interventions in Eritrea's past, but also the influence of modernist discourses so prevalent in the Horn of Africa during the revolutionary period. Donham (1987, 1999) has shown how pervasive and powerful the concept of being and becoming modern had been in the years leading up to, and throughout, the Ethiopian revolution of 1974. His exploration of dynamic and competing views of what constituted "the modern" for pre- and postrevolutionary political elites, urban students, and southern Maale cultivators and evangelical Christians, indicates that modernity as the goal of development was both a singular driving force and yet highly differentiated cultural process in Ethiopia.

Notwithstanding the repeated wars that have been waged to establish the differences between Eritrea and Ethiopia, Eritrea's own revolution was not only entangled with Ethiopia's after 1974, but was similarly influenced by globally diffused ideas and models of modernity. Some of these were rooted in Eritrea's history as an industrialized, urbanized colony. They were also informed by the adoption of socialism as a model for development in other postcolonial African states, most famously exemplified in Nyerere's Tanzania. Eritrea thus developed an autarkic quality wherein the fervent and emotionally weighty nationalism of its population, the military mobilization and capacity of its soldiers, and the ethic of self-reliance was fostered by EPLF as an indigenous movement towards modernity. However, it was unmistakably inspired at various times (and in a few cases logistically supported) by other models and movements, including the Algerian, Egyptian, Chinese, Soviet, Albanian, Syrian, and Libyan. Thus, Eritrea's experience must be viewed not as an autochthonous or exceptional example, but rather a variation on the theme of "Marxist modernism" (Donham 1999) that swept the globe from the 1960s to the 1980s, connecting diverse movements and meanings into the common search for both dignity and a "place-in-the-world" (Ferguson 2006).

From this context, it is one of the most distinct ironies, then, that the independent Eritrean nation-state emerged in a world already radically reorganizing amidst the rise of neoliberalism and the uneven impacts of globalization. Its birth in the global era as a postcolonial, postrevolutionary, marginalized African state, has positioned it uneasily amidst the global system of nation-states. In search of solid moorings, perhaps, the PFDJ government has drawn heavily upon the strategies, policies, and practices that allowed Eritrea to achieve statehood in the first place, including military discipline and "self-reliance." It has also meant that the state's existing tendencies towards isolationism and its obsession with sovereignty would be strengthened and maintained after liberation in 1991, only to become a key factor in the present political-economic and human rights crisis.

By the turn of the millennium, the internal contradictions of Eritrean elite politics that had long been obscured by the seductiveness of its nationalist struggle and leadership (see Connell 2005) had bubbled to the surface. For both the Eritrean state and people, the turning point clearly came with the outbreak of renewed war with Ethiopia over the disputed border town of Badme in the spring of 1998. Small-scale clashes between Ethiopian and Eritrean forces soon gave rise to all-out war between the two states (see Ruth Iyob 2000: 663), which wreaked havoc on the Eritrean economy, devastated much of the country, left hundreds of thousands dead, and displaced close to one million more. The loss of so many young soldiers was one Eritrean families and the country itself could ill afford. At the time of this writing, seven years since the cessation of hostilities, peace remains elusive, and signs of further war flicker ominously on the horizon.

Just as the underlying causes of the border war remain an object of debate (see, for example, Tekeste Negash and Tronvoll 2001; Bundegaard

2004: 48–49), so too does the idea that the war caused either the ensuing political crisis within the government or the wave of severe human rights violations. While the war may indeed have derailed movements towards democratization, the internal repression that followed it was also a product of authoritarian and repressive patterns deeply lodged within the EPLF since the days of the struggle. Moreover, while observers and the state itself noted the resurgence of nationalist fervor among Eritreans at home and abroad that accompanied the outbreak of the war, in retrospect this was the final moment when anyone could assume a unity of interest between the Eritrean state and society.

Our own respective fieldwork in Eritrea highlights the impact of the border war in unique ways. O'Kane was carrying out research on nationalism and land reform in the highland Eritrean village of Embaderho during much of the period when the border war was at its height. The people of Embaderho possessed a set of identities that were based not only on kinship and shared village residence, but also extended to the level of the nation-state. According to the oral history of the village, Embaderho was founded around 1400 CE by migrants from the northern province of Ethiopia. However, any presumed affinity between the people of Embaderho and their counterparts in Ethiopia had been totally destroyed by the experience of Ethiopian occupation during the liberation war of 1961–1991. Many of the village youth left at this time to enlist in the EPLF, and many households displayed martyrs' certificates in prominent positions.

The embedded reality of national identity in Embaderho was demonstrated by the events of the spring of 2000 (O'Kane 2004). After the Ethiopian army broke into the western lowlands, it advanced quickly into Eritrean territory, taking the strategic town of Barentu a few days later. The morning after the news of Barentu's fall reached Embaderho, at the bus stop where people gathered to travel to Asmara, the name of the lowlands town was quietly and apprehensively on everyone's lips. A few days later, rushing to secure the new front line and stop the Ethiopian advance, the Eritrean Defense Forces (EDF) rapidly moved troops from the Zalambessa front to the lowlands. As the soldiers passed through Embaderho, the villagers rushed in large crowds to greet them and provide them with food and bottled water. But this warm reception in Embaderho, as in other communities soldiers passed through, did not signify the uncritical faith of the Eritrean masses in their government. Villagers saw no contradiction between support for the troops of the EDF on the one hand and skepticism or even outright opposition to the government's proposed land reform on the other, which involved nationalization and the subsequent obsolescence of collective village-based land tenure. As one villager stated, "this government is passing." The present government has not yet passed, however, and in the months and years since the Ethiopian invasion it has only strengthened its grip. And despite the end of the border war in December 2000 with the Algiers Agreement, severe criticism of the government emerged amid an uneasy peace. This in turn provoked a cascade of human rights violations that continue unabated to this day.

Hepner witnessed the latter developments throughout much of 2001, largely from the vantage point of Asmara and other urban locations. Interviews with government officials; leaders of the mass organizations known as Unions; clergy of Orthodox, Protestant, and Evangelical churches; university students; and everyday people—many of whom had been guerrilla fighters or who were currently serving in the military—indicated enduring and newly emergent rifts within official nationalism as an ostensibly unifying ideology. Although her research focus was largely on the institutions, material exchanges, and sociopolitical practices that had bound the Eritrean state and society to its diasporic citizens in the United States for over thirty years, nearly every structured and unstructured interaction was dominated by the political concerns unfolding daily. Among these were the canceling of scheduled elections for December 2001 and the banning of all political parties save the PFDJ; the crushing of an independent student organization at the University of Asmara and the subsequent arrest of student leader Semere Kesete, followed by the postponing of the fall semester as the student body was sent to workcamps near Assab; the issuing of an open letter to the PFDJ by fifteen high-ranking government officials calling for democratic reforms and the implementation of the constitution, and the subsequent arrest of those officials and others deemed sympathizers; and the closure of all independent media outlets and the arrest of about a dozen journalists. These developments require a radical rethinking of nationalist political praxis by Eritreans and scholars of the Horn of Africa.

Authoritarianism and Sovereignty in the Modern World (Dis)Order

Fervent nationalist commitment and the quest for modernization were not the only, or even the central, driving forces behind the Eritrean revolution. They were underpinned by the EPLF's entrenched authoritarian tendencies, which found their expression not only in the efficient delivery of services to people in the liberated zones but also in the use of repression against dissident voices within the front. Eritrea's revolution, like other comparable revolutions around the world, has always had its dark side.

At the same time that the EPLF inspired scores of sympathetic observers for its commitment to "the masses," its provision of services and its staunch independence from both superpowers, the leadership crushed without mercy those within the movement who challenged the logic of Maoist "democratic centralism."

This repressive capacity was present even in the optimistic years between liberation and the outbreak of the 1998–2000 war with Ethiopia, evidenced in the new government's detention of former "collaborators" with Ethiopia and loyalists to the ELF. Since the Ethio-Eritrean border war, moreover, internal repression has worsened. Just as one can find no family in Eritrea that has not lost a member in either the liberation war or the border war, no family has been spared the fear and suffering precipitated by the human rights catastrophe unfolding since 2001. At the time of this writing, thousands of Eritreans languish in prison without charge or trial, many of them beloved heroes and veterans of the liberation struggle who raised critical perspectives or revealed unorthodox beliefs. Citing "national security" as its primary concern and looking towards the example set by the US in the War on Terror, the Eritrean government justified its measures and its rejection of international critiques, not surprisingly, in the language of sovereignty, unity, and self-reliant development.

Among other things, Eritrea's contemporary political crisis has forced a reassessment of the revolution itself. Those who hailed the EPLF's ethic of self-reliance during the liberation war believed it would provide the foundation for a postindependence development strategy that might avoid the snares in which most African countries found themselves following the neoliberal turn. Intoxicated by the initial wave of democratization that accompanied the implementation of structural adjustment (the former largely a condition of the latter) in the mid-1990s, optimism had returned to the continent in the form of a putative African renaissance. Among the new leaders heralded by the international media and former US President Bill Clinton was Eritrean President Isayas Afeworki. Celebrated (with racist overtones) as "the African nation that works,"[6] foreign governments and multilateral lending agencies like the World Bank all congratulated Eritrea and welcomed it as an example of ingenuity, tenacity, and uncorrupted moral fortitude. Within the neoliberal camp, Eritrea also represented a tempting natural experiment: a "blank slate" free of debt, run by a new government whose physical and political infrastructure would need to be built from scratch, a country with as-yet-untold resources and a disciplined and dependable population.[7]

A kind of electrified enthusiasm crackled throughout the Northern/Western development communities following Eritrean independence. But Eritrean elites also claimed to see great potential in the fact that independence was attained a full generation after the rest of Africa; it would therefore be possible, they argued, to avoid the mistakes that had brought down earlier aspirations for development in the continent. For a moment, then, Eritrea hung in the balance: would it become a laboratory for neoliberal models of political-economic growth in Africa? Or would it retain its revolutionary nationalist ideals and insist on a "self-reliance" that refused subservience to Northern/Western pressures? In practice, economic policy in postliberation Eritrea combined elements from several economic paradigms. At the same time as it announced the nationalization of the country's land, for example, the Eritrean government pushed for what Tekeste Negash and Tronvoll (2001: 35) call "the primacy of market forces over exchange and interest rates," a policy that stood in open contradiction to that of Ethiopia and that may have contributed to the outbreak of war in 1998. Even before the return of war, however, the central question for Eritrea still remained. Given its small size, often glossed in terms like "unviable," or "weak," with what regional economic community, superpower, or emergent political-economic bloc would Eritrea align itself?

At this point, it is worthwhile to recall the historical emergence of such superpowers and blocs when situating Eritrea. At the dawn of the twentieth century, the world was divided between the colonial regions and the European and North American states that ruled them. The persistence of a few areas that resisted colonial rule (Ethiopia, for example) did not alter this fundamental division of the world. Rivalries between the European powers led ultimately to the outbreak of two severely destructive wars between them; these wars led in turn to the global dominance of the United States of America, the rise (and ultimately, the fall) of the Union of Soviet Socialist Republics, and the rise and apparent victory of new nationalist movements in the vast areas of the world that had been under the sovereignty of the old imperial powers of Europe. The world order that took shape at the Yalta conference in 1945 ensured that a new division of the world between the US and the USSR would dominate the remainder of the century, and it was in this context that former colonies struggle to find and wield their independence.

The two superpowers had, in their very different fashions, developed rapidly through the decisive intervention of the state in their societies. This was especially true (and took a drastic human toll) in the case of Stalin's USSR, but it was also true in the case of the US. The forging of American power that took place in the Second World War was predicated on the expansion of the American state and consumer capitalism in particular (Carroll and Noble 1988: 385ff). Even where societies did not experience putatively socialist revolutions leading to a collectivized economy, the state played a decisive role in economic life. The losers of the Second

World War, West Germany and Japan, were able by the 1970s to challenge the US for economic leadership in the "free world," and did so through different but comparable forms of state-society relationships. Socialist or capitalist, these were all modernist states, dedicated to the administrative ordering of nature and society (Scott 1998), an ordering that required the disciplining of both mass society and the individuals who comprise it.

The new states that broke free from European colonial rule from the 1950s onwards (or were liberated from Japanese rule in 1945) all attempted to pursue programs of economic development. The results of these attempts were mixed at best. The "tiger economies" in East Asia experienced the most growth (Harris 1987). With a few exceptions, the new African states all went through relatively brief periods of high growth, only to find that progress halted and then thrown into reverse.[8] What all these regimes had in common, however, was a political relationship between the masses and the new elites, a relationship that Tom Nairn incorporated into his theory of nationalism (1977). Nairn argued that nationalism was a phenomenon of late developers seeking to compete with the established, modern industrial economies at the core of the world economy. To emulate the success of those economies, the leaders of new states in the periphery had to persuade their citizens to participate in processes of national development, despite severe social costs. Persuasion of this kind required new ideologies, and that of nationalism in particular, such that national identities could effectively supplant those based on kinship relations or village membership (see Chatterjee 1993).

It would be inaccurate to reduce the Eritrean revolution, or any other nationalist revolution, to such a matter of cold calculation by political elites. The leadership of the PFDJ, like the EPLF before it, has always made history in circumstances not of its own choosing, circumstances that ranged from the difficult to the dire. It is not to justify human rights violations by Eritrean movements or governments in the past or present (for even in the worst of circumstances alternatives to repression could have been found) to say that those movements and governments have always had to operate in a wider regional context of threat and hazard. It is precisely that context, combined with the poverty of the vast majority of the population (badly exacerbated by war and environmental degradation) that account for the particular characteristics of the EPLF and its revolution. The apparently positive aspects of that revolution—such as the greater freedoms available to women, the provision of health care and education, and the suggestion of a new and radically different form of development—were accompanied by the centralization of power in an unaccountable authoritarian leadership, and purges of those who threatened nationalist "unity." In order for development to proceed during the revolution, and more importantly, after independence, society needed to be sufficiently motivated and mobilized. The processes by which people became unified subjects as well as trained soldiers were achieved through political strategies that regulated bodies and minds, channeling their energies towards collective goals of modernization and development within a unified sovereign space.

The light and dark sides of the Eritrean revolution, therefore, were always locked together, and their embrace was rooted in the objective circumstances of an underdeveloped periphery. The nature, origins, and dynamic of this embrace, this conjunction of social reform and economic development on the one hand, and censorship, repression and torture on the other, is best understood, we argue, by applying the conceptual triad of development, militarism, and biopolitics. This framework not only helps illuminate aspects of the modernist revolutionary past, but is especially useful in understanding the Eritrean state's orientation towards neoliberalism and globalization.

Development, Militarism, and Biopolitics

Within Eritrea today, it is difficult to separate processes and discourses of development from those of militarism. Both, moreover, require distinct modes of disciplining and controlling bodies and minds. *Militarism* is an ambiguous term at best (Skjelsbaek 1979), one that has been described as a "portmanteau concept covering a number of separate phenomena" (Smith 1983: 18). These include high levels of military expenditure, tendencies towards the use of war and force in military relations, and (most importantly for this volume), and the "militarization of domestic social relations" (Smith 1983: 18; see also Enloe 1988; Green 1995; Lutz 2002). To this we might add the valorization of military life above all other potential ways of contributing to the nation, and in this sense militarism has been a common (though not universal) feature of nationalist movements. The Irish nationalist revolutionary Pádraig Pearse notoriously praised the bloodshed of the First World War, claiming that "the earth needed to be warmed with the red wine of the battlefields" (Townshend 1983: 282). His was by no means the only statement of this kind to be made during the twentieth century. While no Eritrean leader has to our knowledge made such an overt claim, the policies of the PFDJ regime ensure the privileging of the military and predicate national development on the militarization of society.[9]

The most obvious example is the induction of all citizens ages eighteen to forty into both the Eritrean Defense Forces and the national service campaign.[10] As conscripted members of the EDF, young people are trained in the methods and ideology of national defense, and are frequently de-

ployed for development projects such as road building, construction, water-
works, and agricultural harvest. The goals are both national development
and nation-building, while the results are the strengthening of state control over individual lives and national policy. The state news agency recently made very revealing claims about the function of military service
in today's Eritrea:

> The Southern Red Sea region recently hosted the graduation of the 19th round
> National Service trainees as well as the commemoration of the completion of
> several major developmental projects. This dual celebration is a historic event
> that conveys a very important message, i.e., the Eritrean Defense Force are both
> soldiers of development and messengers of peace… As a result of this effort,
> the Eritrean people, rather than respite after securing independence, had cho-
> sen to embark on the nation-building process with intensified efforts so as to
> make up for the time and opportunities they had lost during the years of colo-
> nial rule. Accepting the responsibility of realizing the Eritrean people's dreams
> and aspirations, the Eritrean government set out to cultivate a defense force
> of development with the same iron discipline and dedication of the days of
> struggle for independence. Believing that only an educated and skilled youth
> could succeed in realizing the people's dream, the Government had issued the
> National Service Proclamation in 1994, and through the 19 rounds since then
> had produced hundreds of thousands of industrious citizens who had fully
> acquired both military skills and other professions. The sole objective of the Na-
> tional Service programme is thus to cultivate capable, hardworking and alert
> individuals that could turn the Eritrean people's dreams into reality and do
> away with poverty.[11]

Eritrea is not the first to make use of the armed forces in this fashion.
The case of Israel after 1948 provides one historical precedent for what
the Eritrean state is attempting today (Ben-Eliezer 1995). In the early years
of the Israeli state, the army was not only dedicated to specifically military goals, but also to wider nation-building goals, such as assisting recent Jewish immigrants to settle in the country (Ben-Eliezer 1995: 272). In
so doing, the Israeli Defense Force merged with the Israeli nation, which
became a "nation-in-arms," just as the French nation had become after
the revolution of 1789. In Israel, this isomorphic relationship between the
army and the people was part of a wider ideology of settlement, one that
saw individual pioneers as deindividualized parts of a wider national collective, analogous to the parts of a great machine (Weiss 1997: 815–16; see
also Handelman 2004). Such a point of view is shared by the Eritrean leadership, and it has many other parallels in the twentieth century, especially
in those countries on either side of the Cold War divide which aspired to
goals of "developmentalism."

After the Second World War, the exigencies of superpower rivalry encouraged the emergence of a new economic discipline—development.

Hoben (1982: 349) has defined development as "the deliberately planned, bilateral, multilateral and private efforts to foster economic development and social change in low income countries since World War II." Whether or not those involved in pursuing economic and social change did so in military fashion or not, they had certain assumptions in common. During the second half of the twentieth century, both capitalist and socialist states pursued policies aimed at transforming their societies—and in all cases this was done in ways that concentrated power in the hands of a (usually self-selecting) elite. In the initial decades after the war, import-substitution industrialization was the development method of choice; in the case of the Asian Tiger economies this gave way after the 1960s to a gradual opening up of the national economy to the world economy, but even then the state took a leading role (Rozenwurcel 2006: 3). To do so, it was necessary to intervene decisively in the lives of the people and this in turn required an ideology of developmentalism, which would inspire and legitimize such powerful interventions.

Nor is this something that has disappeared with the rise of globalization and a putatively antistatist neoliberal ideology. Rather, in the contemporary world we can see how the social disruption wrought by the harshest forms of neoliberalism, as in post-Soviet Russia, can bring in its wake the rebirth of a highly militaristic nationalism (Sperling 2003). In an Africa whose postcolonial armies are both armed forces and labor forces (Luckham 1994: 21–22), the opening up of the continent to global economic forces provides new opportunities for the military to remain a key player in economic affairs. Turshen has noted that in Africa the conjunction of globalization and militarization has had severely adverse effects on African women, and by implication on African communities as a whole, effects that include (but are certainly not limited to) "the economic violence of impoverishment (for the majority) and loss of state service" (Turshen 2004: 120). Eritrea's case, involving as it does the work of a functioning state that carries out both human rights violations and development programs with equal precision, is different from the cases cited by Turshen, but it remains very much a case of the conjunction of militarism and developmentalism.

Militarism and developmentalism thus remain intensely biopolitical phenomena. In the context of newly independent developing states, the introduction of modern military technology and organization, as well as the introduction of the new goal of national economic development, required the remaking of subjects themselves. This triggered what has been described as "a process of 'civilising' people as a nation, a class, a race and a gender, specifically through control of 'individually coded bodies—where they work, how they reproduced, even the language they dream in" (Patel and McMichael 2004: 238). Aihwa Ong (1990: 258), for example, defines biopolitics as "the state organization of the population to secure its control, welfare and productivity," as developed through her rich ethnography of women factory workers and spirit possession in Malaysia (1988), a model developmental postcolonial state, and, incidentally, one that was cited by Eritrean politicians seeking a new model after the fall of the Soviet Union. The methods and forms of organization addressed by the biopolitics concept are not grouped together randomly. From the education of individuals in the nationalist ideology of the state, to the training of workers who will be offered to multinational corporations, to the use of torture against those who rebel, biopolitical acts are related to each other in a structured, and structuring, form.

It is Foucault (1979) who has probably done the most to popularize the concept of biopolitics in contemporary social theory, but Agamben has analyzed its most disturbing features. For Foucault, biopolitics arises when life itself becomes the object of structures of power. In his analysis, this change occurs with the rise of modernity in eighteenth-century Western Europe, and he exemplifies it through contrasting, on the one hand, the public execution of regicides before the beginning of the era, and the panopticon prison model on the other, whose spatial arrangements allow for the control of prisoners through permanent surveillance. Importantly, this surveillance is only made possible by the emergence of a new discourse concerning the relationship between life and power. Foucault's analysis implies the view that the subjection of life to power is itself a product of modernity.

Giorgio Agamben's analysis of modernity's underbelly suggests otherwise (1998; see also Norris 2000). He traces the roots of the modern state and its forms of biopolitics back to the beginnings of the Western tradition that shaped the world order into which the Eritrean state emerged in the early 1990s. For Agamben, all the forms of biopolitics cited above—eugenics, the use of national education systems to build willing soldiers or pliable factory workers—are rooted in the deep structure of state/society relations. States from the time of the Greeks down to the early twenty-first century are by definition sovereign states, and the essence of sovereignty, Agamben argues, lies in the power to decide who is and is not a member of the political community whose institutional expression is the state itself. Those that are simultaneously internal to the community, and yet excluded from it, are reduced to the status of "bare life."

Those in this condition exist in the marginal circumstances that Hannah Arendt (1943) saw as the lot of the refugee in the modern world. Expelled from a national or civil community, refugees had to appeal to concepts of human rights precisely because, Arendt argued, they had lost those attributes conventionally assumed to be human. Harrington (2005), meanwhile, has argued that the changes in citizenship law in Ireland since the founding of the Irish state represent particular responses to the changing biopolitical needs of that state. For Harrington, the constitutional referendum in which nearly four-fifths of those who voted did so in favor of altering Irish citizenship so that rights were stripped from the Irish-born children of foreign nationals was a biopolitical act that represented the creation of a new category of "bare life." A more dramatic expression of this category is the fate of those who have fled from the current Eritrean regime only to be returned by the states where they sought asylum. There have been persistent and well-documented cases where such individuals have been tortured at the behest of the Eritrean state, including among other methods the use of the "helicopter," in which the victim is tied up with his arms and legs behind his back, often for days at a time.[12] Far from irrational acts of violence, the motive in such egregious abuses is to demonstrate the state's power over the individual, and to restore the breach in the state's definition of the proper organization of the national polity (see Sluka 2000; Scheper-Hughes and Bourgois 2004).

This then, is the tragedy and paradox of contemporary Eritrea. While the government has indeed chosen to resist subservience to Northern/Western pressures and thereby avoid becoming an "apparent state," its modes and methods for retaining sovereignty have relied upon its capacity to deploy coercive, often brutally violent, power among its own people. These forms of power and the modes through which they are organized are deeply rooted in Eritrea's own revolutionary nationalist past and remain oriented towards modernist notions of independent statehood. But they are also clear responses to the political-economic pressures of neoliberal globalization, which sectors of Eritrean society at home and abroad appear to increasingly embrace as an alternative to the current configuration. All inspired at one time by the progressive aspects once contained in the Eritrean revolution, the editors and contributors of this volume nonetheless believe that an understanding of the current crisis, and Eritrea itself, requires both new analytical tools and a recontextualization of the roots of that crisis itself.

The Contributions in this Volume

While theoretical concepts and debates should not distract us from recognizing and confronting the gravity of structural violence, armed conflict, or human rights violations (rather quite the opposite), we argue that the concept of biopolitics allows us to simultaneously track how repression and violence in contemporary Eritrea have emerged out of the conjunction between the methods of political organization related to the nationalist revolution of 1961–1991, and the particular variant of development that was adopted after the country's independence. The chapters in this volume address not so much overt resistance, which has become all but impossible in Eritrea today, but rather the ways in which the contemporary Eritrean state, itself "a shifting complex of people and roles" (Herzfeld 1997), has sought to reshape national (and transnational) subjects through the strategic nexus between biopolitics, militarism, and development. They also address the ways in which everyday people are enmeshed in this nexus, and how they struggle within and against it.

Tekle Woldemikael analyzes the ways in which the Eritrean government, like the EPLF before it, makes use of one of the most potent weapons in its arsenal—the public spectacles that offer to the peoples of Eritrea a government-approved national identity. Trapped in conditions of hardship and uncertainty, citizens both at home and in diaspora react by participating in the state's spectacular fetishization of nationality, especially in the carnivalesque moments that commemorate the most historically significant date in the country's history: Independence Day. Tekle Woldemikael's portrait of a regime that engages in deliberate and consciously planned reshaping of identity among its subjects evokes a particular kind of modernist power analyzed by Handelman (2004) in Israel, for whom bureaucratic power over a population is maintained at least partly through the use of public spectacles that entrench a "national taxonomy" of identity and hierarchy (or egalitarianism) among the masses.

While Tekle Woldemikael shows how people become intoxicated by the political messages conveyed through sensory engagement with the bureaucratic spectaculars in the urban core of Asmara, both Michael Mahrt and Amanda Poole show how the lived experiences of state-sponsored nationalist identities are significantly more complex and always incomplete, especially in the rural villages where much of Eritrea's population resides. The Norwegian anthropologist Kjetil Tronvoll (1998) has argued convincingly that the modernizing project of the new Eritrean state represents a threat to the only institution that has ever really stood between the peoples of the highlands and disaster—the kin-based village community. To wit, Michael Mahrt's chapter investigates points of contradiction between the tenacious local-level identities of land, lineage, and lived experiences with political change, versus the new identities and political formulations proffered by the state. Through a thick ethnographic description of rural conceptions of space, place, and time, Mahrt shows how relationships between the state and rural communities are in practice much more ambiguous than official discourse on Eritrean nationalism would suggest. One of the implications here is that in practice, the nature of Eritrean national identity has not yet been fully determined, despite the state's idealization of rural life and its claims to the historic mobilization of the *hafash*, the masses.

Similarly, Amanda Poole draws on recent ethnographic research on resettlement and rural development to explore how refugees formerly displaced in Sudan and now resettled by the Eritrean state experience and speak about national development, work, and service as compared to "stayees," or those who were not displaced throughout the thirty-year war. Poole shows how the new state, its official nationalist ideology, and its practices of development have confronted an older pattern of communal life and work, one based on mutual aid and assistance. The village community of Hagaz suffers the loss of its young people and its internal autonomy, but clings stubbornly to its independence as it contends with state policies around resettlement, agricultural development, and food security.

Tanja R. Müller and Jennifer Riggan each examine the role of education in the new dispensation, the ways in which it is related to the militarization and mobilization of society, and how the new cadre of teachers and students experience and respond to the policies of the state. In her account of contemporary educational policy and students' aspirations at the university level, Tanja Müller analyzes the Eritrean state's self-declared claim on the country's educated younger generation as it simultaneously decentralizes the country's only institution of higher learning, the University of Asmara, and reconsolidates administrative power over the minds and life chances of Eritrea's best and brightest. The state's claim is made as if the youth were a national resource to be exploited for the greater good, and the wider consequence is to trap Eritrea in a "negative dialectic" in which the intended outcomes of national development will not be forthcoming. Enriching this portrait of the growing frustration of Eritrean youth and the militarization of education is Jennifer Riggan's analysis of how the same state policies that underpin the restructuring of the university are also restructuring education at the secondary level, while folding educational achievement simultaneously into the military and its processes of homogenization and massification. Drawing on interviews with young teachers mandated to equalize educational achievement among their younger students while themselves serving in a military capacity, and analyzing interactions between teachers, students, and government officials, Riggan describes how the policy goal of "avoiding wastage" converges with both militarization and development strategies while undermining the goals of nationalist education itself.

As noted above, a consistent theme in the contributions to this volume is that of the resistance inspired by the state's deployment of its power.

In circumstances where that power is as brutal as it is efficient, however, resistance can take only limited forms. This is highlighted in Magnus Treiber's chapter, which chronicles how urban youth in Asmara struggle to negotiate autonomous spaces for individual expression and strategies for personal control in a time of military conscription and wanton imprisonment. Under conditions wherein the regime makes enormous demands on the lives of individuals, the quest for autonomy, whether through social interactions in bar scenes or through ecstatic religious worship, becomes an act of resistance. Treiber reveals the cultural work required by "internal exile" or "resistance in the head," as well as the real risks of escape and physical exile for which so many Eritrean youth are pining.

In their dreams of a "good life" in diaspora, some of these youth may one day join their compatriots now scattered around the world, often through the desperate quest for asylum. Their fate as asylum seekers, and the new opportunities presented by their navigation through Western legal systems, is analyzed by Tricia Redeker Hepner. She argues that recent asylum seekers enter into a transnational political terrain long dominated by EPLF/PFDJ, where they not only struggle to claim their rights under national and international law, but also contend with considerable problems of surveillance and threats to themselves and their loved ones by the Eritrean government. In passing through the asylum system, however, Eritreans gain new insight on the political environment from which they have come and begin thinking of themselves as new kinds of rights-bearing subjects. Hepner suggests that these experiences are important factors in the stimulation of a new global Eritrean movement based on human rights, as Eritreans worldwide carve out spaces for autonomy and engage in efforts that aim to transform both cultural and transnational political patterns.

Finally, Greg Cameron's comparative analysis of Eritrea as a developmental state not only contextualizes Eritrea with respect to other developing nations across the political spectrum, but also provides insight into the probable fate of the PFDJ regime's "revolution from above." He suggests that the attempt to repeat the experience of the East Asian developmental states is likely to fail, not only (or even mainly) because of the hostile nature of the political environment within Eritrea and the Horn of Africa, but also because of the inherent flaws in any attempt to repeat the developmental models of other times and other places. Trapped amid the contradictions between the biopolitical control its managerial elites would demand, and the ways in which the individuals living under those elites would resist that control, Eritrea's future seems to recede further into uncertainty. Thus, Cameron demonstrates the gap between the Eritrean state's putative developmental goals and the real consequences of the form state intervention in Eritrean economy and society takes. Finally, in their conclusion, editors O'Kane and Hepner reflect again upon this uncertainty, particularly with respect to Eritrea's struggle for sovereignty as part of a globally resurgent fixation on national security and autonomy amidst the unpredictable pressures of a globalizing world.

Notes

We wish to acknowledge our appreciation of all who participated in this project, especially the authors whose work appears in this volume, the Eritreans who shared their experiences, Dr. Christopher Clapham for his critical feedback, Dr. Victoria Bernal for her interest and participation, and Lily Harmon-Gross for editorial assistance.

1. Numerous news articles quoted Ali Abdu's statement, directed towards US Assistant Secretary of State for African Affairs Jendayi Frazer. For example, see Jeffrey Gettleman, "Eritrea Defiant on US Diplomatic Pressure," *International Herald Tribune*, 18 September 2007. http://www.iht.com/articles/2007/09/18/africa/eritrea.php.

2. Throughout this book, Eritrean and Ethiopian names appear as the person's given name followed by his or her father's name. This is consistent with practices in the Horn of Africa, where a person's given name is used as the primary name, even in formal settings. Eritrean and Ethiopian authors' names thus also appear in the Bibliography alphabetically by given (first) name, rather than by father's (last) name.

3. Shabait.com, "Eritrea; President Isaias Afwerki's Interview With the Local Media—Part I," *Africa News*, 23 November 2005.

4. See, for example, "'You Have No Right to Ask': Government Resists Scrutiny on Human Rights," Amnesty International, AI Index: AFR 64/003/2004.

5. Such a view is obviously simplistic and self-serving in its failure to account for Eritrean culture as an internally differentiated "open system" in which ideas and practices associated with democracy and rights have not been present for a long time, but have undergone further change and vernacularization in response to contemporary conditions.

6. Joshua Hammer, "Eritrea: Back From the Ruins," *Newsweek*, 26 February 1996, 40; see also James C. McKinley, Jr., "Eritrea: African Success Story Being Written," *New York Times*, 30 April 1996; "Eritrea," *Time*, 30 March 1998, 41.

7. Paul B. Henze, for example, counseled that an independent Eritrea could only achieve economic success through a clear separation between economics and politics; whether this was ever an option in the context of postindependence Eritrea or the wider context of the Horn is questionable, however (Henze 1990: 10).

8. As Ferguson (2006: 13, 11) indicates, "The economic and political reforms of the last two decades were meant to bring African states and economies into line with a standard global model. But the ironic result of the structural-adjustment era has been the creation of an Africa that is actually more different than ever from the imagined global standard. … The idea that deregulation and privatization would prove a panacea for African economic stagnation was a dangerous and destructive illusion. Instead of economic recovery, the structural-adjustment era has seen the lowest rates of economic growth ever recorded in Africa (actually negative, in many cases), along with increasing inequality and marginalization."

9. It is worth noting, however, the appearance of a billboard of sorts on the outskirts of Asmara showing the image of Eritrea, its southern border dripping with blood, accompa-

nied by the faces of a young soldier and an older fighter of the guerrilla generation, and the Tigrinya words "Dobna b'demna: awet n'wefri warsai yikeaalo," which translates, "Our border by our blood: victory to the courageous heirs to the struggle and those who made independence possible." This statement recalls another of Pearse's remarks: "Bloodshed is a cleansing and sanctifying thing" (Townshend 1983: 282).

10. The upper age limit for the conscription of young women was subsequently lowered to 27. One can speculate that this was an important strategy for insuring the successful reproduction of the nation.

11. "The Eritrean Defence Force—Soldiers of Development and Security," Shabait.com (Asmara), December 2006, http://allafrica.com/stories/200612131015.html. Accessed 26 April 2007.

12. See, for example "'You Have No Right to Ask': Government Resists Scrutiny on Human Rights," Amnesty International, AI Index: AFR 64/003/2004, 30–31. See also "Eritrea: Conscientious Objection and Desertion: A documentation by Connection e.V. Germany, War Resisters International, and the Eritrean Anti-Militarism Initiative," http://www.wri-irg.org/news/2005/eritrea-en.htm.

— *Chapter One* —

PITFALLS OF NATIONALISM IN ERITREA

Tekle M. Woldemikael

Introduction

Every year on 24 May, Eritreans celebrate Independence Day with great fanfare and revelry.[1] This is a celebration of the day the nation became a reality, after thirty years of armed conflict with Ethiopia (1961–1991). On that day a nationalist guerrilla movement, the Eritrean Peoples Liberation Front (EPLF), took power, making Eritrea an independent country from Ethiopia. In 1994, EPLF's third congress was conducted in the town of Naqfa, wherein the guerrilla movement transformed itself into the only party in the country, renamed itself the People's Front for Democracy and Justice (PFDJ), and assumed absolute control of the state. Ever since then, nationalist leaders and the state-controlled single party have propagated a form of nationalism that is increasingly aimed at controlling the culturally plural Eritrean society, bringing it under the party's firm hegemonic control so that society can be reconstructed in ways the party leadership considers desirable.

This form of nationalism can be characterized as an integral nationalism (Alter 1994) with the aim of producing an integral state (Young 1994). It also has historical roots in the celebrated EPLF, which acted as a total institution (Goffman 1961) by controlling every aspect of the guerrilla fighters' lives during the nationalist war. The EPLF, and now the PFDJ, have aimed to make the public succumb to its unbridled hegemony and identify with the state totally. One of the mechanisms the state uses to accomplish social control has been through sponsoring, planning, directing, and orchestrating the 24 May Independence Day celebration.

However, the joy participants feel in participating in nationalist holidays is a small reward in return for the enormous demands the Eritrean nationalist movement makes on the people. This article examines how the state manipulates the public to participate in 24 May Independence Day as a national holiday, and how and why the public participates in the state-organized celebrations. I argue that the 24 May celebration serves multiple ideological functions for the state and society. These include providing the state with a sense of broad popular support for its rule, thus allowing the government to believe in the ideological illusion that state and society live in seamless harmony, while at the same time providing the people (the *hafash*, or "masses") with psychological release from the dire economic and political plight that characterizes contemporary life in Eritrea. This project of the state, however, will be "ultimately undermined and defeated by what Achille Mbembe aptly terms the 'the historical capacity for indiscipline of society'" (Young 1994: 248). In the case of Eritrea, the unruliness of the "masses" has taken different forms, from internal self-criticism within the ruling party, to open disapproval of, and resistance to, the regime by Eritreans both at home and in the diaspora.

The Independence Day Celebration: 24 May 2005

In May 2005, the official and unofficial celebration of Independence Day had a carnival-like atmosphere. The celebration lasted for over ten days, with each day devoted to special activities. Among these were speeches by the president, parades by uniformed men and women, singing by renowned performers, musical theater, students' dramatic plays, acrobatic performances, circuses, and cultural shows by representatives of all recognized ethnic groups in Eritrea. There was also continuous dancing and jubilation by the spectators. Sponsored by a government organization, the National Holidays Coordinating Committee (NHCC), these activities are set up to promote the celebrations and galvanize public participation in the festivities in order to reproduce indefinitely the experience of liberation in 1991.

One of the ten days of celebration, 23 May, was designated as that of the Independence Day Carnival Parade. During this day, the main avenues of Asmara were filled with people from different age groups, religions, and ethnicities, all dressed in different outfits, parading in the streets of the city, clapping and dancing and performing to music. Here is a description of event by Meron Abraha, a journalist for the government website, www.shaebia.org:

The parade open[ed with] a long procession with a marching band up at front [that] made its way through the Independence and Martyrs Avenues and reached Bahti Meskerem Square. ... Taking part in the parade were small children from the various kindergartens in the city, elementary as well as secondary school students, Sunday school students of the Catholic and Orthodox churches, members of the clergy in their unique attire, the followers of the Islamic faith, and representatives of all the district administrations of Asmara. ... There were also some cultural groups dressed in the clothes of the different ethnic groups, who portrayed the culture and traditions of their respective nationalities. There were also youngsters, dressed in the colors of the national flag, performing different acrobatic, aerobatic and circus performances in the parade. The public expressed admiration: men clapping their hands and women ululating and sometimes dancing to the tune of the music around.

The carnivalesque atmosphere in Eritrea can be linked to what Achille Mbembe called the banality of power in postcolonial Africa. Mbembe wrote, "Ceremonies and festivities constitute the pre-eminent means by which the *commandement* speak and the way in which it dramatizes its magnificence and prodigality" (Mbembe 1992: 9). According to Mbembe, the banality of power includes the predictable, everyday routines in which power is exercised as well the obscene, vulgar, and the grotesque aspects of life that are intrinsic to all forms of domination and power, and are the mechanisms of confirmation or deconstruction of the power structure (Mbembe 1992: 1–2). Mbembe was inspired by the work of Mikhail Bakhtin on Medieval Carnival and focused especially on Bakhtin's analysis of laughter, comic composition, profanity, and parody. Mbembe centered his analysis of public spectacle on what he called the grotesque aspects of the body such as the mouth, the genitals, anus, and things related to the belly such as eating, drinking, and belching, and took them to express the banality of power in Africa. In the case of Eritrea, the banality of power takes the form of carnival as described by Bakhtin: there is a concentration of bodies of both leaders and followers into the public arena where they rub one another's shoulders in close proximity, where they enter into "a free and familiar contact," and where a new interrelationships between them may possibly be worked out (Bakhtin 1984: 123). Peter Biles, a BBC journalist who covered the 24 May 2003 celebration, described how different bodies, including the president of the country, were involved in a public display of the banality of power in Eritrea:

> In carnival mood, tens of thousands of Eritreans partied into the early hours of Saturday to mark their country's 10th anniversary of independence. ... In the capital, Asmara, they thronged Liberation Avenue, the main street characterized by its palm trees and Italian-style cafes. ... As popular Eritrean songs

blared from loudspeakers, Asmara's well-heeled young set danced and war veterans in wheelchairs were pushed by their relatives or friends. ... Shortly after midnight, Eritrea's president, Isaias Afewerki, appeared beneath an arch of flashing party lights. ... Although he was flanked by bodyguards, police and soldiers, the atmosphere was surprisingly relaxed. ... President Isaias, dressed in a blue safari suit and black sandals, set off to walk the entire length of Liberation Avenue.

He waved, often with both hands held aloft, while the crowds cleared the road to make way for him. ... People cheered loudly and whistled, and the police beat back groups of excited young men who tried to close in on the rear of the presidential procession. ... Few heads of state would have felt confident enough to have embarked upon such a public walk-about at night, but Eritrea has always been different. (2003)

However, behind the festivities and celebrations, we have to look at how the ruling party operates using different technologies of power (Foucault 1978). The government's celebrations are planned to manipulate the public to participate in the ceremonies and experience the madness and temporary euphoria that the festivities induce. Even more important is how these festivities are produced through technologies of power or biopower (1978: 140). By technology of power or biopower, Foucault meant the "numerous and diverse techniques of achieving the subjugation of bodies and the control of populations" (1978: 140). The Eritrean state, through the various micropolitics of the state, uses technologies of power in an attempt to produce nationals who will obey, follow its programs, and respect its authority and disciplinary power. The Independence Day celebration is one of the mechanisms used by the party in its attempt to produce docile bodies, subjects who fit into the ruling party's image of nationhood.

The National Holidays Coordinating Committee (NHCC) planned the weeklong celebrations within Eritrea and around the world through its branches within the various Eritrean diaspora communities. A description of the plan published in the government's shaebia.org website reads:

According the National Holidays Coordinating Committee (NHCC), the weeklong celebrations will include various programs highlighting the historic event cultural shows at the Bahti Meskerem Square, cultural and musical performances in the main streets of Asmara, marching bands, dramas, photograph exhibitions, Independence Day carnival, community get-togethers and fireworks. Different sports activities including mass sport and Independence Day Marathon will also be carried out. So far, soccer matches, cycling as well as car and motorcycling competitions have already been conducted in connection with the Independence Day Celebrations. ...

The streets of Asmara have also been decorated with lights and flags, thereby creating a festive mood. Private businesses have also decorated their restaurants, shops, boutiques and the like. ... Similarly, Eritreans around the globe are making extensive preparations to celebrate the joyous occasion. Thus, Eritreans residing in different European and American cities will conduct various activities, including children's sport festival, cultural and artistic shows among different age groups from 21 to 28 May 2005. ... The activities that will take place in Washington and its environs would also feature similar progress. Walta Cultural Troupe, consisting of 11 popular singers, has already arrived in the US to give the event added splendor.

In 1991, the celebration of Liberation Day was a spontaneous act. Since then, it has become ritualized through the active sponsorship of the state. There have been 24 May celebrations every year since 1991, but after that year the government has sought to capitalize on the holidays and celebrations. The celebration of Eritrean independence might have remained a purely spontaneous and popular affair, one carried on without the intervention of the government, but we will never know this for certain. Taking advantage of popular responses in the early days of liberation, the celebration of 24 May has become a top down practice. Thus, although each annual celebration has had its unique aspects, the celebrations have become more formal and ritualized with the passage of time. For example, the independence celebrations of 1992 were more ritualized than those of 1991. The state organized the festivals, which consisted of marches, speeches, art shows, visits from foreign leaders, prayers in churches and mosques for the martyrs of the nationalist war, and dances and musical performances. Even more formal were the 24 May 1993 festivities. Although the referendum was conducted between 23 and 25 April of that year and Eritrea was officially declared a sovereign nation on 27 April, the government delayed declaring Eritrea formally independent for a month because it wanted to announce it on 24 May. Thus, it made the festivities of Independence Day coincide with the declaration of Eritrean independence. Hundreds of thousands of Eritreans in different towns and regions of the country, and Eritreans in exile, celebrated that day.

For the government of Eritrea this is a show of solidarity and support from the public. According to Eritrean traditions, support is shown when people attend one another's weddings, funerals, and other events; showing up to celebrate Independence Day also indicates to the government that the people are behind them, that they have not lost touch with their supporters. This sentiment was aptly expressed in the Independence Day Carnival of 21 May 2005 by Meron Abraha, when he stated, "Stressing the importance of conducting such a carnival, the organizers note that since 'freedom was attained by the people for the people,' the people were naturally involved in the carnival" (Meron Abraha 2005).

Thus, the public is manipulated into legitimizing the system in a highly planned and orchestrated manner. This involves declaring that day a national holiday, shutting down all the shops and workplaces, and sponsoring nationally famous singers and dancers who perform for the public for free. Everything comes to a standstill. In every town, village, and neighborhood, there are the PFDJ-run organizations that seek out talented individuals who might perform for the holiday. Once selected, they practice with others and prepare for the event. The leaders of neighborhood organizations are expected to encourage or pressure their communities to come out for the day. There are veiled threats of reprisals if a person refuses to participate. The only show in town is the government-sponsored celebration. During festival days, there is nothing to do except go to the celebrations, ceremonies, and parades. Performances are open to the public and they are done quite professionally. People are encouraged to join in and dance and participate. Celebratory speeches are given by the president. People who participate in the revelry are clearly in throes of joy, waving Eritrean flags; many are interviewed and their statements broadcast on the radio and television repeatedly. Overall, the experience seems to lead to some form of amnesia and forgiveness among the public. As Peter Biles (2003) wrote about the 23 May Parade, in which President Issayas walked among people publicly,

> President Isaias' appearance was all the more unusual because his government has attracted strong criticism in the last two years and his opponents say he now heads a repressive regime that lacks any genuine popular support. ... However, there was no sign of that discontent as the residents of Asmara came out to celebrate the anniversary. ... In fact, they seemed eager to thank the man who for many years led the fighters of the Eritrean People's Liberation Front in their armed struggle for independence from Ethiopia. ... In a young nation such as Eritrea, the strong sense of nationalism, forged from 30 years of conflict, cannot be over-emphasised.[2]

The manipulation of diaspora Eritreans is more subtle. The hegemonic intent of the government and the party is hidden from the public. The best musicians and dancers are sent to entertain them. The public comes voluntarily to meet, socialize, relax, and celebrate with other compatriots. They are often socially isolated and alienated from their host societies. In addition, they lack the independent organization necessary to pursue their communal concerns outside of the control of the Eritrean government. In the government-organized celebrations of independence, the diaspora public comes, dances to the music and songs, has a good time, and momentarily forgets it lives in diaspora.

But at the same time, through this participation, the dancing and revelry can serve to relieve the public's inner tensions and disappointment (Fanon 1963). Mbembe refers to such interactions as relations of "promiscuity" or "convivial" tension between the *commandement* and the target population, resulting in mutual "zombification," i.e., robbing each other of their vitality and leaving them weak (Mbembe 1992: 4–5; Richman 1992: 116). After the festivities, Eritrean people are left with the sense of solidarity with the ruling group, while the ruling group feels it has found a way of gaining back people's trust in its effectiveness and power. Of course, all this is illusory. Instead of zombification implying that people become something like the walking dead, the celebrants in Eritrea—rulers and ruled alike—are seized by temporary euphoria in which they forget all the failures, frustrations, and disappointments of life for that moment. It is also true that the local people are not alienated ethnically or culturally from the ruling class. The ruling class maintains kinship, friendship, or personal connections to the people, especially the most vocal and politically significant group in Eritrea, the Tigrinya speakers.

But it should be pointed out that these events themselves construct consent and to some extent forgiveness and forgetfulness. This is supported by Bakhtin's analysis of carnival: "Carnival is the place for working out a *new mode of interrelationship between individuals.* … People who in life are separated by impenetrable hierarchical barriers enter into free and familiar contact on the carnival square" (Bakhtin 1984: 123). It is also similar to the collective consciousness created by "ritual activity" and "mythological thought" that Durkheim wrote about in 1912 (1998). Durkheim wrote, "Collective consciousness … has the effect of disengaging a whole world of sentiments, ideas and images which, once born, obey laws all their own" (1998: 91). The Eritrean public at home and abroad feels good when they attend and participate in these celebrations. There is plenty of food and revelry; one feels as on a drug, or possessed by some type of temporary insanity or madness. This is the moment the public lets its hair down; some of its inner tension and trauma is relieved and released. As Fanon pointed out in *The Wretched of the Earth* (1963), public dancing with such energy and emotion serves a therapeutic purpose. In Fanon's own terms, the people's release

> takes precisely the form of a muscular orgy in which the most acute aggressivity and the most impelling violence are canalized, transformed, and conjured away. The circle of the dance is a permissive circle: it protects and permits. … Men and women come together at a given place … fling themselves into a seemingly unorganized pantomime, which is in reality extremely systematic, in which by various means— shakes of the head, bending of the spinal column, throwing of the whole body backward—may be deciphered as in an open book the huge effort of a community to exorcise itself, to liberate itself, to explain itself. (1963: 57)

When the participants are in the dance hall, moving their shoulders and heads and arms and legs to the rhythm of the drums and music and dance

of the other, they enter into a trancelike state. Every worry and disappointment they have is temporarily forgotten and forgiven. Such amnesia leads
to a "feel good" attitude, to a perhaps more forgiving outlook and a reduction in the despair and disappointment they feel towards the Eritrean
leaders and government. Under such conditions, the public does not want
to hear negative things about the government precisely because it cannot
afford to do so. It wants something that will be soothing and comforting.
The party and the government know that very well and provide the medium for it. So at the end of the day, the issues of human rights and other
problems are pushed down to the subconscious level and the consciousness of the public seems positive towards the nation, the leaders, and the
flag, and they feel hate and disdain for the detractors and those who are
perceived as enemies of the nation. Such gross manipulation of sentiment
functions to maintain the system, and allows the state to avoid answering
critical questions about its policy and actions over the last few years.

Pitfalls of Nationalism

The May 2005 spectacle in Eritrea disguised the dire political and economic straits in which the nation found itself. All the celebrations took
place while the human and civil rights of the local population were violated on a daily basis. The most surprising aspect of the May 2005 celebration was that it came amidst Eritrea's deepening economic and political
crisis. As the International Monetary Fund (IMF) reported in 2005,

> Eritrea remains one of the poorest countries in the world, with a per capita
> GDP of about $130 and a Human Development Index ranking of 156 out of 177
> countries. More than half of the population lives on less than US$1 per day and
> about one third lives in extreme poverty (i.e., less than 2,000 calories per day)
> (IMF 2005).

In 2005, the United Nations Children's Fund (UNICEF) reported that
Eritrea was in a critical economic situation and in need of external economic help due to four consecutive drought cycles and high level of malnutrition. "All six regions of Eritrea had malnutrition rates higher than 10
percent, and three of them, the rates were above 15 percent" (IRIN 2005).
In addition, the Ethio-Eritrea border war of 1998–2000 had not been fully
resolved; tensions and the possibility of another border war flaring up
loomed large in the horizon. The war and the continuing tensions, endemic
drought, and inadequate rainfall had put Eritreans on the verge of a major
famine and grave danger. As though to defy the abject poverty and the
looming famine, the government paraded its 250 imported new tractors

that it hoped would enhance agricultural productivity and tackle famine in the future. Under the title "New Tractors to Boost Agricultural Production," the government website shaebia.org reported, "The Government of Eritrea has imported 250 new tractors in an effort to enhance agricultural production. The tractors were shown to the public on Thursday in a parade along the main avenues of Asmara and through the Bahti Meskerem Square, where a huge crowd gathered to watch a cultural show" (www .shaebia.org, 21 May 2005).

However, the Eritrean economy was then at its weakest point after fourteen years of independence. The government suffered a terrible shortage of foreign currency. According to the IMF, "Foreign reserves declined in 2003 to equivalent of about 2 weeks of imports" (IMF 2005). Every year, Eritrea's imports greatly exceed its exports. For example, in 2005, the estimated value of imports was $676.5 million f.o.b. and of exports was $33.58 million f.o.b. (i.e., a ratio of 20 to 1) (CIA World Fact Book 2006). In 2006, the estimated value of imports went up to $701.8 million while the estimated value of exports went down $17.65 million. The ratio of imports to exports was almost double of the year before, rising from 20 to 1 to a shocking high of about 40 to 1 (CIA World Fact Book 2007). Thus, the economic deficit of the country has been staggering. To mitigate the situation, the government has passed a policy regulating foreign currency, much of which comes into the country as remittances. According to economist Tekie Fessehatzion, "In no other African country are remittances as important to the national economy as in Eritrea, where remittances compromise slightly less than one-third (30 percent) of the GDP" (2005: 168). In addition remittances consisted of more than 26 percent of the per capita income of Eritreans in Eritrea in 2002. "As percentage of GDP, remittance flows exceeded net official development assistance to Eritrea for all years since 1993, with the exception of 1995 and 2002, which were years of extreme drought and food shortage. When combined with Official Development Assistance (ODA), remittances provide two third of Eritrea's GDP for the years 1995–2002" (Tekie Fessehatzion 2005: 169). It is alarming that the government of Eritrea relies so heavily on the Eritrean communities abroad. Because of the economic crisis, the government has passed regulations to control the flow of foreign currency, including cracking down on merchants and private investors who it claimed were responsible for the economic difficulties. With the single-party government, the Peoples Front for Democracy and Justice (PFDJ), taking full charge over all economic activities, the private sector has been practically stifled. Then, in a hasty attempt to weaken the merchants, the PFDJ opened fifty shops to sell groceries and food items in 2005 (Agence France-Presse 2005). In effect, the party has been acting as a private enterprise, monopolizing all investment.

Other forms of repression and control in the public sphere have also worsened. Severe religious repression has resulted in the targeting of evangelical and Pentecostal groups, especially in the past several years. Even the majority Orthodox Christian Church has not been spared. All private newspapers were banned in 2001 and numerous journalists have been arrested since then. Eleven senior government officials were arrested in 2001 and remain in prison without charge or due process. Young people have been required to serve in the military with no or little compensation. Most of them have been serving beyond the required time period, some of them for over ten years. Today, there are 200,000 soldiers in a nation of 4 million, i.e., one of every twenty Eritreans is a soldier.

The politics of self-reliance is another mechanism the state uses to control society. Various religious and other NGOs have been kept out of Eritrea, and the state used this method to consolidate its power and prevent outsiders from observing conditions in the country. NGOs have been weakened and largely serve the interest of the state, and are therefore unable to create a base outside governmental control. Religion has been a big factor in Eritrean politics, and the state has co-opted the old and existing religions in its zealous persecution of the new religions that threatened the established religions of Islam and Orthodoxy. With the established religions now under its control, the new regime denied any civic organizations that might emerge outside of its purview. The first victims of this were religious minorities, especially Pentecostals and Jehovah's Witnesses.[3] The conservative sides of the Orthodox, protestant, and Catholic churches, as well as Islam, have since submitted themselves to the control of the state.

What we are witnessing currently in Eritrea is the pitfalls of excessive nationalism of the kind that Frantz Fanon described. Fanon warned that once independence was achieved in the formerly colonized countries of the Third World, the national bourgeoisie that came to power would become the instrument of global capital, using its position to enrich itself and serve as a intermediary between capital and the ex-colony. Instead of being a champion for the liberty and freedom of the people, the bourgeois class identifies itself as the guardian of the nation's interests, and whatever benefits it is also assumed to benefit the people. Fanon attributes this failure to the inability of the national bourgeois leaders to move beyond nationalism. He argued that the national bourgeoisie is incompetent, with limited capacity and ability, mired in class interest and self-interest, seeking only to perpetuate itself and to benefit from its position of power and its linkages with international powers and capital (Fanon 1963: 148–205). Using Fanon's insight as a point of departure, we can see that the Eritrean nationalist aspiration for greater liberty and freedom has been betrayed in the years since Eritrean independence. The nationalism that was to liberate the people has turned into a vehicle for their manipulation and domination.

Towards an Integral Nation-State

The new Eritrean state aims to establish absolute state power by bringing the whole society under the hegemony of the party, in order to transform and reshape that society in accordance with its own vision. The PFDJ has been trying to discipline the Eritrean population and create a mode of citizenship characterized by submission of individuality, culture, traditions, political aims, and human rights to the state's demands without resistance. It aims to produce civilians who are docile bodies, who can be transformed into malleable and more efficient agents of the state's nationalist dreams; in the words of Foucault, "[a] body is docile that may be subjected, used, transformed and improved" (1979: 136). Under such a scheme, the whole society would be a huge organization working in harmony within a single administrative structure. The party aims to become a large-scale solidarity group, encompassing the entire population. The human and material cost of maintaining this enterprise would be confounding.

I suggest that the state's desired end product is an integral nation-state (Alters 1989; Young 1994), wherein the state and society are gelled into a seamless unity and where distinctions between state and society and nation would be erased. The state has not been completely successful and has not achieved its goal, partly because the party lacks the capacity to accomplish its vision, and because culturally pluralist societies often are not easily manipulated and controlled by totalizing nationalist efforts (Young 1994).

This hegemonic practice of the PFDJ has historical roots in its predecessor, the celebrated EPLF, which acted as a total institution controlling every aspect of social life. One can think of the guerrilla movement as a prison or cage—a cage of the Goffmanesque type, one that forms a "total institution." Erving Goffman stated that the total institution "may be defined as a place of residence and work where a large number of like-situated individuals, cut off from the wider society for an appreciable period of time, together lead an enclosed, formally administered round of life" (1961: xiii). It is an institution where all the aspects of the life of individuals under the institution are controlled and regulated by the authorities of the organization. The concept of total institution has been applied to prisons, mental hospitals, boarding schools, concentration camps, and boot camps (Goffman 1961) and may also be applied to the EPLF, a guerrilla movement. Initially the soldiers of the nationalist fronts were volunteers. The innovation of President Issayas Afeworki as a guerilla leader and his group was the creation of a movement, the EPLF, from which members could not escape or leave. If you were a member of the EPLF, you were highly controlled in ways that led scholars like David Pool (2001) to view the front as a rational organization. However, EPLF's organization was always based on absolute domination over the individual members, who had no time for privacy and free movement (Pool 2001). These nationalist excesses were important in creating a nation called Eritrea.

After independence, the EPLF evolved into a dominant single party, the PFDJ, and sought to continue its policy of acting as a total institution, and to impose its definition of what the nation should be. In its 1994 National Charter, the PFDJ asks itself the following question: "If we are to succeed in achieving our objectives, what kind of organizational structure and organizational principles should the Front have?" It answers its own question in the following way:

> The detailed answer to this question should be left to the constitution, but the basic ideas are as follows: ... Given the Front's extensive objectives and the structure of our society, ... given the absence of any positive experience of a multi-party system in the country, the Front, as during the liberation struggle period, should as much as possible be broad-based, embracing all patriotic Eritreans who have at heart the welfare of Eritrea and its people. ... At the same time, organizationally and procedurally, the Front must strive to attract and actively recruit all citizens who are interested in the unity, peace and prosperity of Eritrea, and want to become active in politics. Basically, the Front should be a reflection of the unity of the people of Eritrea, and the guarantor and promoter of such unity. The Front must be the center of political gravity in Eritrea guaranteeing peace and stability, promoting and strengthening nation-building, healthy democracy and political progress (PFDJ 1994).

As can be seen above, the PFDJ sees itself a movement/party/government, a trinity, one in three and three in one. It desires the public to succumb to its unbridled hegemony and identify with it totally. Thus, in the case of Eritrea, nationalism is not subtle and banal, manifesting itself in how the institution operates (Billig 1995). It is a "hot nationalism" (Billig 1995; Hutchinson 2005); it is "grotesque," à la Achille Mbembe. It requires centrally controlled public declarations of national loyalty and celebration. This large-scale solidarity (Calhoun 1998) does not tolerate criticism or diversity of views. Even within the party, there has been a gradual purging of members who have dissented or questioned policies of the leader and the party.

Celebrations, holidays, and other activities are used to remind the public that there is a nation and its leader is to be identified with the nation.

The nation is objectified in the person of the nationalist leader, Issayas Afeworki, and in the army, the party, and the various government agencies. In public, the leader's ideas and policies are to be defended and considered as the statement of the nation, the views of the party are always correct, and the party represents the people. If a person of Eritrean origin is found to be in a conflict with Ethiopians or other nations, he or she is to be supported because he or she is Eritrean, regardless of the merit of the reason for the conflict. The state, the leader, the party are all representations of popular will (Gramsci 1971). Any critical statements against the policies, actions, and statements of government, the leader, and the officials are deemed as anti-Eritrean, and therefore, opposed to the nation. The body of the president is the human representation of the nation, the speech of the leader is the speech of the people, and the feelings of the president are the feelings of the nation, for he is devoted to the people, to the nation. He has the national interest at heart with no trace of personal interest. Even when he makes a mistake, he does so in the interest of the nation, for he is the nation and the nation is him. The same goes to the nationalist party that replaced the EPLF.

Recently, Issayas Afeworki has himself systematically replaced any person or individual who can challenge his power or authority with individuals who have little social base within the front or whose loyalty to him is unconditional. The patterns of consolidation and centralization of power in the person of Issayas is similar to many postindependence African and Third World countries. Dan Connell has referred to this as the move from collective leadership to individual dictatorship (2004). Instead of seeing it as a process of consolidation of power, Connell sees this as betrayal of the revolution, an interpretation with which I disagree. It has always been this way, except that now it is happening on a national scale in which Eritrea is an actor in the international stage, unlike the EPLF, which was an isolated and obscure nationalist movement.

The party, as a total institution, aims to construct an integral state. Crawford Young defines an integral state as "a design of perfected hegemony, whereby the state seeks to achieve unrestricted domination over civil society. Thus unfettered, the state is free to engage in rational pursuit of its design for the future and to amply reward the ruling class for its governance service" (Young 1994: 249). The mechanism for producing an integral state is integral nationalism. Integral nationalism is radical, extreme, militant, aggressive, and excessive. According to Alters, "integral nationalism casts off all ethical power, obligating and totally subordinating the individuals to one value alone, the nation" (Alters 1989: 20). The end product would be an integral state, where the state and society are gelled into seamless unity and distinctions between state and society and nation would be nonexistent. In Eritrea, the nation under the control of single party attempts to control the entire population and bring it under its tight control, reshaping them to be firm supporters and reorganizing society and culture in the vision of the party and the state.

Stuart Hall wrote about ethnicity as a cover story, as something different than its content, to show the variability and flexibility of the meaning of ethnicity (1989: 15). Craig Calhoun's (1998) insight that nationalism is a rhetorical or a discursive formation is similar: the terms *nation, race,* or *ethnicity* are used as cover stories for varied activities and practices of disparate groups, and in much the same way, nationalism is a cover story that can have different contents and programs within it. It can be an instrument for resistance against intolerable conditions, or it can be a cover for abusive and oppressive actions or programs. We can only judge nationalism by its practice (Brubaker 1996: 7). In Bourdieu's *Logic of Practice,* he writes that the structures as well the process of structuring are in reflexive interaction, giving structure and agency an interactive role in producing and reproducing social structures and practices, habitus (Bourdieu 1977). Nationalism can be both a structure and a structuring force (Brubaker 1996).

By embracing nationalism, nationalists succumb to the limitations of its structure and its structuring logic, habitus. So the logic of nationalism becomes a prison that does not allow people who use it as a vehicle to gain power to escape its limitations. Thus, national identity, like all forms of identity, becomes the cover story (Hall 1989) or the vehicle (Brubaker 1996) with logic of its own. Nationalism can also be used to claim arbitrary and undemocratic actions of the national bourgeoisie. Without realizing it, the nation as represented by the PFDJ is creating an integral state, a state that is potentially destructive to the autonomous and culturally plural life of Eritreans.

Conclusion

Nationalism is a double-edged sword. It can be a tool for bringing about a greater future or it can be a destructive force, one that is unable to produce new heights of human liberty and dignity. The Eritrean state and the ruling party, and many Eritreans at home and abroad, have wrapped themselves in a shawl of nationalism to such an extent that they are blind to the dire situation their country is in. They see the current excesses of nationalism in Eritrea as an end in itself. These excesses were important in creating a nation called Eritrea. But they are also detrimental to the evolution of civil society that respects the human rights of the people. The fact is that nationalism is a powerful force that needs to be tamed and used in specific moments to prevent others from annihilating and destroying human life. But unbridled solidarity based on religion, land, language, or common history or memory can lead to human misery and suffering (Malkki 1995a).

In a situation where the oppression is total and people have no other mechanism of organizing the populace, nationalism becomes an effective method of protest because nationalism creates wide-scale solidarity. This sense of solidarity can be mobilized and deployed in confrontation against totalitarian systems. But often nationalist movements tend to mistake the nationalist struggle as an end in itself and stop their pursuit for greater human equality and dignity and liberty. Instead, they worship the nation, creating myths of national uniqueness and superiority. The national forms become an imperative that dictates their actions. They seek national glories and worship themselves as unique, forgetting that the embrace of nationalism was a tactical and not a long-term strategy or an end in itself. The nation becomes the basis for self-promotion and worship, in the manner of idolaters who create idols to stand for gods. But idols are not to be worshiped and considered as real. Marx wrote of fetishism of commodities in capitalism; here we have fetishism of nationhood. The Eritrean case illustrates this social reality.

A historical perspective can be useful to explain this sad situation. Eritreans had very limited freedom to protest under Ethiopian rule (1961–1991). This was especially true under the Derg, the group that overthrew Emperor Haile Selassie and established a Marxist-Leninist state in Ethiopia in 1974. As was true in many parts of the world during colonial and postcolonial rule, joining the armed nationalist movement in Eritrea was an effective method of protesting Ethiopian rule. Eritrean nationalism created wide-scale solidarity. This sense of solidarity was mobilized and deployed to confront the totalitarian regime of Mengistu Hailemariam of Ethiopia, leading to the defeat of the Ethiopian army in 1991. Class struggle may have been an effective way of getting rid of the totalitarian regime in Ethiopia and the inequalities in society, but nationalism in Eritrea, by blurring the differences between classes, created a huge imagined community ready to act in unison (Anderson 1991). That was the value of Eritrean nationalism.

After independence, the nationalist movement in Eritrea wanted to continue its policy of acting as a nationalist movement that controls every aspect of the society under its control. Its experience as a guerrilla movement became resource for creating a mythical and ideal past of harmonious, faultless, and integrated relationship between the movement and society. This is not uncommon in nationalism. In *The Break-Up of Britain*, Tom Nairn expressed the view that a society needs a strong national identity and that

> it is through nationalism that societies try to propel themselves forward to a certain kind of goal (industrialization, prosperity, equality with other people, etc.) *by a certain sort of regression*—by looking inwards, drawing more deeply upon their indigenous resources, resurrecting past folk-heroes and myths about themselves and so on (1997: 348).

But he also observed that substance of nationalism is ambiguous. The ambivalent nature of nationalism is

> like the old Roman god, Janus, who stood above gateways with one face look forward and one backwards. Thus does nationalism stand over the passage to modernity, for human society. As human kind is forced through its strait doorway, it must look desperately back into the past, to gather strength wherever it can be found for the ordeal of 'development' (Nairn 1977: 18).

After independence, the PFDJ sought to impose its definition of what the nation-state should be by using the recent past of glorious success "against all odds" (Connell 1997) and mythologizing that experience and drawing lessons from it. In the process it mistook the nationalist struggle to be an end in itself and suspended its pursuit for greater human equality, dignity, and liberty. Instead, there is veneration of the nation in Eritrea through a myth of national uniqueness and superiority (Tekle Woldemikael 2005b). The national form has become an imperative that dictates the actions of the nationalist leaders. The nation has become the basis for self-promotion and delusion of grandeur for the president and the ruling party. In doing so, it aspires to create what is known as an integral state (Alter 1989; Young 1994).

Notes

1. The title "Pitfalls of Nationalism" is derived from Frantz Fanon's chapter title "Pitfalls of National Consciousness" in *The Wretched of the Earth* (Fanon: 1963).
2. BBC News (2003/05/24 www.new.bbc.co.uk/go/pr/fr/-/2/hi/africa/2935752.stm)
3. It is to be noted that the guerrilla movement, the EPLF, was against these groups from a very early point, because they were seen as having the potential to undermine national sentiment. It even listed them as antiprogressive religions in its National Democratic Program in 1977 and National Charter of 1994.

— Chapter Two —

WAR, SPATIOTEMPORAL PERCEPTION, AND THE NATION
Fighters and Farmers in the Highlands

Michael Mahrt

Introduction

Commentators have often remarked upon the impressive support the Eritrean liberation movements received from the rural populations in the areas they operated during the liberation war (1961–1991). There is no doubt that this support was vital for the movements' eventually successful struggle. Many also see a direct link between this support and the overwhelming vote in favor of independence in May 1993, assuming that support for the liberation movements also meant support for the cause they were fighting for. The former Eritrean Peoples' Liberation Front, now in government, has done much to strengthen the idea that the independence struggle represented the desire of the Eritrean people for self-determination and the right to live in a free Eritrea. This is a political idea that is repeated endlessly in much of the media and marked in the state's orchestration of national days, such as Independence Day and Martyrs' Day. This very demonstrative display of nationalism, dictated from above, actually raises questions about the validity of nationalist mobilization. Why is it necessary to keep repeating the mantra of "one people, one heart," and continually reinforce the idea of one nation, one people in so many other ways?

Just as many outsiders were enthusiastic about the struggle in Eritrea, many have been disappointed with the subsequent developments. The former liberation movement and now government has increasingly suspended civil rights and are, in the view of most independent observers, oppressing the very population that supported them during the difficult years of liberation struggle, whose freedom and general interest they were purportedly fighting for. The oppression and suspension of the most fundamental civil liberties through the introduction of roadblocks with ID checks, imprisonment of political opposition, suspension of the private press, clampdown on certain religious groups, and of course the much-dreaded national service requirements, are all measures introduced in the name of security, as at least one writer has pointed out (Bundegaard 2004). How did it come to this? Why is there a need to oppress and control a population that was supposedly supporting the very movement that is now in government? Why are "the masses" suddenly considered a security problem in need of draconian control?

In order to understand that, it is necessary to adopt a more anthropological approach and analyze the nature of the support given to the liberation movement during the liberation struggle. What was that support based on, and what were the motives for it? Among most commentators there seems to be an assumption that the support was based on a common understanding between the liberation movements and the population regarding the cause the movements were fighting for. This is the official nationalist version, in which a united people of Eritrea unanimously demanded independence from Ethiopia and a government based on national self-determination. In this chapter, I will examine the liberation war from the perspective of rural highland farmers, taking into consideration the further impact of the border war between Eritrea and Ethiopia (1998–2000). I base my analysis on fieldwork conducted in the highlands in 1994–1995 and 1999–2001 and subsequent shorter visits throughout 2002–2006. I argue that the particular rural population I was studying did not support the liberation movements because they represented Eritrean independence and self-rule—i.e., the nationalist cause. Rather their support was qualified, and indeed strategic, and rested upon ideas of good governance. Using analytical concepts from Benedict Anderson (1991), Tuan (1977), and Deleuze and Guattari (1986), I support my argument by showing how the liberation war was perceived within a particular spatiotemporal understanding that did not correspond to the nationalistic perception of a limited, sovereign geopolitical space. I also show how the liberation war as a spatial practice fitted into preexisting ideas of the relationship between movement, violence, and state power.

History and Times Past

When reading about Eritrea, and indeed when visiting the country, it is hard to miss the importance of the liberation war. Asmara maintains some very distinctive monuments in its honor, most notably the oversized sculpture of the famous *shidda*, the plastic sandals ubiquitous among the liberation fighters. However, when one travels to the rural areas, the liberation war is much less visible, and indeed much less present in everyday discourse. This is not to say that events of that time are not discussed or are unimportant to rural people. It is just that it is not talked about as the liberation war, or the struggle (*qalsi* in Tigrinya), as it is referred to among the fighters and in urban areas. In the following we shall get to a better understanding of why that is so. Let us start with an examination of how time is talked about in relation to events and periods in the past.

The use of numerical systems to indicate time—i.e., years, dates, etc.— universalizes time, and thus reduces the importance of the local. For example, 1 September 1961 is a universal date, applicable all over the world, meaningful to anyone who lived through it wherever they were. It provides a wider reference point, one that connects otherwise separate events and is in that sense neutral and universal and applicable as a reference for events in any given place. On the other hand, the use of specific references to local events, persons, etc., to indicate periods of time, as in the examples I will go through below, localizes time and puts a strong emphasis on the local meaning of time. Furthermore, an analysis of the specific usage of terms reveals the understanding of locality and spatial understanding as well. I shall explore this in detail here with regards to the different discourses surrounding the understanding of the time of the liberation war in Eritrea, and in particular the difference between the official version, so to speak—that is, the discourse of the liberation movement, now government—and that of the rural highland population.

The official version of the liberation war has been authored and adhered to by an intellectual and mainly urban elite. All too often commentators rely primarily on data and interviews gathered in the capital, Asmara, and/or among former liberation fighters. The bulk of Eritreans, the rural population that comprises 80 percent of the total by some estimates, is spoken for by these urban intellectuals schooled in the official version of recent Eritrean history and politics. The former Eritrean Peoples Liberation Front (EPLF), now in government and known as the Peoples Front for Democracy and Justice (PFDJ), or at any rate the leadership, consisted primarily of people from the larger urban areas of Eritrea, mainly Asmara but also Keren, Mendefera, and Massawa, many of whom were educated at the main Ethiopian university in the capital Addis Ababa. An example of this bias in the data is Bundegaard's assertion that the time of the liberation war is commonly referred to as "the struggle" (Bundegaard 2004: 29). This is true only in Asmara and among fighters and educated people. Among the rural population it is not so; although they are aware of this name, they use their own naming of periods of time. To them the liberation struggle began in the time of Haile Selassie, *gezie Haile Selassie;* it continued in *gezie Derg,* or the Ethiopian occupation after the revolution of 1974. The current time is known as *gezie Shaebia,* indicating the time of the EPLF/PFDJ. This is in accordance with a common way of naming periods of time. *Gezie Tilian* (the Italian colonial period), *gezie Engliz* (the years of British Military Administration), *gezie Haile Selassie, gezie Derg,* and *gezie Shaebia* therefore all denote the periods of various governments in recent history and provide the reference for related events.

One among many incidents from my fieldwork illustrates this. I was sitting with a group of five or six older men in the courtyard of my neighbor's house, drinking the millet beer left over from the wedding of his daughter the day before. I was trying to find out whom I should most appropriately address as *Aboy* (literally, "my father," a polite way of addressing older men). In the context of this, Ghebremariam tried to figure out how old he was. The following is a near-verbatim rendition of the conversation that followed:

Ghebremariam: I think I am at least fifty-five years old.

Tsahaie: When were you born?

Ghebremariam: I was born the year the English left.

Tsahaie: If you were born the year the English left, then we can count the years since then. When the English left there was the time of Haile Selassie. First the Federation lasted ten years and then after that another twelve years. That's twenty-two. After Haile Selassie came the time of the Derg, who were here for seventeen years. That's thirty-nine. And now the Shaebia have been here for ten years so you must be forty-nine.

At all times, this was the way to place any event in time for the villagers. The reference points used were the political regimes of the day. Although most people are aware of the numbering of years, using the Orthodox calendar, they simply prefer dating events according to other indicators of time periods. The time of "the struggle" was never used as a marker of time during my fieldwork.

The difference between this way of talking about these crucial years and that of the official version is striking. To the villagers, the major political changes are changes of regimes that serve as markers of time, helpful in compartmentalizing time into smaller segments. Although great changes occurred in the political geography in living memory, in particular the Ethio-Eritrean federation of 1952, annexation of 1962, liberation of 1991, and independence of 1993, these are not significant enough events for the villagers to use as the preferred markers of time. To the liberation movement and government, however, those are exactly the pivotal events. Within nationalist ideology, the federation and annexation were key moments that sparked the struggle. The struggle in itself was the process through which the nation achieved its goal of liberation. Thus, in that particular discourse, the nation passes through these stages of federation, annexation, and struggle in an almost teleological way.

The terminology used for time and place is similarly revealing of these differences in understanding history. In the official, government-sanctioned version, the period before the start of the liberation struggle is known as the colonial period, and the terms *"gezie Haile Selassie"* (*gezie* meaning "time") or *"gezie Derg"* are not often used, though they are also not specifically avoided. The term *struggle* indicates a particular understanding of that part of history as a time with a political purpose rather than a particular political regime. The phrasing is within the standard (i.e., *gezie qalsi,* "time of struggle"), but it is clear that this is a different concept altogether. What defines a period of time for nationalists is not who is ruling but the state of a particular geopolitical area, i.e. occupied or liberated. There is the time before the struggle, and the time of the struggle, and the time after liberation. Where the villagers use the time markers to help them place events, the political marking of time is quite the reverse. Rather than helping place events in time, events define those times. In the nationalist scheme, the defining moment of the (allegedly) first shot fired by Idris Awate in the liberation struggle, and the day the Ethiopian soldiers were driven out of Eritrea, mark the beginning and the end of the struggle, and the achievement of *natsenet,* liberation.

Benedict Anderson (1991) has described this process as the creation of empty homogenous time in nationalist discourse. It allows for a vision of the nation going through time, struggling to break free, as it were. The nation as such is not questioned, and the struggle is simply the process by which the nation arrives at its destiny. What defines a period of time is the political state of the nation—i.e., occupied, liberated, struggling to get free, etc. This is incidentally also why, in the official version, not much emphasis is put on the changeover from Haile Selassie to the Derg. This was indeed a dramatic change in terms of political environment, military alliances and strategies, security measures, and administration. From the viewpoint of nationalist discourse, however, Eritrea was still occupied by Ethiopia and the struggle thus continued.

The time after liberation is known in Asmara, among the government and the urban educated elites, simply as *dehri natsenet* ("after liberation"). To the government and the educated elite, the time now is simply the time after the pivotal event of liberation. To the villagers, however, this is the time of a particular government that has replaced the previous government. It is the time the villagers refer to as *"gezie Shaebia"*; to them, what matters is not that a rearrangement of the geopolitical space has occurred, but that a new government is now in control of the area in which they live. They could never use the time of the struggle as a marker, for it would make little sense lexically, as it is a singular term for a unique period, unlike the use of the rulers' names that are similar terms, metonymically denoting similar things. But more than that, no relevant concept underlies the idea of a time of the struggle. The struggle is a transformative period and as such unique. It indicates that an indefinite period precedes it and another, different indefinite period succeeds it, and that something or someone goes through this transformative period. That something is the nation in the nationalist discourse. The nation was occupied, went through the struggle, and emerged liberated.

Although it was a time of hardship, violence, and life indeed was a struggle, the term is not used by the villagers because they do not perceive the nation as an entity in the way that the nationalist discourse objectifies it. To understand this more clearly, we shall now turn to spatial perception and later how it relates to war and political power.

Continuity and Space

During May 2000, the third offensive in the border war, as it is known, intensified in the area where I was conducting fieldwork. As the Ethiopians were advancing across the Mereb river, which marks the border between the two countries and lies around fifty kilometers from my fieldwork site, we heard and saw the shelling from the frontlines and watched the displaced people pass through the area on their way further into the countryside. I watched as a few people were making their preparations to depart, as indeed I did myself. Some were burying their most valuable belongings, others tried to send their children to stay with relatives in the capital or elsewhere considered safer. Most, however, simply packed a small bag, and made ready to run if the Ethiopians managed to breach the defenses on the steep hillsides outside Adi Quala.

I was talking to an elderly man about how this time compared to the times when they had to flee their village during the liberation war. He told me that this was different. This time, he hadn't even burned his ID papers, he told me, because there was no use. The Ethiopians were coming and they were going to kill you just because you live here, the old man told me:

> Before, we would burn our papers if we thought a battle was coming our way. If the Derg found you with papers from the Shaebia [EPLF] or the Jebha [ELF],

then they might kill you or take you away. And if the Shaebia or the Jebha found you with papers from the Derg, you knew that they would punish you. So we always burned our papers if we heard that there was a battle coming closer.

During the liberation war both the government and the liberation movements issued identity papers to people. The possession of any of these papers was potentially incriminating, and could get the bearer in serious trouble. People were questioned as to their loyalty to one or the other of the groups vying for the power in the area. As another old man told me: "Whenever we would chance upon a group of armed men while traveling in the *berekha* [wilderness], we would either say 'long live Eritrea' or 'long live Ethiopia,' depending on which group they were." When I asked how they could tell them apart, he said, "That was easy, they had different hairstyles, different uniforms, and they spoke different languages. The Ethiopians, even the Oromo people, would speak Amharic, you know ... (imitating the sounds of Amharic) ... , and the *shifta* [literally "bandits," referring to the liberation movements] would speak Tigrinya or Tigre, or sometimes Arabic."

People in the village do not talk about the liberation war as a continuous time period, but in terms of the actual incidents affecting them, such as the one above. Two incidents in particular were singled out repeatedly, however. The first was an actual battle between the EPLF and the Ethiopian government troops in the village, from which the residents had to flee and spend several days wherever they could find shelter, whether in other villages or sleeping rough in the bush. In another case, a group of Ethiopian government troops were camping in the village. At night a group of armed men approached the camp. Thinking they were liberation fighters, the Ethiopian soldiers shot at them and a long nightly battle ensued (the effects of which were still visible; the roof of my house had a hole and the wall was pock-marked from bomb fragments). There were casualties on both sides, but the next day it was discovered that the approaching group was actually another batch of Ethiopian soldiers. Unaware that their comrades were camping in the village they too had mistaken that group for liberation fighters. When this mistake became apparent, the soldiers of both groups took out their anger by randomly killing young men from this village and neighboring ones. The excuse they used was that they should have been told what was going on, and because the villagers failed to do so, this was proof that they supported the liberation fighters. Seven randomly chosen young men were executed on the spot. When I asked when this happened the answer was: "*gezie* Derg."

The generic word used to describe these types of things is *kuinatat* (plural, the singular form is *kuinat*). This can be translated as "the situations," or more precisely the "happening things." It is literally a neutral term, but in vernacular use it is most often connected with undesirable and disturbing situations. More importantly for the present argument, they are local. They affect a particular place and the people that happen to be in that place.

Although most people were aware of the hostilities between the liberation groups and the government, and that these unhappy incidents were related to this hostility, they were not seen as part of the liberation fight, or the "struggle." Although the liberation movements did try to give their version of the political situation and what they were fighting for, most people understood this in the context of what was seen as the traditional fight between those in power and those resisting that power (i.e., the *shifta*).

Such violent situations as described above were viewed as something accidentally affecting the area for various reasons, e.g., its location on the edge of the escarpment separating Seraye from Akele Guzai provinces; its proximity to Mendefera town and the road from the Ethiopian town of Adwa to the Eritrean capital, Asmara; and so on. Events in other areas were only relevant insofar as they affected the people themselves, or relatives and friends in those places. They were not seen as part of the same ongoing struggle for the nation's liberation, but as part of the current living conditions of their area. These conditions were reminiscent of similar problems that, according to the villagers, had always affected their areas.

The liberation fighters, as indicated in the first quote of this section, were generally referred to as *shifta*, which translates roughly as "bandits." An older man told me that it was only later, after the Shaebia came to power, that they began to talk about them as *tegadelti*, "fighters." A *shifta* is someone who no longer lives in his village, but instead in the *berekha*, the wilderness, and he survives by stealing, begging, and robbing. The reasons for leaving a village to become a *shifta* were most often refusing to pay taxes to the rulers or fighting within the village. A *shifta* would often stay away from the village for as long as it took his family to settle his issues with either another family in the village or with the government. This could take months or years, and meanwhile that person would wander around the highlands, stealing where he could and then changing his area before anyone could come after him. He would avoid villages where relatives or friends of his opponents lived, and often several *shifta* would join together in bands. In this way, most people saw the liberation fighters as just another form of *shifta*. And as such, they were having issues with the government and were constantly moving from place to place, as they were conducting guerrilla warfare. It was within this context of movement in particular that the liberation fighters were seen by the villagers as *shifta*. It was not because they were stealing—most often they were not—but because their way of living, their antagonistic relationship with the government, and in particular, I argue, their use of space was similar to that of other roaming *shifta*. Even the *shifta*, who were not liberation fighters, would have frequent clashes with government forces. In similar fashion, the liberation movement could cause momentary problems in particular areas.

Political and Economic Space

The often violent types of changes in power relations were always structurally apart from the daily life of villagers, which was governed by different rules, such as those revolving around the agricultural seasons, marriage arrangements, religious ceremonies, inheritance rules, and the like. Prior to 1991 the main relation villagers had with any government was through taxation, and especially tithe in the case of rural economies, such as the one in which I did fieldwork. The right to collect tithe in any area was known as *gult*. In many works on Eritrean and Ethiopian land tenure, this is confused as a type of land ownership (see for instance Joireman 2000). However, based on the material I collected during my fieldwork, and even on the actual descriptions in those works that describe it as ownership (see for example Jordan Gebre-Medhin 1989; Tekeste Negash 1987; Teshale Tibebu 1995), it is more correct to refer to *gult* as a right to collect taxes in certain defined lands. The most authoritative work on the subject also points out: "Nothing … suggests that *gult*-holders typically involved themselves in the agricultural management of their lands" (Crummey 2000: 200). However, even here one may object to the use of the possessive pronoun. *Gult*-holders did not own land in the sense of being able to freely dispose of it as they liked under the law. The main right *gult*-holders upheld was the right to tax the land to which they held *gult*. This right was enforced by the *gult*-holders and indeed it was the resistance to this that often caused individual farmers to become *shifta*, as mentioned above.

The acquisition of *gult*-rights was a matter of political maneuvering within the political system of the time. Prior to Italian colonialism this took place within the context of the overall Ethiopian kingdom, headed by the emperor, but under the control of various kings and princes with varying degrees of independence. Under these kings and princes were further layers of noblemen who controlled *gult*. Often such noblemen would have ambitions to overthrow their superiors or increase the lands from which they could extract taxes. When this was pursued clandestinely and illegally, it was with the use of *shifta*. When done legally and sanctioned by the kings or even the emperor, it was done by the conscription of soldiers from among the villagers.

The political organization of villages was important as well. Although it varied from place to place, the usual structure involved a *chica-shum,* a kind of chief of the village, who was usually from one particular lineage. There would also be a *danya,* or lay judge, that dealt with all types of civil and criminal cases, ranging from petty theft to arson and murder (but did not involve crimes against the government, such as tax avoidance and disobedience of any kind). Apart from this, villages had what was known, and still is (though in a changed form), as *baito.* This is a type of village parliament where villagers would debate issues of concern to them all. However, these individuals were exclusively male heads of households, or *gebar.*

The economy of the village was and still is organized around the household as the main independent productive unit. As soon as someone married, he[1] would seek to set up a house, however modest, and work his own lands. Although details of the often very complicated land tenure systems in the highlands of Eritrea and Ethiopia are beyond the scope of this paper, suffice to say that all rested on the principle of patrilineal descent, and that the complicated rules often gave rise to fierce legal and sometimes physical fights over the right to work a particular piece of land.[2] When land was distributed, the right to work the land rested with the male head of household, and all decisions were his and his alone. Bauer (1985) has described the fierce individualism and economic independence among highland Tigrinya-speaking farmers in Northern Ethiopia, and the same applies to the Tigrinya-speaking farmers in the neighboring Eritrean highlands.

The important point to make is that changes in government tend to follow principles that are unrelated to the day-to-day life in the villages, which revolves around localized economic and social activities. These activities are solidly founded in land. Almost all aspects of life in villages are somehow related to land issues. Furthermore, these are sedentary relations with the land. In most cases, a man will have rights to land only if one of his patrilineal male ancestors, one to seven generations back, depending on the area, resided in and worked the land of the particular village in which he claims land.

To the villagers, therefore, governments are opposed to their own type of life. They are itinerant, coming from outside; and their succession to power is not related to the land to which they are linked, nor their ancestry, but rather to violence and the ability to build powerful alliances. This does not mean that villagers are unconcerned with matters of the central government and who holds power. Indeed it matters a lot, but mainly in terms of how they rule, not who they are, or where they are from. Their legitimacy does not derive from their origin, but from their governance and their violence. Even today, older people will tell you that the best government they had were the Italians. In terms of interference they were less troublesome than later rulers, and as many liked to tell me with a cheeky grin, unlike the British, they liked the local girls, and unlike the Ethiopians, they treated the girls well. In addition, it should be mentioned that the Italians brought with them opportunities for cash income and alternative work to tilling the land at a time, where shortage of agricultural land was becoming an issue (see Tekeste Negash 1989).

Returning our attention to the village in which I worked, the killing of seven innocent boys and young men by Ethiopian soldiers, described above, was a turning point for most people. It was a moment when they decided that the regime of the Derg had reached the point where support for its rival to power was the only solution. Many now saw the EPLF as a better alternative to the Derg and thus worth supporting. They brought with them ideas of fair treatment of the farmers, and the promise of law and order, and of freedom from the kind of terror and oppression brought by the Derg.

The crucial point, however, was not one of a national Eritrean identity. There was no geopolitical imagination to support the idea that legitimate claims to power originated within borders, little more than lines drawn on a map. The political aspirations of the EPLF appealed to villagers simply because they were seen to be capable of better, and more just governance. They were supported for pragmatic and not nationalistic reasons. The extraordinarily disciplined behavior of the fighters, who rarely if ever stole, raped, or killed the farmers and indeed often assisted villagers with farm work when there was a lull in the fighting, contrasted sharply with the Derg soldiers, who became increasingly hostile to the rural population, in particular after the EPLF took the vital port town of Massawa. Increasingly out of supplies, the Derg soldiers took to looting, raping, and as we have seen, random killing. In the eyes of the villagers, and as most would agree, this did not amount to good governance, and the EPLF appeared better organized and better disciplined and hence a better alternative to the Derg.

Where the nationalist rendering of the liberation movement sees all these events, the fighting and so on, as part of the overall struggle for independence, the villagers saw them as isolated incidents that were a regrettable part of living conditions in their area. Although the villagers heard the political rhetoric of the liberation movements, whenever fighters remained in the village or vicinity long enough to form relations with the people there, the idea that they were fighting for a national liberation was not readily accepted. To the villagers the *shifta*, or liberation movements, were vying for political power, trying to replace the current government, as the current (Derg) had replaced the previous (Haile Selassie), which again had replaced the previous (the English), and so on. This type of government opposition and eventual overthrow and its relation to the *shifta* has a long history in the area. I will not delve too deeply into that here, but suffice to say that *shifta* were often tools used by kings trying to destabilize a rival king or overtake an area or indeed a route to power.

The change of power at all levels throughout the history of highland Eritrea and Ethiopia has almost always been violent. Prior to Italian colonialism there was the "era of the princes," which was a long period of perpetual conflict between different princes vying for power. Though this ended with the victory of Tewodros, Eritrea then quickly became the object of interest for the Italians, who again took the area by military force, and had their ambitions checked by losing the famous battle of Adwa in 1869. In living memory, only wars have achieved changes of power, except for the handover from the British Military Administration to the Ethiopians through the Federation. More importantly, governance is always closely linked with military power. Those in power are those with the military strength to obtain and retain that power. Finally political power in terms of governance and taxation is structurally apart from the life of the village, in particular in the way that it is not related to the economic use of land: in its strong focus on military power, the government uses land in ways very different from and indeed in many ways opposite to how land is used by the rural population.

War, Space, and the Nation

Benedict Anderson (1991) describes nations as imagined communities, but other communities are also imagined in the sense of each individual not necessarily knowing all within that community (e.g., religious communities, professional communities, etc.). Hence Anderson qualifies this by arguing that nations are not just imagined as communities, but also as limited and sovereign. *Limited* is not solely to be understood as geographical limitation, but is closely linked to that. For example, a man born in Jordan and having never ventured outside that country may still feel himself to be a Palestinian. This is possible because nationalism defines a limited group of people, which again are defined by their particular relation to a limited geographical space—a relation that cannot be reduced to physical presence or even nativity. The limitation argument thus refers to the mechanisms of identity and how that relates to a particular form of spatial imagination. The idea of sovereignty is the idea that the people thus identified are those that have legitimate rights to that geopolitical space, and thus refers to the political aspects of nationalism.

In line with Yi-Fu Tuan (1977), I argue that place is created through spatial practice, and through the practical experience of space. This includes interpretation of space, place, and of other actors' spatial practices (Tuan 1977). War is, as Deleuze and Guattari (1986) point out, above all a spatial practice. For the villagers, war is one of the more powerful ways that space is experienced, and in particular how space, violence, and political power are linked. It is therefore the experience of war as a spatial practice, as seen from the villagers' viewpoint, that we shall focus on now, in order to better comprehend the relationship the rural population had with the liberation movements and have with the idea of Eritrea as a nation-state.

War deals with the distribution of people and material in the land according to strategic principles; it is about movement in space (Deleuze and Guattari 1986). This was clearly perceived by the villagers during the liberation war. The fighters were perceived as *shifta*—as people who are not settled, but move around in the landscape. Their use of space is governed by strategic rules, i.e., avoiding areas where they might run into enemies, not staying very long in each area to avoid having the villagers unite and come after them, etc. They display much of the nomadic and violent attributes of the "war machine," as described by Deleuze and Guattari.

In contrast, the villagers' use of land is centered on opposite principles, namely the distribution of land to people (rather than people in land) and settlement rather than movement. This is the creation of place out of space and its ongoing maintenance of this. As Tuan (1977) points out, the creation of place from space is through the practical interaction with space. This means that different interactions with the same space create different places that may overlap fully or partially. The daily labor of tilling the land, walking to neighboring villages to drink coffee and share gossip, the late night walk up the hill to partake in the church service, etc. all are part of the creation of the land the villagers inhabit as place. It is a place laced with history and historical references are used in everyday discourse, from the stories of the origin of the village, over the naming of everyone who ever lived there and worked the land, to the extraordinarily detailed knowledge of who grew what crop on which plot many, many years back.

The military use, in contrast, is temporary. It creates temporary places with strategic importance. Their use as a place with a name ceases once the war moves on and it can be disregarded. These places may be used later on in nationalist discourse, with fond memories of battles won (such as the battle of Afabet), or dark memories of atrocities witnessed (such as She'eb). But they are then what Tuan calls "mythical places" (1977), that is to say, places created as fixed in time and serving purposes of creating stories that reach beyond the place itself. They are no longer places of war with strategic importance, but rather an integral part of the establishment of a nationalist mythology. As such they have entered into the service of the sedentary power in Deleuze and Guattari's terminology. This is what is happening at the moment in the current emphasis on the liberation war for the creation of Eritrea as a nation. It is no coincidence that the national currency has been named after one of the most important places for the EPLF during the liberation war, the town of Naqfa.

I am in no way arguing that villagers do not recognize borders and that this is why they do not adhere to a nationalist perception of the liberation war. Indeed physical, geographical borders are of utmost importance to the villagers. Many of the fights that lead to villagers choosing to become *shifta* occur when someone transgresses the boundary between one agri-cultural plot and the next. A popular saying even has it that when it comes to land, even women will join the fight (of one village against another).[3] The right to work the land, however, is completely different from the right to govern the land. It is thus not that the villagers do not imagine that rights can be held to land within defined boundaries, but that the legitimacy of different rights is based on different forms of logic. In other words, the right to govern is not derived from inheritance, or origin, but has traditionally been derived from war. As mentioned above, Tuan points out that places are created by the practical experience and interaction with space. The right to live and work the land in a particular village relates to the economic interaction with the land, as understood within a particular understanding of inheritance, kinship, marriage, etc. The right to govern relates to the military and political interaction with land. So the creation of boundaries in one does not imply that this mechanism applies to the other.

It is worth going a bit further along with Deleuze and Guattari's argument here. They argue that the relationship between the war machine, as they call it, and the state is a dynamic relationship between movement and sedentary power. Once the state appropriates the war machine as the military, it turns it against that which threatens it—against the nomadic groups, against movement, because movement is the main threat to sedentary power. Alternatively the state turns the military against other states to express the relation between the states (Deleuze and Guattari 1986: 113).

The war is outside the sedentary village life, it is movement, it pops up here and there, because it follows the principles of distribution of people in the land, a principle of movement and of motion. One could say that war in the pure nomadic sense, employed by Deleuze and Guattari, is the destabilization of place by the nomadic aspect of the war machine. It changes places by treating everything as space. When the battles were approaching, the normal rules of the place cease to apply. During one particular bad time, most of the villagers left the village, taking only their cattle and a few belongings with them. They left, not knowing what to return to, or indeed who would return. The normal life centered on sedentary activities is disrupted by the arrival of the war, and only resumed once the war had moved on. The place is disrupted by this. Upon return from flight, houses may have been burned, grain stores looted, and crops destroyed. This was very much the experience of the liberation war for the villagers. Although the latter part of the liberation war—in particular after the EPLF captured Afabet in 1988—more and more resembled a conventional war, the area I worked in only saw it as guerrilla war, a very mobile form without clear frontlines. The war would take place in a literal sense when it arrived in the village as in the examples mentioned above. This is how, I argue, the liberation war was not seen as a nationalist war for the villagers. It was a war for political power, and was not related to the villagers, except when it influenced their lives, such as when it took place in or near the village.

In contrast to this, the border war (1998–2000) was a fixed war with frontlines. It was no longer the state fighting mobile *shifta*, but one state trying to take over another—including the villagers living inside it. This was a clear example of the state having fully appropriated the war machine as military and two states using it against each other to express their relationship. From the viewpoint of the villagers, what happened was that they clearly understood that they were thus being aligned by default with the state, not because of political allegiance, but because of geopolitical identity, defined by space and not by social relations. The villagers no longer just lived in a state—they had become part of the state. In other words, the threat to the sovereignty of the state became a threat to them as citizens, and as such, one of the imaginations described by Anderson (1991) was imposed upon them violently.

Conclusion

Thus to conclude, we return to the short story of the old man choosing not to burn his ID papers as Ethiopian troops advanced towards the village in 2000. His motivations for not doing so reveal his understanding of the difference between the border war and the liberation war. During the liberation war, the issue was the right to govern. This right has historically been obtained through violence. The different groups vying for power relate to the villagers, the old man included, as potential allies or enemies of their candidacy.

During the border war, however, the people living on the land were now the targets of the violence. It did not matter anymore what allegiance you had—you were defined by your presence in the territory, and as such, you became a target. The support the liberation movements enjoyed during the war of independence was a strategic survival choice. In the past, it made sense to support those that were in control of the area you live in; today, supporting those that might provide the best kind of governance continues to make sense. During the border war it was clear that such a choice was no longer open to the villagers: it had been made for them by the political shaping of the geographical space they inhabited. The community of the nation, to paraphrase Anderson's term, never was more clearly imagined than at the moment when people realized that they were going to be targeted, not because they got in the way of a fight, or because they supported one group or the other, but because they belonged to a community defined by a limited geopolitical space.

The support that the liberation groups received, I would argue, was not a straightforward support for the cause of Eritrean self-determination or liberation of the country. Rather, it must be understood within the context of particular perceptions of power and geography, politics and space. To the villagers, political power comes from the outside, and is gained through violence. It is closely related to the activities of *shifta*, people who choose to live a violent life outside of the village. In this triangular relationship, between government, *shifta* or liberation fighters, and the villagers, it is the *shifta* and the governments that come and go, violently. The *shifta* come and go as nomads, in the sense described by Deleuze and Guattari (1986), and the governments as itinerant power holders, achieving that status through the use of military force. The villagers remain in the land and deal with the rulers and the other actors strategically. The support that developed for the liberation movements was not based on an agreement on the geopolitical aims, i.e., the "liberation" of Eritrea, but on a belief that the liberation fighters were serious contenders for political power and held more credibility in terms of the benefit they could bring to the villagers. The villagers did not care much where the borders were drawn or indeed where the rulers were from, but much more about the quality of governance.

It is within this context, I believe, that the increased militarization of Eritrean society, the border war with Ethiopia, and the ever-increasing political control over the population should be understood. The border war and the intensified control are not just parts of a struggle for political power or the preservation of independence from the outside threat. These two goals were achieved at the official end of the struggle in 1991. But there is one struggle that was not won at that time, and which continues today. That is the struggle for the political idea of Eritrea as a nation.

Notes

1. I deliberately use the male pronoun, as the traditional rules favor male inheritance of land (though with exceptions that space does not allow me to go further into). There is a new land proclamation from the government, but it had yet to be implemented at the time of my fieldwork.
2. For more detailed discussions, see Nadel 1946, Ambaye Zekarias 1966, Markakis 1974, Bauer 1985, Tekeste Negash 1987, Jordan Gebre-Medhin 1989, Teshale Tibebu 1995, Tesfai G. Gebremedhin 1996, Tronvoll 1998, Hendrie 1999, Crummey 2000, Joireman 2000. The work of Crummey is of particular value.
3. This is considered a particularly strong saying due to the fact that most women upon marrying move to new villages, traditionally quite far from their home village. They are thus fighting for the land of a village where they are considered outsiders, as they are from a different family.

— *Chapter Three* —

THE YOUTH HAS GONE FROM OUR SOIL
Place and Politics in Refugee Resettlement
and Agrarian Development

$\mathcal{C}\sim$

Amanda Poole

In October 2006, the UN cited Eritrea for breaking the ceasefire accords with Ethiopia and moving armed troops and tanks into the temporary security zone—a tense strip of land that has divided the two countries since the end of open conflict in 2000.[1] The Eritrean Information Minister provided the rejoinder that the military was there "to pick crops." "If the harvest is not taken," he claimed, "it will be lost with severe consequences for our food security" (*BBC News* 2006). Whatever other motivations it may be masking in the convoluted politics sustaining the border dispute, this claim is consistent with a powerful discourse in Eritrea that explicitly couples national sovereignty and food security. In fact, soldiers *are* frequently deployed in agricultural labor on both state-owned and smallholder farms. According to UN figures, Eritrea has only produced an average of 30 percent of its cereal needs over the past decade" (Harris 2006), and the attainment of food security is one means to legitimize the nation's right to sovereignty. Leaving aside the unsubtle calculus of harvesting crops and claiming sovereignty within disputed border lands, food security and national sovereignty have been at the center of rural development projects of the Eritrean state since independence in 1991, legitimizing state interventions into agrarian production. Consequently, national news articles on rural development cast community-level activities like soil and water conservation into an explicitly political project of nation-building: it is through such community-building activities, claimed the state-led press, that "the people are playing a vital role ready to safeguard the sovereignty and national integrity of their Nation" (*Eritrea Profile* 2005b).

This intersection of community work, food production, and militarization also reverberates throughout local landscapes in Eritrea, if in strikingly different ways. I begin with a brief vignette from my fieldwork in a community where I researched refugee resettlement and rural development in 2004–2005.

It was a windy afternoon when I met with Idris and Abdella, farmers from a village at the edge of Hagaz, a town in the western lowlands of Eritrea that had been one of the pilot sites for the resettlement of refugees returning from Sudan after independence in 1991.[2] The dry wind pulsed through the surrounding hills, kicking up dust that settled in a fine film on the surface of our tea. It was *menchelos*, the strong wind at the end of summer that could destroy crops if it came too early, or too late, but was required to dry the sorghum and millet in preparation for harvest. Although the wind was timely in following the rain this year, some of the plots around us yielded only sparse stalks. These men were in their sixties and had been raised here, farming and rearing livestock on land that had been lost to the refugee resettlement program. They began, like many of my interviewees did, with nostalgia for a lost landscape of plenty: "The past was better than the present because there were a lot of animals. Even the farming was well and good," explained Abdella. They described the land as having been "fat" and "wet." "But gradually in the course of time the land gets more and more barren, just like a human being, who gets older and older." Idris agreed, but linked the loss of soil youth and fertility to a lack of capacity to care for the land and practice desired cultivation:

> It is impossible to practice successful communal work on our farms, because all the youngsters with energy are at the front. … The elders here are weak, they cannot work on something that needs a lot of force. Their sons went to the front. If you check all of the houses, you can only find women and aged men in each house. This is the reason why some of the farmland is not properly cultivated. If we are not able to provide the land with fertilizers or cow dung, and make terraces, the crops will not grow as desired. We need help from the government to provide us with fertilizers. This land needs help. If we don't get any help from the Ministry of Agriculture, our fingers alone will not have the power.

The power to build community, secure livelihoods, and continue subsistence practices across generations in a landscape facing the erosion of fertility and youth on both material and symbolic levels—these are immediate concerns among people in Hagaz. However, these processes unfold in the local context of resettlement and broader state-led development in different ways for local farmers and returned refugees. When the first few thousand returnees came to Hagaz under the official repatriation program in 1994, they were allocated plots for housing at the northern edge of a small but growing town. They were returning from Sudan, where as

many as 300,000 Eritreans lived as refugees during the struggle for independence. Some of the refugees were returning to their hometown, but
many arrived to a place and region they had never lived in before, and to
a nation they had imagined from afar for as many as thirty years. By the
time I began my research in 2004, Hagaz had grown to incorporate three
villages, including that of Idris and Abdella. Elsewhere, I have explored
the frailty of the "returnee" and "stayee" categories; in this chapter, I examine the ways local farmers and return refugees engage differently with
concepts and practices of agrarian labor, both mandatory state-led labor
known as *ma'atot*, and self-initiated, traditional community work known
as *wofara*. Shifting practices of community work in the context of postconflict resettlement expose the need to interrogate how agrarian politics become central to ways that people reestablish ties to landscape and
community after periods of violence and displacement—a process that is
tightly enmeshed with questions of power and agency of rural producers
in the context of postcolonial state-making. I draw from my ethnographic
research in Hagaz to explore how local idioms of youth, fertility, and development, connected to practices of community work, become a medium
through which different members of the Hagaz community negotiate
claims to belonging, and call into question the meanings and practices of
sovereignty over national lands.

Sovereignty and Biopolitics in
Eritrean Agricultural Development

In this chapter, I use the concepts of biopolitics and sovereignty to understand people's negotiations with the state and shifting practices of community labor. Foucault's (1978) model of biopolitics—the techniques of
governance concerned with fostering the life of the population—maps
neatly onto the appropriation of labor for food production in Eritrea. However, coupling biopolitics with sovereignty provides a means to explore
the complex ways that agency takes shape beyond the boundaries of the
biopolitical projects of the state and the increased militarization of society,
landscapes, and agrarian production. Drawing from Agamben (1998), biopolitics do not supersede an archaic form of sovereign power as Foucault
argues; rather, they have always been bound up with sovereign rule, so
that sovereignty originates in part with the production of the biopolitical
body that is able to take shape over the figure of bare life.[3] These concepts
are opened up by ethnographic research in compelling ways. Hansen and
Stepputat (2005) focus our attention on "issues of internal constitution of
sovereign power within states through the exercise of violence over bod-

ies and populations." At the same time they question "the obviousness of the state-territory-sovereignty link" by revealing the ways they are socially constructed. Following this, Donald Moore (2005) points to the ways that state sovereignty comes up against other nodes of sovereignty in rural spaces, nodes that are both "selective and situated" within the always-contested terrain of "place, power, and cultural politics."

Agrarian relations are an important medium through which place, power, and cultural politics are constituted by communities negotiating the demand to rework social ties in the postconflict context. Looking critically at issues of food security and production in Africa, Pottier (1999) reminds us to consider the multiple concerns that shape farmers' production decisions, and the ways that agriculture itself becomes an "idiom for social expression." In this vein, recent studies of agrarian change in Africa write against unilinear models of causality, and point to the need to examine multiple trajectories of social change that often center on questions of social identity and are rooted in historical socioeconomic conditions. Consequently, Englund (1999) views the shift in Malawian communities from communal work parties for beer and food to paid piecemeal labor not as the necessary decision of individual rational actors in the face of agricultural modernization and the growth of a cash economy. Instead, paid piecemeal labor in these villages reanimates traditional practices while exposing and reaffirming social and familial relationships — calling for a "more nuanced understanding of personhood and sociality." Also, while refugees in this area faced exploitation under this piecemeal labor system, for some these labor relations became a means of transitioning from "strangerhood" to "solicitude" and belonging. Similarly, Kea's (2004) work in the Gambia operates in conversation with gendered analyses of agrarian labor in West Africa (Carney and Watts 1990, 1991; Schroeder 1999) to analyze social differentiation *between* women as they actively reinforce host/patron and stranger/client categories in order to secure their claims to increasingly scarce resources of land and labor. Kea describes these micropolitical struggles as fraught with both tension and opportunity as people "continuously reconstitute their social networks and relations" in order to access resources "in a context where they cannot depend on the state, on financial institutions, or even on family and friends" (2004: 378).

These studies push us to consider the ways that identity and social relations shape the micropolitics of agricultural labor relations in the shifting political economy of rural African communities. However, as I explore below, the interactions of farmers and return refugees in Hagaz expose the ways that agrarian micropolitics are also inextricably bound up in negotiating translocal identities and processes — in this case, the meanings of citizenship and national belonging.[4] To this end, I examine how local farmers and return refugees in Hagaz engage differently with concepts and practices of community work on the land—practices of labor that provide one medium of constituting place, power, and belonging in the Hagaz community. These practices, I argue, expose fissures in the state-led nationalist discourse by shifting concerns to the local moral economy and people's inabilities to build stable livelihoods and pass on traditions of subsistence-based production to future generations. *Moral economy,* while having a long history in scholarship and debates about peasant production, refers here to the significance of social arrangements of reciprocity in meeting subsistence needs among rural producers, and during times of political economic change, the struggle "over norms, values, and expectations related to the livelihoods of subordinate classes" (Neumann 2002: 37). Consequently, the multiple forms of labor animated by community members in Hagaz suggest that biopolitical regimes themselves may generate the possibilities of "selective and situated" sovereignties in the production of food. I return first to the different kinds of community work, *ma'atot* and *wofara,* and they ways they are communicated by official discourse. I then trace how these different forms of labor are animated in discussion and practice between farmers and returnees.

Agrarian Development in National Level Discourse

Framed through the language of self-sufficiency and "love of work," traits espoused by the revolutionary parties during the thirty-year national struggle for independence, agrarian labor in Eritrea becomes part of a biopolitical project concerned with crafting subjects and consolidating sovereignty—linking the body politic with national territory. On one level, this principle is manifest in the large-scale conscription of youth and adults into the military and national service campaigns. In an article in the government-run English newspaper, *Eritrea Profile,* a Ministry of Agriculture official described the role of students in performing requisite summer service by harvesting the fields of elderly people whose children are martyred or in the military: "We are making them responsible citizens of the future. It is like treating the tree so that it will give a good service ultimately" (Siltanyesus Tsigeyohannes 2005). These students were not only crafted as citizen-stewards of the land, they were also represented as "the nation's children," in this case, substitutes for missing kin, those sons and daughters conscripted into military service and absent from their families and their roles in local, village, and lineage-based agricultural labor.

The coupling of food security with national sovereignty through biopolitical regimes of conscription and work parties has specific meaning in the region's environment and history. Food insecurity was one argument used against Eritrean independence following Italy's loss of the colony in the aftermath of World War II (Alexander Naty 2003). Since independence, the Eritrean government has justified its rule and right to sovereignty by displaying the solidarity of its people and embracing concepts of self-reliance in the face of aid dependence and the circulating discourses of vulnerability, dearth, and dire need. "The key to economic emancipation is work," claimed a September 2005 anonymous commentary in the *Eritrea Profile,* and the shared responsibility to "prevent relief aid from becoming a disease and an addiction, which gnaws at the body of the nation" (*Eritrea Profile* 2005c).[5] Here, emancipation applies to the national body, which is linked to disciplined work and self-sacrifice in the efforts to conserve and develop agrarian resources as well as re-create an imagined national landscape of verdant fertility, lost during long years of colonial appropriation and violence.[6] In an *Eritrea Profile* interview with a Ministry of Agriculture official, land and people are more explicitly linked through the rhetoric of duty and common national identity that obligates people to attain their "right of living" on the land, which, the official reminds us, "wherever it is, belongs to the government" (*Eritrea Profile* 2005b). In fact, all land is legally national territory since the Land Proclamation Act of 1995. This act, although it has only partially been implemented, overwrites a mosaic of traditional tenure regimes.[7] Equating 'right of living' with national duty on national land collapses different forms of labor into an ideology of working for the nation (or perhaps working for the government, as the Ministry of Agriculture official's statement provokingly suggests).

Articles and images in the *Eritrea Profile* and on *EriTV,* the sole national television station, frequently highlight the various achievements made by the government in cooperation with local communities towards developing land and water resources, and describe rural development specifically as the cornerstone of the government's development priorities. Consequently, the Independence Day celebrations in 2005 involved a parade of new shining red tractors down Liberation Avenue, the center of downtown Asmara, that were destined for prime agricultural areas. Many front covers of the newspaper during my year in the country displayed President Issayas Afeworki on field visits to rural development projects, eyes shaded by a wide brimmed khaki hat as he surveyed the progress of committed communities in distant regions—through media coverage, linking these areas to the nation-building project through visual representations of the gaze and presence of the state. This visual depiction of agricultural production and fertility also becomes an iconic image of an independent Eritrea under the leadership of the party. EriTV frequently intersperses its programming with long panoramic vistas of fields of grain along with the industrious activity of national service workers digging catchments or performing other agrarian labor activities.

Community-level projects of agrarian development are often enacted in *ma'atot*. Officiated by local administration, all able-bodied people are called to perform mandatory labor in the interest of agricultural or infrastructural development. In growing towns like Hagaz, performing *ma'atot* is a prerequisite to getting the proper documentation that allows people to claim rations or food aid. Consequently, *ma'atot* is one means of tracking the population and making it legible, as people are registered and then conscripted into community work. *Ma'atot* draws on the traditional practice of community self-help, *wofara*.[8] Researchers have noted the persistence of *wofara* among Eritrean refugees living in Sudan as well as return refugees, and the ways it was practiced across ethnic and religious groups in the maintenance of Eritrean identity and livelihood in the creation of communities both materially and symbolically (Sorenson 2000; Bascom 1999). It was often relayed to me that when someone needed help weeding or harvesting, or repairing a home, community members would be called together and the host would prepare food and drink for them. *Ma'atot* was contrasted to *wofara* because it was initiated by the state and did not contain the same norms of reciprocity—as one person described it, *ma'atot* was "a word coined by the government, just calling youngsters to work, nothing in return." While *ma'atot* was obligatory for most, *wofara*'s continued prevalence in the community, and between different kinds of community members, became a more contentious and tenuous matter.[9]

Local Narratives of Work and Community

When the first few thousand people came to Hagaz from Sudan under the official repatriation program in 1994, a project operated jointly between the Government of Eritrea and the United Nations High Commissioner for Refugees (UNHCR), they were allocated plots for housing at the northern edge of a small but growing town. By 1996 the pipes were installed to pump underground water from beneath the seasonal river bed, and the road was tarred that ran through town to link the Eritrean capital with Sudan. By the time I began my research in 2004, there were nearly 18,000 people in Hagaz, which had grown to administratively incorporate three villages to the north. The population of Hagaz was made up of diverse groups of local "stayees" and return refugees who settled in Hagaz both spontaneously and under the official repatriation scheme.[10] Most of the original inhabitants of the region were Blin and Tigre, both Muslim and Christian. Although many of the returnees were also originally from surrounding areas, nearly every other Eritrean ethnic group was represented in the current population, particularly a number of Tigrinya residents who had chosen Hagaz as the resettlement site closest to the highlands.[11]

The community took shape through a municipal zoning project that was to become a model for other Eritrean communities in the context of postconflict development planning. The stayees who came from the northern villages had lost farm and grazing land through rezoning that allocated land for refugee resettlement and urban expansion. Returnees gained this housing land if they were registered and returned under the organized repatriation program—coming back on their own initiative risked losing access to limited land allotments.[12] This process constituted regimes of spatial disciplining informed by idealized notions of modern urban and agricultural development that valued sedentarization, individual titles to houses (all land being national property), and the rationalized zoning of housing and productive activities.[13] Consequently, the informal homes of some of the oldest settlers, many of whom had been forced to relocate to Hagaz by Ethiopian administrators in the 1970s and 80s, were slotted for relocation—from the cacophony of conjoining compounds, tall palm trees, trails, and huts to regimented plots at the southern outskirts of town, a large area nearly bare of vegetation and spotted with few concrete houses between the markers for roads and compounds that have yet to be built. The old settlement currently occupied by these community members stretches along the seasonal river, on land that was rezoned for the expansion of irrigated garden plots. Other parts of the old settlement, adjoining the center market area, have been rezoned in the anticipation of modern houses that would one day be constructed by "returnees"—Eritreans living abroad in the diaspora. In the typology through which the experience of return takes shape, "return refugees" occupied a category quite distinct from "returnees," and were granted land at the northern outskirts of town—an area commonly referred to as "the refugee camp," shortened to *measker* in Tigrinya.[14] *Measker* lay separated from the rest of town by a dry river bed, across which only one electrical line extended to a single wealthier household to form an island of light in an otherwise darkened conglomeration of cement buildings, huts, and shelters.

None of the returnees were allocated farmland, though some had access to ancestral land in their father's villages, and others entered into rental arrangements with local farmers, which I address below.[15] Local rain-fed farms were typically planted with pearl millet and sorghum, with occasional groundnut production. Wealthier community members were able to rent irrigated plots along the dry river bed, where they grew produce for the local market, usually citrus fruit and vegetables such as onions, okra, and a spicy green known locally as *jirjir*. Farther to the south, larger plots of land had been allotted to commercial farmers who typically grew onions, and were at that point diversifying into citrus fruits and animal feed.[16] Although they may not have had access to farmland, most community members reared poultry and/or some livestock, particularly goats that shared grazing resources with surrounding villages. Recent years of drought have heavily impacted farmers and those practicing animal husbandry—increasing the difficulties that people experience with deepening poverty in a climate of inflation, economic stagnation, loss of labor through conscription, and underemployment.

Returning to Abdella and Idris: we sat on low stools outside Abdella's hut. Looking south, past the patchwork of crops and beyond a dry sand floodplain, we saw the houses of the return refugees, people they described alternately as "strangers" and "brothers" as they talked about the changes in their lives and landscape. I asked them how *wofara* happened in their community. Both men shook their heads. First Idris explained that communal work was still important for weeding, because most people lacked the capacity to hire workers. Then Abdella described how communal work was stifled not by poverty, but by the loss of kinship and community networks brought about by conscription and national service: "We the old people are here to do the communal work, to help each other. The people with money can hire workers. Otherwise, there is no communal work as such—at least at this time, because the youth died in the battlefield, while those alive are still at the front." Farmers from a neighboring village corroborated these sentiments, one of whom stated of communal agricultural work: "There is almost none. In the past people had a lot of camels and oxen, so they helped the poor people. Now everyone is the same, so you can say there is no *wofara*."

When we returned to the subject of cultivation, these men explained that their capacity to produce food has declined through loss of labor, land, and fertility. Abdella told me, "At this time, we farm every piece of land, but in the past, we had a lot of land and would fallow it for one or two years. Besides, the best land was where Hagaz settlers were allocated housing. This land is dead." In the depiction of lost fertility, and literally, lost land, people crafted claims to place at the same time that they described an erosion of youth from the soil and from the village community. In the farmers' descriptions, this loss of fertility became entangled with a loss of village-level solidarity and autonomy—in contrast to the memory of previous times, when people were not only able to practice communal work, but were able to "prepare our food here, rear our cattle here. It wasn't like now."

Past times, however, also denoted the ways in which farming became an overtly political act during the Eritrean struggle. Area villagers were forcibly relocated to Hagaz by the Ethiopian military in order to drain the countryside of support for Eritrean fighters. Many farmers described their displacement and their struggles to produce food in the context of colonial occupation and violence. For example:

Idris: They told us, warned us, to come close to the Ethiopian flag.

Abdella: Even though we moved to towns, we were able to farm our lands, by some means or another.

Idris: We used to come to our farm during the night, hiding ourselves from the Ethiopians. Then we would pick our crops and fill the sacks. Then we would go to the river and dig a pit to hide our sacks of crops. If they found the crops they would burn them. We were living unsecured. We passed a very hectic and unsecured life. We were in a bad and threatening situation. But what to do? We didn't leave our land though.

These stories were corroborated by the narratives of men and women forcibly relocated to Hagaz during the conflict but who had remained in town, many of them still maintaining familial farmland outside of town. Some however, stressed the inability of people to produce food during periods of intensified conflict and forced resettlement. In the experience of rural agrarian production, the loss of people due to the conscription under current policies recalled earlier periods of forced migration and conscription. One older farmer who had relocated to Hagaz explained: "The drought appeared when the Derg set its foot to Eritrea. So people fled away. Their animals were destroyed. The younger joined the field. People got fewer and fewer, so it is natural that the work will get harder and harder until they stop working." Current agricultural practices exist in a markedly different context—where farmers and other community members described the daily security and freedom from the bouts of violence that had permeated life during years of Ethiopian rule. However, as farming at times took the shape of active resistance to state repression during colonial times in the oral history accounts of villagers around Hagaz, today, these productive practices have become a means by which people place themselves within and remove themselves from the state and its projects of mandatory labor in agrarian development; village and kinship-based subsistence practices, they suggest, are not equivalent with food or labor provided by the state.

Despite, or perhaps because of, the attenuation of the farmers' abilities to maintain practices vital to local communities and landscapes, they maintained expectations about the role of the state—especially its accountability in providing fertilizers and tractor service. At the same time, however, they identified the state's lack of capacity to provide the means for people to craft secure livelihoods for themselves through continuity with long histories of working the land, traveling with cattle, or accessing markets now cut off by closed, patrolled borders. Two different kinds of mobility are implicated in this context: traditional mobile livelihoods that involved the diversification of production and mobility in search of seasonal resources, and migration out of necessity in the face of collapsed production and the monetarization of farm inputs—particularly in the form of tractors that have become critical replacements for lost labor of humans and livestock.[17] However, mobility and employment outside of national service and other state jobs have been severely curtailed by government policies that restrict the spaces where many groups of people may legally work or travel. As Abdella asserted: "First of all we need peace and security. If there is peace, we can go wherever there are natural resources. We will work hard and eat. We can work with our hands." Now however, at a time when proper work has been constrained, mobility in search of wage labor has become fraught with danger, mostly due to state policies restricting mobility and private sector employment opportunities in the context of conscription and the constant threat of renewed warfare. Abdella continued: "Now, the farmers are searching for manual work by going far from their villages. In the towns they get money so they can hire tractors to farm their land. Some of them return with some amount of money, while others get lost. They disappear. So the people are risking their lives."

These restrictions on agrarian production and pastoralism, along with a slimmed space (both politically and economically) for earning the subsidies provided by wage labor, are entwined with deep ambiguities over the modernization of agriculture in the context of state repression. Consequently, not only do *wofara* activities exist in contrast to mandatory *ma'atot* programs, they are also contrasted to mechanized labor. For example, numerous farmers in the area expressed a desire for equitable access to the few tractors available to plough land before planting. Many however, described the disadvantages of relying on tractor service: it was difficult for some to secure timely access in order to plant when desired, and it was often difficult to find the money to pay for tractor service—particularly in the context of escalating fuel prices. Also, many farmers indicated that the scarcity of oxen and labor forced them to rely on tractor services that were less desirable on stony soil than these traditional forms of plowing that "cut the land as desired": "the oxen cuts the land until the land turns to furrows that can contain water. But the land plowed with tractors never draws water. The water floats over the land and flows away." This statement also refers to the practice of *goso*, or replowing the land by oxen after the crops have sprouted in order to create the furrows necessary to hold rainwater after the brief but violent downpours. Ironically, the few tractors available in the area were leased from commercial farmers; state-owned tractors were not available around Hagaz. However, the broader process of mechanization was often described by farmers as linked indelibly to state policies of agrarian development along with the creation of conditions that force farmers to rely on tractor service. Consequently, in some cases, mechanized farming was described to me as a vehicle for deepening a crafted dependency on the state. When I was traveling with a Hagaz resident to his home village late in the summer, we paused our bicycles by a vista of lush fields, some thick with sorghum and pearl millet, others fallowed and filled with tall wild grasses. People farm out of a hope for the future, and out of a sense of tradition, he told me. Then he speculated that grain would soon be threshed by state machines, paid for by the people. "Why not do it traditionally?" I asked. "The people have no choice," he replied. "The youth are all in the military. They don't have the power to do it themselves. It makes them more dependent on the government."

Despite the challenges facing rural producers, Idris was firm about wanting his children to continue farming the land, acknowledging how change is inevitable, but that practices of production should continue. Abdella's response was more ambiguous. He cast his open hand towards the fields around us. "What are they going to farm on this land? Nothing! There is no future here," he insisted. "We have no hope from this land." I asked if he would relocate, but he explained that he would remain here, in this place. There are good things about it: it is better for the animals, the air is fresh, it is close to the brush where they harvest wood. "Maybe things can change," he said finally, "the place will fill with grass. The wild plants will return."

The desire to sustain subsistence livelihoods, and pass them on to future generations, raises a critical point of disjuncture between discourses of food security and what Marc Edelman (2005) describes as "food sovereignty"—the ability of rural producers to have some power over the means of production and markets, rather than simply being provided with adequate access to food commodities. Accordingly, this notion of the power to work the land through continuity of generations casts a valuation for a traditional, lineage-based land tenure system against the state's land nationalization. Also, it suggests how local idioms and practices of work drive social processes in ways that draw on the hope and optimism of community building—things that escape biopolitical mechanisms. Consequently, these farmers contrasted state claims on labor with a focus on autonomy and collective good, however attenuated—suggesting the possibility of rebuilding particular kinds of social ties and reclaiming or rejuvenating land through infusing it with meaningful labor.

Return Refugees and Community Labor in Hagaz

These statements on the atrophy of *wofara* by local farmers paralleled the common claim of people residing in town, particularly among the returnees living in the main part of Hagaz, who contrasted *wofara* among Eritrean communities in Sudan with Hagaz. "Sudan was better," claimed one returnee, "Maybe you work in a small shop, you sell tea, or you work on a farm. Here, there is no work, so no one is working together." Often return refugees, none of whom were allocated farmland under the repatriation scheme, critiqued the inability of people to support themselves through wage labor in light of both inflation and state policies that have closed off spaces for independent business—a condition that inhibits locally initiated community labor.

Although they discussed the lack of salaried work opportunities in the country, return refugees often claimed both community labor and a general "love of work" as a part of their identity as Eritreans in a way that differed from narratives of local farmers. Returnees living in *Measker* (mostly those who returned under the organized repatriation scheme) generally agreed that *wofara* was less common in other areas of town, but that this practice persisted in their neighborhood through a strong sense of cooperation, compassion, and community identity unique to those who shared the experience of exile. A community leader from *Measker*, explained, "This cooperative work is mostly done here [in *Measker*] in this time. For example, in other parts of town you don't see much *wofara*. But these people, they work it cooperatively. These people were refugees in Sudan, so they have passed a miserable life, and now here they came organized, so these are one people." As Sorensen (2000) suggests, *wofara* persisted as a means of crafting community sustainability and cohesion across ethnic groups among Eritreans living in Sudan, even as the particular kinds of work done through *wofara* shifted in relation to local conditions that shaped people's livelihood strategies. In addition to the type of labor performed, practices of *wofara* in Sudan and in resettlement replicated and expanded forms of social reciprocity traditionally rooted in village kinship relations (Tronvoll 1998). This observation points to the suppleness of traditional self-help practices as they are mobilized in the search for continuity and cohesion. In the context of resettlement to Hagaz where returnees were often only able to access farmland through rental or sharecropping relations with local farmers, *wofara* generally shifted from agrarian labor to domestic work (particularly with housing infrastructure). However, in marked difference to these earlier studies, *wofara* as it was practiced in Hagaz became a means of building and maintaining solidarity between particular groups—specifically those who experienced exile and resettlement to new communities in Eritrea. Consequently, *wofara* became an important medium of both social integration and differentiation between community members. As I describe below, returnees mobilized this practice to distinguish themselves as belonging to a particular civic community that valued local labor and self-help, at times in contrast to local landowners.

Other returnees who repatriated outside of official aid channels and so live outside *Measker* — many of them still waiting for housing land — agreed on the unique nature of "the camp," and contrasted it with other Hagaz neighborhoods. "Yes, the people in the refugee camp help each other. They are compassionate," claimed Kedija, a Tigre woman who came originally from the Semhar region in the northeast of the country, where she said *wofara* was also practiced with a spirit of "brotherhood." She fanned the charcoal under a clay *jebena*, or traditional coffee pot, as we sat beneath the overhanging thatched eaves of her hut, sheltering from the breathless afternoon sun. Kedija described people in the Hagaz center as more divided: "If you have a problem, if you are able to take care of yourself, that is OK. Some people say I am from Semhar, so they don't help me. They help the people to whom they belong. If this is so, how can they agree? How does unity come? Can you sympathize with each other?" Kedija also explained that she turned to other returnees in *Measker* for socializing, rather than her immediate neighbors. "While we were in Sudan, we used to have common interests. We, the people who emigrated together, consider ourselves as if we were created from the same womb."

One returnee woman living in *Measker* drew on idioms of work and labor to distinguish the capabilities and identities of return refugees during the construction and modernization of Hagaz. The returnees were distinctly hardworking, she suggested, and it was due to their labor that Hagaz grew from a village of huts into a town of proper cement brick homes. She explained that it was also due to this labor that return refugees crafted a claim to place: "The refugees or the people who came from Sudan are more hardworking than the people who were here. When we came here there were only huts with no brick compounds. But when we arrived here, we developed Hagaz. We came here and lived in places wherever the *Beni Amer* didn't live.[18] The people who came from Sudan want to live in a nice house, in a nice place. They are very hardworking. But the people who were here are not active. If the worst comes, we can build a single house with bricks. We came here thinking it is our country."

Returnees described themselves as skilled and willing to work, but unable to support themselves through wage labor in light of inflation, conscription, and state policies that close off spaces for independent business. A returnee man from *Measker* explained: "It is because there is no work, people are coming for this aid … so if there will be any sort of work, people will not take aid … people came from Sudan with artisan skills. People who are coming to Hagaz bring with them skills they wouldn't have obtained here. Some are computer literate, some are mechanics. In fact, exile is a great teacher. To be a refugee means to learn."

While the farmers described their loss of sovereignty over local land and production through their inability to properly work the soil and practice traditional forms of *wofara*, many return refugees reappropriated the category of *refugee* and linked it to other national identifiers, such as "love of work" and sacrifice for the country. In doing so, they made claims of belonging to a national territory through a shared past of suffering during the conflict, and to the land within Hagaz they have worked to develop. However, the contrast between *wofara* and *ma'atot* remained salient in ways that exposed the meanings and significance of locally initiated *wofara* labor in building and maintaining social relationships through supporting individuals and households in the community. A divorced mother of four, Brikty was raising her children in *Measker* after having returned to Hagaz in 2001. She was quick to assert that the government, particularly in its manifestations as the National Union of Eritrean Women (NUEW) and National Union of Eritrean Youth and Students (NUEYS), does not do *wofara*, which by definition arises from, and is practiced by, the local people.[19] Brikty reaffirmed the "feeling of oneness" of people in *Measker* and the ways this sentiment was reinforced through *wofara*, when she would call her neighbors to help her repair her home in exchange for some food or beer, and they "would work well together." However, she also stressed that the people of *Measker* are unique not only in local solidarity performed through *wofara*, but also in performing citizenship duties such as *ma'atot*: "They are very active in whatever the government says. People from *Measker* go to meetings first, and are not late in doing what the government wants. They want to be first in everything."

Brikty, like many of the returnees I spoke with, demonstrated complex, sometimes contradictory notions of belonging. The sentiment of active citizenship according to the demands of the state and local administration was similar to the claims of belonging expressed through the physical development of Hagaz, the modernization of the community via the returnees' skills, solidarity, and love of work. However returnees may re-knit collectivities and build community, they do so both within and outside of official state mediums—participating in *ma'atot*, but drawing on *wofara* as a distinct and important practice that reaffirms local social relationships through reciprocity and asserts the particular solidarity of refugees that was fostered in the experience of exile and return. In doing so, lines of belonging and identity are redrawn in ways that do not mesh seamlessly with the biopolitical project of nationalizing citizens and territory through labor on the land. On the one hand, a notion of national labor becomes a means to emphasize differences between people in the community—particularly between returnees and stayees. On the other hand, while return refugee families animate the practice of *wofara* in "the camp," their critique of the lack of salaried work collides jarringly with the powerful expectations with which they returned to Eritrea regarding their own agency within the project of national development and their efforts to secure individual and family livelihoods in an independent country. These frustrated expectations were expressed in stories of skills and job experiences that people had anticipated using when they returned to Eritrea, eventually to find little foothold in the tight economy, the difficulty accessing farmland, and government restrictions on employment and trade. So certificates of training and past employment from Sudan remained wrapped carefully in plastic and cardboard, to be displayed with a mixture of pride and regret in interviews with a foreign researcher. A growing number of young people from both returnee and stayee families were looking for places where they might have the power to create the kinds of futures they imagine, risking their lives to escape back over the Sudanese border.

Finally, it is important to detail that while most local farmers lacked money to pay for agrarian labor, some did hire returnees from town as well as rent them land—relationships that draw important connections across these community groups. While *wofara* seemed to be spatially specific, occurring between neighbors who may not share kinship, ethnic, or religious commonalities, agrarian labor relations (both paid and in exchange for access to resources such as oxen or rented land) provided a means for people from *Measker* to connect with local farmers. At the time of research, the effect of these relations was to put land in production that otherwise people may not have had the capacity to farm—a situation that many farmers described as a positive contribution to crop production and to their own household incomes.[20] Consequently, in the context of diminished labor under programs of national conscription and service, the presence of return refugees refracted the ambiguities that farmers expressed over changes in their lives and farming practices: alongside modern changes like labor-saving tractors and mills, came a loss of land, social continuity, and local-level autonomy.

Conclusion

In the attempt to follow Hansen and Stepputat's (2005) call for "embedded and emic understandings of what sovereign power really means," it becomes necessary to look at the local effects of the increased militarization of society on agrarian landscapes and food production in Eritrea. More than this, however, it allows us to see that although farmers and return refugees in Hagaz may perform both mandatory national service and *ma'atot* in a simultaneous disciplining and production of the national citizenry and landscape, these community members are never just that.[21] As the stories from Hagaz suggest, the terms along which communities are "repositories" for national values are subject to negotiation. This takes shape in the gaps between the power of the discourse and projects of national/food security, and the realities of people's inability to maintain food sovereignty in local spaces. It also takes shape in the difficulties that return refugees face in building stable livelihoods and communities, even as they may claim national belonging through communal work.

In this context it is helpful to draw from the idea of selective sovereignties developed by D. Moore (2005). There is something seductive about the notion of plural sovereignties, the autonomy of local, traditional places. According to Moore's formulation, however, selective sovereignties, while they may appear to be about preserving the local, are always about negotiating with the translocal in struggles over material and symbolic relations to place. In Hagaz and villages that have been enveloped by the resettlement area, people craft claims to local places through the constant negotiation of nationalist visions around citizenship and the ability or inability to work and create communities. It is through the farmers' reputed withdrawal from *wofara* that they describe the erosion of village-level sovereignty rooted in kinship networks that provide cultural continuity, and rooted in rights to land that has since been partitioned. And it is through the returnees' active animation of *wofara* practices that they claim rights to belonging in a national territory, though it may not be on the terms that they had imagined.

Cederlof and Sivaramakrishnan (2005: 27) argue, "Notions of community pose obstacles to national imaginations, and yet clearly serve as the building blocks for them. Investment in and ambivalence with regard to notions of community, especially regional or local forms of community, are the stuff of contested nature because the definition of nature has turned on defining the associated community." In the case of Eritrea, "contested nature" involves the cultivation of a fertile sovereign nation, where citizens in rural areas fulfill livelihood duties through communal work on national land. However, these kinds of labor—communal, paid, traditional, and supple—refuse to be collapsed, and expose the ways in which the struggle for continuity and order exceeds the slimmed but commanding visions of the state. Biopolitics is a useful lens to analyze the nation-level discourse and agendas in linking subjects to territory, and exposing how militarized agriculture works on the levels of both social and material production.

However, as the youth erodes from soil and communities, and local moral economies are violated, biopolitics as an analytical framework falls short of accounting for the multiple ways that people seek spaces outside of the state's nationalist vision through which they might reinvest the land and community with meaningful labor.

Notes

1. The UN delineated this twenty-five-kilometer zone running the length of the border within Eritrea, although the villages around which the dispute originated in 1998 were granted to Eritrea.
2. I use pseudonyms to protect the identities of the community members who worked with me in Eritrea.
3. Agamben uses the term "bare life" to denote those that lay outside the boundaries of the political community but are subject to the exercise of authority.
4. A number of studies detail the complex entanglement of local and translocal processes surrounding resource use and land claims. Donald Moore's (2005) ethnography on struggles over land in Zimbabwe offers a compelling analysis of the ways in which local resource struggles are also always translocal in that they engage with regional or global sociopolitical relationships and nodes of power. Furthermore, in the context of South Asia, Cederlof and Sivaramakrishnan (2006) propose the concept of "ecological nationalisms" to explore how nature is not only a fixed locus for resource struggles at the local level, but is also often the ground where contested identities are mapped onto struggles for rights mediated by place attachments, and mired in the politically potent language of intimacy, stewardship, and national belonging.
5. Although I lack space to do this here, there is much to be analyzed regarding the contentious relation of the government of Eritrea with international aid and development organizations. See Hayman 2003. For a study on the tumultuous relationship between the government of Eritrea and international organizations involved with resettling refugees after independence, see McSpadden 2000.
6. Pauline Boerma (1999) provides an insightful study of the ways in which memories of deforestation in Eritrea become linked to colonial appropriation and violence in people's narratives, and fuel the government's focus on reconstructing a fertile past landscape that may not have existed to the extent that people describe in their memories of place. In my dissertation, I draw from this research and use it to develop the concept of national environmental imaginaries in order to describe the roles played by people's memories of place and perceptions of environment in current political and moral critiques of governance.
7. For a recent review of land tenure policy in Eritrea and its critics, see Tesfai 2003.
8. In this paper I will continue to use the Tigrinya term *wofara* for the sake of consistency, although the Tigre term *kewa* was often used by Tigre and Blin community members.
9. The only ones who seemed to escape *ma'atot* in Hagaz were those who could claim infirmity, or the very few families wealthy enough not to need food aid.
10. Stayees include landowners from villagers in the area, along with a large number of migrants from other villages both within and outside the immediate region. Many of these settlers were forced to move to Hagaz by the Ethiopian military in efforts to consolidate the rural population for surveillance and to remove the support base for Eritrean fight-

ers. More recent settlers include villagers from drought-affected areas. During the year I lived in Hagaz, nearly ninety households had relocated to the main residential area of town from surrounding villages in search of water and food aid.

11. Aside from returnees, there are a growing number of Tigrinya residents who have relocated to Hagaz in order to participate in commercial farming ventures or in administrative positions, while others have been involuntarily appointed to Hagaz for national service (positions that include teaching, military, etc.).

12. Spontaneously repatriated refugees had variable access to housing land—some were able to gain it with relative ease through the administration, while others reported to me that they had been waiting for years.

13. This process has correlates in other postcolonial African projects of state making and resettlement. For resettlement schemes informed by high modernism and state developmentalism, see Scott 1998. Also useful is Alexander, McGregor, and Ranger's (2000) rich historical and ethnographic treatment of resettlement and state-society relations in Zimbabwe's Shangani Reserve.

14. The difference between "returnee" and "return refugee" was a subject of fierce debate within the Ministry of Land, Water, and Environment—stalling the publication of at least one policy and research document regarding the negative environmental impacts of refugee resettlement. I explore this debate more fully within my dissertation.

15. Other pilot sites included farmland for return refugees as part of the resettlement package. However, Hagaz was denoted as an urban area, and returnees were expected to either work outside the farming profession, access farmland from ancestral villages nearby, or rent land from local farmers.

16. In this chapter, I focus primarily on rain-fed farmers. Commercial farmers were also profoundly impacted by the militarization of agrarian production—an issue addressed in other sections of my dissertation.

17. Stepputat (2001) adopts the term "mobile livelihoods" from Olwig and Sorensen (2001) in order to describe "the social and spatial practices of people involved in migratory movements," and to "lift … the concept of 'livelihood' out of its locally-bounded context."

18. *Beni Amer:* The name given to the population of related ethnic groups that inhabit the border between Sudanese and the Eritrean lowlands.

19. Officially, NUEYS and NUEW are national organizations that exist independent of the government; however, there are multiple complex relations between them and the state. Most people I talked to in Hagaz linked these groups to the government and the sole ruling party, the People's Front for Democracy and Justice (PFDJ).

20. More empirical studies are needed to determine the ecological impacts of resettlement in lowland areas, including Hagaz. I am currently analyzing GIS data to track changes in land use in the area since independence as one means of assessing shifts in forest and brush resources along with the expansion or contraction of farmland on marginal hillside areas.

21. Simon Turner (2005) analyzes political subjectivities in a Lukole refugee camp in Northern Tanzania, demonstrating that refugees "are constantly working on constructing their own political subjectivities—their own sovereign decisions. In other words, sovereignty is complex and multilayered in the camp as are the means of exercising it."

— *Chapter Four* —

HUMAN RESOURCE DEVELOPMENT AND THE STATE
Higher Education in Postrevolutionary Eritrea

Tanja R. Müller

Introduction

Education policy commonly has objectives beyond the area of education, comprising a combination of political, social, economic, and pedagogic concerns (Psacharopoulos 1993; Green 1997). Within revolutionary societies such as Eritrea, education is regarded as an important instrument to promote social change. The rationale behind education as a tool for societal transformation is twofold: the formation of conscious citizens motivated by collective goals, coupled with the transmission of skills necessary to overcome underdevelopment and achieve self-sustaining growth (Arnove 1994; Müller 2004; Pham Minh Hac 1998).

One focus of formal education systems in revolutionary settings thus centers on creating a more just social order (Collins 1987; Müller 2005). At the same time, and in line with developments in other developing and transitional countries, education policy centers on the fulfillment of human resource needs, often stipulated by a national development plan (Buchert 1998). The prototypical example for the success of a strategy to achieve the latter is Singapore (Castells 1992), regarded as a model by the Eritrean leadership (Müller 1998). Other examples include South Korea and Taiwan (Hoogvelt 1997), and on the African continent with varying degrees of success Mauritius, Botswana, Tanzania, and Uganda, among others (Desta Asayehgn 1979; Mkandawire 2001; Kwesiga 2002). Most of the latter can, like Eritrea, be to varying degrees described as developmental states (Mbabazi and Taylor 2005; Mkandawire 2001).[1] Castells points out the often-overlooked similarities between revolutionary states and developmental states: in both cases, the state "substitutes itself for society in the definition of societal goals" (Castells 1992: 57). He then argues that in cases where the societal project remains confined to a transformation of the economic order, a developmental state is the outcome, whereas if a fundamental transformation of the social order is also envisaged, one can speak of a revolutionary state.

This distinction is here regarded as rather artificial, as the legitimacy of any developmental state arises from the commitment of its population to the transformation of their social, political, or economic order, a societal project that is not short of being revolutionary. Thus, for a developmental state not simply to be a dictatorship of development requires a political leadership quite comparable to the leadership of revolutionary mass movements, able to provide an ideological framework for state policies that might otherwise demand unpalatable sacrifices. And while, as Hall (1996) rightly points out, consent to the project of the state or the governing elite is not maintained only through ideology, dominant ideas become a "material force" and play an important part in carrying that project into the future.[2]

In the context of this chapter, a developmental state is thus defined as having two components: one ideological and one structural. At the structural level, it "establishes as its principle of legitimacy its ability to promote and sustain development" (Castells 1992: 56). At the ideological level, the governing elite "must be able to establish an 'ideological hegemony', so that its developmental project becomes, in a Gramscian sense a 'hegemonic' project to which key actors in the nation adhere *voluntarily*" (Mkandawire 2001: 290, emphasis added).

The focus here is on the ideological component of the Eritrean developmental project. When looking at postindependence Eritrea, one finds a state whose legitimacy is firmly based on the past and on a ruling elite. The latter, in line with liberation movements in other parts of the globe, employs selective narratives and invents new sets of traditions in order to establish not only an exclusive postindependence legitimacy but equally "the sole authority of one particular agency of social forces" (Melber 2003: xiv–xv; see also Müller 2006b). In this case the authority is the former liberation movement, the Eritrean People's Liberation Front (EPLF), renamed the People's Front for Democracy and Justice (PFDJ).

In addition, strong notions of inclusion or exclusion have been developed as key factors in shaping national as well as personal identities. What has been called "personal nationalism" (McCrone 1998: 40), understood as an active process of affirmation of one's national identity, is of prime importance in a nationalist revolutionary culture like Eritrea's.

This affirmation is often based on militaristic rituals, as more generally within the hegemonic Eritrean narrative the nation and the state appear as one. The material form of this oneness is the mass-conscripted national army. It is here where the synthesis between the citizen and the state is experienced concretely and any distinction between state and civil society disappears. Most visible in this agenda is the mobilization of youth within the nationwide national service campaign that was introduced in 1995. The campaign then consisted of six months of military training plus one year of civilian reconstruction activities, and enjoyed great popularity at the time. And while the ideological underpinnings stressed predominately the service aspects, the military element always remained a crucial part.[3]

Therefore, those who define themselves outside the military collective are ultimately regarded as betraying the nation (see for example Assefaw Bariagaber 2006b). It should not be forgotten, as Buck-Morss argues, that the nation-state and revolutionary classes can trace their origin to the same historical event: the French Revolution, which invented on the one hand the utopian discourse of equality and of the "people" as sovereign, but also produced arguably the two most catastrophic forms of modern political life: revolutionary terror and mass-conscripted, nationalist war (Buck-Morss 2000; see also Arendt 1990). In a country like Eritrea, where 44 percent of the population is below fifteen years of age, those contradictions are bound to come into particularly sharp focus. The majority of the current young generation has no experience of the armed struggle that lies at the foundation of the country's narrative. But they grew up in what can be described as "a moral and political zone of indistinction" where the political is thoroughly embedded into everyday life practices (see Agamben 1998; Müller 2008). At the same time, Eritrea has since 1991 moved from being closed off in a remote corner in the Horn of Africa to being exposed to the wider world and the opportunities this global environment has to offer. This global exposure, together with the disappearance of the (liberation) war that formed part of the thread which held the revolutionary project together, is bound to weaken the ideological hegemony of the political leadership, and questions about the personal versus the communal are bound to be formulated in a new light (see Bernal 2006; Müller 2005).

How, then, does this young generation relate to the hegemonic narrative of the ruling elite, and how is the balancing act of asserting personal and national identities played out in practice among them? To discuss those issues in more detail, the focus here is on young people in higher education, those who are groomed to one day become the new elite and thus carry the torch of the Eritrean revolution into the future. This is also a crucial stage in the process of social reproduction in terms of the imposition of the dominant culture as legitimate (Bourdieu and Passeron 1997). At the same time, whether envisaged as such or not, education opens up avenues for new forms of agency on an individual level and thus acts as what Bourdieu calls a "strategy-generating institution" for personal liberation. The following draws on data collected between 1998 and 2006 among students at Asmara University and the College at Mai Nefhi.[4] Of particular concern is how the state project as applied to education policies and human resource development initially succeeded at both reinforcing personal nationalism and opening up spaces for personal liberation, but of late has become a tool of oppression. These dynamics, if they are to continue, will not only jeopardize the state's developmental agenda but may lead to the Eritrean polity in its present form becoming unviable.

Education and Human Resource Development until 2001

Similar to other settings where education plays a particularly important role in achieving wider objectives of the state, two factors characterize human resource development policies in Eritrea: a high degree of centralized educational planning accompanied by an integrated approach towards economic development and human capital formation, and considerable emphasis on the social and moral dimension of education.

The education system that emerged in postindependent Eritrea draws heavily on the nationalist "Revolution School" set up in the 1970s by the EPLF in the first liberated areas of the country. At the same time one can find many features that resemble the administration of education under the previous Ethiopian regime. This is not the place to discuss in any detail the exact workings and structures of that system, as the focus here is mainly on tertiary higher education (Müller 2006a, 2006b).

Concerning the latter, the role of higher education within the national human resource development strategy broadly follows the pattern advocated by Thompson and Fogel (1976) for educational development in developing countries, in which higher education is strongly embedded in the national community as a whole instead of being an elitist institution removed from the realities of the majority of the population. The role of the university herein is that of a "developmental university" (Coleman 1994: 334), an institution first and foremost concerned with the "'solution' of the concrete problems of societal development" (Coleman 1994: 334). Such a university sets out to "ensure that the development plans of the university are integrated with or linked to national development plans" (Coleman 1994: 343). This is exactly how Dr. Wolde-Ab Yisak, former president of the University of Asmara (UoA), used to cite the mission of the university: "We [the university] should play a leading role in the process of nation-building and social transformation" (Dr. Wolde-Ab Yisak, interview 13 June 2001).

Within the centralized human resource development planning in Eritrea, this had certain implications for the workings of the university. After having passed the matriculation exam, subjects of study were allocated, and students' personal priorities were given only cursory concern in this process. Dr. Wolde-Ab Yisak, together with all the ministries, drew up a list in which areas human resources were most urgently needed. Accordingly, it was then decided how many students should be admitted to which departments.[5] For postgraduate studies, the university drew up staff development plans and facilitated sending students abroad for education at the master's or PhD level. In that way it was expected that the country's human resources would be used in the most efficient way. In addition, summer work programs and compulsory university service before graduation, both intended to foster social solidarity, have always been part of the process of higher education.

The success of such a strategy depended largely on a shared vision between the goals of the official policy side, embodied by the government and the university administration on the one hand, and the people, the individual students, on the other. Without such a shared vision, the problem of "brain drain" plaguing many African countries, whose university graduates leave for the industrialized world where salaries are considerably higher, is difficult to avoid.

The Eritrean government claims as one of its major assets that "the culture of governance in Eritrea is the close relationship between the people and the leadership" (Ministry of Education 1999: 3), implying a popular propensity to follow government policy without resistance. And indeed, when looking concretely at the lives of university students in 2001, a majority appeared to be willing to use their educational qualifications not only for individual fulfillment but at least partly to comply with the government's plan for them. The following will discuss possible contradictions that might emerge in the lives of individuals using narrative data collected in multiple in-depth interviews among a group of twenty-nine women students during the academic year 2000–2001.[6]

Human Resource Development versus Personal Aspirations

In the tearoom of the University of Asmara in 2000, one topic surfaced regularly in students' conversations: how to avoid becoming a teacher. Often, when students were denied their first choice of subject, they were put into the Secondary School Teachers (SST) department. Equally, many students who studied applied sciences were sent for teaching. The latter was due to the university requiring that most degree programs include four years of academic study and one subsequent year of national service, where students are allocated to a relevant ministry and work for a symbolic salary. Only after students have completed this service year will they graduate.

Students resisted becoming teachers in all sorts of ways. For example, that is why Sultan chose plant science: "When I joined the university, I really wanted to study medicine, but in freshman year my marks were low," she explained. She could have gone for biology and continued in the medical field from there, "but at the college of science they will make you become a teacher." She hated the idea of teaching, so she chose plant science (a subject for which her grade point average (GPA) was enough) "and also some medicine is made of plants, so there is some connection" (Sultan, interview 11 October 2000). In general, when students knew their freshman GPA was too low to join their department of choice, they compromised their aspirations in order to resist becoming teachers.[7]

This overregulation of educational opportunities not only implies a lack of personal choices, but equally a lack of decision-making power over one's future, as Hannah explained:

> We don't have private life. ... Whenever you decide something there are a lot of things you have to consider. ... Even if I get a scholarship ... my going out is not sure. ... Now I can decide minor things, but for the future ... our future is trapped, limited. ... You have to get permission from the government to do whatever you want. ... I mean, sometimes you get scholarship from abroad and the government does not send you there, it is frustrating, but it does not discourage me, I have to try and see what happens. ... I'm hoping things will get better (Hannah, interview 6 November 2000).

This is the other side of a policy that centers strictly on perceived human resource needs of the country. The university in general does not encourage people to get their own scholarships, but wants them to be sent through university channels.

The attitude expressed by Hannah, in which certain drawbacks in one's individual life are accepted as part of what being Eritrean means—an attitude which has been described as an outcome of the EPLF's successful endeavor in forging an Eritrean nation (Ottaway 1999; Schamanek 1998)—surfaces in different ways in the lives of different people.

The story of Mehret, who grew up with the EPLF in the Revolution School and was thus socialized within its culture, demonstrates particularly well the trade-offs potentially faced by young Eritreans at the University of Asmara and how individuals grow to accept them.

Mehret — Child of the Revolution

Mehret was one year old when her parents decided to join the liberation struggle. Her mother took her to the liberated areas, where she grew up first in a children's home and later in the Revolution School. She finished schooling after grade seven and was assigned to teach children in grades one and two. It was only after liberation that Mehret could continue her education while still working as a teacher. She completed secondary schooling successfully in 1995, determined to join the university. After a year of pleading her release from teaching duties with the Ministry of Education — accepting the legitimacy of the ministry's claim on her service — she was finally allowed to join the UoA.

That in itself did not end all the frustrations for Mehret, but it did change her attitude on how to deal with them:

> When I completed my freshman studies I wished to join geology, and I had the grades to join, but I was told I must join this educational faculty. I was not happy. ... At that time, the students in the faculty of education had a meeting with Dr. Wolde-Ab, there were many who didn't like this faculty and they were asking him questions. ... In one of his speeches he said, 'You know you are intending to study something and you are finding obstacles, at this time what we are doing is we are preparing for the needs of the country, not for the needs of you, so if you are ... brilliant enough and if you are strong, you don't become successful through finding all your needs but it's how do you become successful even if there are obstacles, that's what makes you strong people' ... and that influenced me, I can say. ... Most of the time I was rigid: I am going to do this, this, and this; if not, I become frustrated, but from then onward I want to say 'I'm going to do my best and work as hard as I can in the area which I am exposed to, then I am going to try as successful as I can to continue with the chances I can get'. ... so that's the way which I prefer to go (Mehret, interview 13 October 2000).

Mehret, while accepting the institutional plan for her life, developed an approach to overcome her own powerlessness and used it to find individual fulfillment. This approach still guided her life in later years. Mehret had for a long time dreamed of continuing her studies in biology, preferably genetics. But while preparing to go abroad for further study, she explained why she thought differently about it later:

> I have to complete my master's, and hopefully also PhD some day ... but I want to come back and live and work here in my country, do something useful, so there is no point for me going to study genetics, as I can do my research abroad, that's fine, but when I am back here, there are no facilities for this kind of research, I can only read things from books and search the internet, that is a bit pointless and boring. ... So I had to change my focus, I will have to do something where I can carry out research activities here, so I will try to do my

master's in something related to educational biology or early childhood development, as this is a problem in Eritrea (Mehret, interview 26 May 2001).

How Mehret and her fellow students come to accept the obstacles put into their way seems on the face of it to vindicate the EPLF's claim about the "closeness between the leadership and the people"; or observations like Ottaway's that within the Eritrean population, despite their frustrations people are willing to go along with much interference into their personal lives as long as it helps the overall development of the country (Ottaway 1999). But even at the time this did not mean that the student generation would largely follow the script written by the political leadership for their future lives, as the following section will reveal.

"I want a good job": Ambitions for an Uncertain Future

When asked about the long-term future, the women in this study all came up with very personal visions of what they were trying to achieve. Three issues featured prominently in these visions: the well-being of one's (extended) family; the continuation of further studies or alternatively starting a business; and, eventually, marriage and having a family of one's own.

A majority of participants mentioned as one of their first priorities after graduation to help their families financially. Sarah put it like this: "When I finish my BA degree, I will work for at least two years and help my parents. ... After that, maybe I will decide for myself" (Sarah, interview 18 October 2000). The same is true for Esther: "I always feel so [responsible for my family], even it forced me to have good results in my [studies] ... because that is the only way to join a good job then help my parents, after that I then go to my own life" (Esther, interview 08 November 2000).

Together with supporting one's family financially, being able to continue their education or start their own business was the prime ambition for the majority of participants. Simret was a law graduate. Her father was a successful consultant in this field, and she wanted to follow in his footsteps: "I don't want anything, also not marriage, to interfere into my career life. ... I like to work and besides, I do not want to be dependent on anyone, I like to be dependent on myself only" (Simret, interview 04 December 2000). Samira, a graduate in accounting and management, was equally determined to have her own business. She said, "I do not mind doing [university] service for free for one or two years, I feel I want to give my country something," indicating her acceptance of the obligation to contribute to the communal good. But after that, "I want to continue with my business plans, probably start some import-export business" (Samira, interview 31 October 2000). This strong vision of an individual professional career was otherwise rare to find. The majority of women had a rather vague notion of the "good job" they wish to have in the future, which is regarded very much as being related to the possibility of continuing their education.

Rahel described the need to continue one's education: "Everyone is getting the BA degree … so you have to be different, that's master's degree or PhD degree" (Rahel, interview 24 October 2000). Similar concerns are voiced by Esther, who says, "because nowadays, everybody is trying to have MA, then I will be the lower one … and therefore, I have to have MA as well" (Esther, interview 08 November 2000). Even with all the restrictions that may lie ahead, all women said they only wanted to go abroad for education but not to live there, "especially when you are educated, you have a very good life here" (Hannah, interview 06 November 2000).

In that sense, the Eritrean human resource development strategy in 2000 seemed to have been successful in building up human capital in Eritrea. Even though many of the students interviewed might not work in the particular field in which they were educated in the future, creating certain areas of shortages in human capital for some time to come, and despite their very individualist, material, careerist, and conventional ambitions for the future, the participants were united by the fact that they saw their future connected to their country. They accepted their social obligation to serve the state and wider community.

Very few participants took their individual career ambitions or advancement as far as openly considering leaving for the diaspora. In contrast, many felt they wanted to contribute something to the development of Eritrea, as the examples of Almaz and Rahel show. Almaz stated, "I want to return to Eritrea. … There are no [people in my field] in Eritrea, I mean what is the benefit of this university training students and no one is returning back … so I want to really work here in Eritrea" (Almaz, interview 22 November 2000). In a similar spirit, Rahel wanted to return after having completed her postgraduate education abroad:

> I will come back. … Other than bringing Indian teachers to this university, you can do it yourself, and if you get educated and you came here you … are getting some kind of growth and development in your life, also if you came here you help your country to develop … both of you [you and your country] are getting advantage (Rahel, interview 24 October 2000).

Among those interviewed in 2000, only two felt they would eventually like to leave Eritrea: Azieb and Rihab. Whereas Azieb cited notions of personal freedom from cultural restrictions as her motivation to leave, freedom for Rihab was strongly related to the political:

> I don't know if our government is going to give us a chance to participate in actual political activities. … They have to realize … they can't rule the country

forever, there must be elections, but I don't know, is it going to happen? ... I don't want to live here for my kids in the future, I want them to grow up more easy. ... Maybe Eritrea is going to be good, it's a matter of time. ... Maybe if some change, or a miracle happens to Eritrea I would like to stay here (Rihab, interview 26 April 2001).

This last statement points to the fact that while in terms of human capital development the centralized development strategy of the Eritrean government in the area of formal education might be regarded as successful, the implications might be different for social solidarity within Eritrean society. Personal freedom has been the main issue in these minority statements. Resistance to restrictions of that freedom, moreover, were bound to become more important in the future, as the Eritrean government failed to offer its people the opportunities they desired. The ultimate resistance for a university student to the government's plan and with it a rejection of nationalist social solidarity is shown by leaving the country and depriving it of the benefits the investment in a student's education should have brought. The results of a survey carried out among an equal number of male and female students in spring 2001 revealed a propensity towards precisely this dynamic.

Among the respondents of the 2001 survey, 80 out of a total of 357 aspired to work and live abroad. While this is still a relatively low number, it was cause for concern. Dr. Wolde-Ab Yisak, the university president, felt at the time that while on the one hand graduates leaving the country had not yet been a problem, it might soon become one: "I think before the conflict with the Ethiopians [referring to the 1998–2000 Eritreo-Ethiopian border war], the return rate was more than 85 percent. ... Now after the

Table 4.1 | Survey Respondents by Long-Term Plans and Sex (Multiple Responses Possible)

In "ten years time" I want to:	No. of students		
	Female	Male	Total
Work in academia	17	45	62
Work for the government	29	35	64
Work in the private sector	85	96	181
Work abroad	34	46	80
Stay at home and have a family of my own	3	11	14
Have a family and continue my career	80	55	135
Missing	1	1	n/a

Source: Survey Data, SPSS Spreadsheet

conflict [started], lots of people have tried to find excuses, so our return rate has been lower than fifty [percent]" (Dr. Wolde-Ab Yisak, interview 13 June 2001).[8]

When the survey was conducted, only one student answered an open question at the end by writing: "I don't care about Eritrea, but I can only dream about myself, because the condition of Eritrea does not allow my dreams; I have a vision, we will be winners at last and the constitution of Eritrea will permit participation and citizenship ... and the dictatorial government of Eritrea is not to stay for ever; death for EPLF and PFDJ." Although probably few students would formulate their opinion in such harsh words, many are frustrated and alienated—a process that started in the summer of 2001, when the potentially oppressive features of Eritrea as a "hard" state came into the open.[9]

The Trip to "the Coastal Areas"

I left Eritrea on the day after the university graduation ceremony in July 2001 and returned in November of the same year. On the campus of the University of Asmara, one could sense a subtle change in the atmosphere among students. What had happened during the summer?[10]

Not many students were willing to talk apart from one sentence that seemingly summed it all up: "I have been to the coastal areas." It referred to an event that proved to be a turning point. Students were quite suddenly required to do an additional round of national service during the summer months, justified by the still-difficult situation after the end of the fighting phase in the 1998–2000 Eritreo-Ethiopian war.

Many of their families experienced financial hardship as a result of the latest war and had banked on their sons and daughters earning some money during the summer months. Thus, very few students appeared on the announced day to board the buses that would take them to their station of duty. In a separate development, the leader of a students' union, which had been formed independently from the official, government-sanctioned body that dealt with youth-issues, was arrested and accused of initiating unrest.

All students were then requested to gather at the national stadium and threatened with "grave consequences" should they fail to do so. Others were rounded up in their dormitories. The whole batch was then driven to Wi'a in the Danakil desert, an inhospitable place at the best of times and therefore unbearable in the middle of the summer heat. After two students died from heat-related conditions, the remaining students were transferred to Ghela'elo, a place of similar climatic conditions but on the coast and with better facilities. During their stay, students were told that they were there to make their contribution to the nation and that they had to help in road construction activities. While some students did indeed help to collect stones for road building, it was clear to everybody that this trip was the punishment for not obeying the first order to report for service.

The incident ended with a measure that brings the oppressive dimension of the Eritrean polity into clear focus: to be allowed to return, all students had to sign a letter in which they apologized for their behavior and stated that they had been arrogant and failed to serve their people willingly. In sharp contrast to the usual workings of Eritrean policy measures that target the collectivity of the nation or particular groups like youth, here the individual was singled out. Each student had to sign individually and it was made clear that those who did not comply would not be allowed to return to Asmara in the foreseeable future. Quite literally, the choice was between giving in to the state's agenda or risking one's well-being by remaining indefinitely in a geographical location that puts one's health at risk.

Back in Asmara and with the beginning of the new academic year, things appeared normal on the surface. But for those who had been sent to "the coastal areas" this was a rupture that would not be forgotten easily. The father of one of the students summed up a more general feeling: "How can you send young people, who are only exposed to the highland climate, down there at a time when even many people who normally live there leave because of the heat?" he demanded. But most of all, many students were just deeply hurt. Just over a year before, when the war with Ethiopia had resulted in a military confrontation that saw large parts of Eritrea overrun by Ethiopian troops, those same students had refused to continue their studies and demanded to be sent to help defend their country at the frontline. And now they were regarded as dissidents at best and traitors to the nation at worst.

This is not to suggest that the government meant to cause serious bodily harm, and the unfortunate death of two students was more an accident than anything else. Equally, there was no systematic machinery of oppression in place. To the contrary, the soldiers whose task it was to guard and cater for the students reportedly felt sorry for their plight and treated them well. But nobody questioned the rationale behind the official interpretation that what was happening was a just punishment for an action of betrayal.

Tellingly, only very few of their lecturers at university raised their voices in support of the students. One lecturer who did so passed away shortly afterward. Even though his death was due to natural causes, many students believed that "they," as the political leadership suddenly became referred to almost everywhere, killed him because he spoke on the students' behalf.

Looking at the wider picture, the episode narrated above might seem of no great importance. But it exemplifies the dynamics that unfold once a hegemonic project loses its attraction and developmental politics turn pernicious in order to retain control. The events in the coastal areas must also be put into the wider context of continuing war and unrest.

Until 1998, when the border war with Ethiopia erupted—the fighting phase of which ended with a number of international agreements in 2000— people gave the government the benefit of the doubt. The predominant sentiment was expressed in sentences such as: "They have been fighting for thirty years, give them a chance to run the country now." The PFDJ-led government thus commanded significant social and political capital, and in spite of their frustrations, most of Eritrea's citizens were prepared to go along with interferences into their lives as long as it helped the overall development of the country (Hirt 2000; Ottaway 1999).

The war and its conduct, however, have proved to be transformative events, a "rupture" for the postindependence polity. Not only could the political leadership at times not guarantee the state's territorial integrity, but equally, many of the gains made in terms of development were put into jeopardy. At the same time a lively debate emerged, even within the ruling party, about the government's hegemony and national configuration. This was not to last, however, and was followed swiftly by a government crackdown. The private press was closed, journalists were arrested, and a group of eleven members of the Central Committee of the party, all EPLF veterans, were put into incommunicado detention where they remain to this day. The oppressive features of Eritrea as a "hard" state were there for all to see (Assefaw Bariagaber 2006b; Müller 2006b).

In line with the general observation that education is one of the essential terrains of social reproduction, it was here that many of the consequences were felt most severely. To quell future dissent before it started, the government imposed structural changes within the education system aimed at enforcing loyalty. Mechanisms to ensure the latter have been modeled on the military structures that characterized the liberation movement prior to Eritrean independence. At the same time, however, the hidden dimension of any oppressive project had begun to emerge: the generative challenge from within.[11]

(Further) Militarization of Formal Education

The events during the summer of 2001 proved to be a catalyst for the militarization of formal education, especially at its higher levels. Starting with the academic year 2002–2003, all students in the last grade of secondary schooling, newly introduced as grade twelve, were required to transfer to Sawa, a remote location in the western lowlands of the country, which doubles as the military training camp for national service. Countrywide matriculation exams are also held in Sawa. Those who pass those exams are no longer transferred to Asmara University, but are sent to a newly built campus in Mai Nefhi to complete their freshman year. The Eritrean Institute of Technology at Mai Nefhi, as it is officially known, is located only a few kilometers south of Asmara. But built on an open field site, it feels isolated and remote. Run jointly by an academic vice director and an army colonel, Mai Nefhi in many ways resembles more a military camp than a place of higher learning. Students, at least in theory, need permission to leave the campus, and in private conversations it is often referred to as "the camp."

In line with the rationale behind those changes, at the time of writing the University of Asmara, at least on paper an institution where academic freedom was respected, was being dissolved. Its faculties were in the process of being relocated to different locations all over the country. The official justification for those measures was a move towards greater decentralization of higher education. In practice, the different faculties are to be governed by different branches of the respective ministries in the future and are thus exposed to direct political control and interference.

Indeed, with hindsight the dissolution of the University of Asmara follows a long-term plan devised even before the events in the summer of 2001, but those events have considerably speeded up its implementation (see also Müller 2008). It was in the following year that no students were sent to the university for their freshman studies for the first time. From then onwards, slowly but steadily the foundations were laid to tighten the screw around the university and dissolve it. This process went hand in hand with ever more power being concentrated in the Office of the President, for whom the university was never an institution that merited much attention, but rather a place where youth were potentially being alienated from core nationalist and political values (see Reid 2005). Following this logic, national service requirements for university students have been tightened in different ways from 2002 onwards. Different batches of students were called to Sawa for additional military training instead of being sent to do their year of expertise-related service, as part of a general government drive to reinforce discipline and patriotic commitment among the student community. Even when sent to work in their professions, service rarely ended after one year as originally stipulated, but often continued indefinitely.

In this overall environment of state control, the only options for resistance seem twofold: either inward migration or, as more and more young people admit to in private conversations, "to get out," to leave the country for a life in the diaspora.

The latter has been made almost impossible for many people of national service age in general and students in particular, who are commonly denied exit visas to leave the country. But as in any oppressive environment, counterdynamics do emerge. On the one hand, many youth find their "way out," be it via Sudan or even Ethiopia, or for women by marrying a foreign national, or in asking for asylum abroad in the course of an official visit. But also those who stay have found ways to create a niche for themselves. Students who in the past would have been sent abroad for further studies now work for the few international nongovernmental organizations still operating in the country. They earn by local standards a high salary, even though they hardly ever work in any position that carries responsibility in line with their education. Not all of those have fulfilled their service requirements and are thus living under threat of being picked up by the military police. But then, many have also developed strategies of their own to evade being caught (Reid 2005; author's observations 2006).

Similar dynamics were observed in 2006 among the students at Mai Nefhi.[12] In informal talks with different groups of students it became clear that the majority rejected "being kept here, of course it would be better to be in Asmara", but developed their own way of dealing with it. Some went home to Asmara every weekend, which is forbidden officially, but can still be arranged. They were well equipped with mobile phones and other gadgets that allow them to keep in touch with their peers and make arrangements to meet their friends. When asked about their future aspirations, the common answer was to do as well as they could in their education and then get "a job in the private sector and have a good life." The statement of one student sums up a general feeling: "Of course we would like to have a choice, what we study, where, but we don't have a choice, we are forced to study here. ... It should not be like this, but we will make the best of it for our future when we are out of here".[13]

Implicit in this statement, and in many other private conversations the author held in Eritrea during her most recent visit in 2006, is a turn towards private and individual fulfillment. This undermines one of the very foundations of Eritrea as a developmental state, the propensity towards social solidarity.

Concluding Remarks

On the surface, one could make the case that the consolidation process of Eritrea as a developmental state has been a success. It has been argued that one fundamental task of such consolidation is control over population movements (Herbst 1990). If judged by these criteria, the control by the Eritrean government over the movements of its citizens is indeed remarkable, in terms of control over emigration, the "exit-option," as well as in terms of internal population movements. This control extends in different ways to the Eritrean diaspora, who for example by and large pay a two percent tax of their income to the Eritrean state. Most remarkable, however, is that this control has not much weakened despite increasing economic hardship, which has exposed the failure of the "promise of development" that commonly serves to legitimize any postrevolutionary leadership (Fouad Makki 1996).

But, looking into the future, questions need to be raised about the viability of the Eritrean developmental project. The gulf between those running the Eritrean polity, mostly members of the generation of ex-fighters, and the ambitions of younger population groups, especially those with some degree of higher education, seem to the observer to widen by the day (see also Reid 2005). The modern ambitions that have been created by the Eritrean revolution can, in today's globalized world, not be suppressed indefinitely by sending people to Sawa or denying them exit visas. Sawa used to be the place where the torch of the armed struggle and the defense of the country's sovereignty were passed on militarily and ideologically to a next generation willing to carry that torch. In the Eritrea of today, Sawa first and foremost symbolizes state control over the lives of its youth, a control that is increasingly being rejected and evaded. The Eritrean political elite has been described as frozen by its own image of the past, the key parameters of which are sacrifice, struggle, and hardship (Reid 2005). An informant put it to the author like this in 2002: "Sacrifice, that is what those ex-fighters always stress, not the positive, that we reached our freedom, or future goals, what determines their mindset is sacrifice."[14]

Indeed, the primary objective of the present leadership seems to be to mold the next generation in its own image through hardship and sacrifice. That goes as far as the belief that the 1998–2000 war with Ethiopia was not so much a disaster that should and could have been avoided, but a more superior way to teach the coming generation the ethos of the armed struggle than any school curriculum. The Eritrean case thus serves as another example for the forceful repetition of past structures of domination inherent in every revolution (Erdheim 1991).

But the Eritrean political entity, in spite of having shown its oppressive features of late, depends on the propensity of its members to willingly serve the common good to succeed. Eritrea's most valuable asset after liberation has been the degree of social solidarity within the nation that has led to impressive achievements in terms of human development in general and education and human resource development in particular. This developmental agenda is bound to fail in the future as the measures taken in the course of the militarization of formal education not only damage national development, but perhaps more crucially erode the country's human resource development strategy.

It is simply not sustainable in the long term that the country's brightest graduates, instead of helping build capacity within the country, work in clerical positions for international nongovernmental organizations or spend their time devising "exit" strategies in terms of how to best leave the country. As has been pointed out elsewhere, good human resource development creates loyalty and commitment. In Eritrea, not only are civil servant salaries much lower than those in the private sector, but, following its agenda of absolute control over society, the majority of senior positions are held by individuals who more often than not lack professional expertise but are loyal to the political project of the government (Mussie Tessema and Soeters 2006).

While until quite recently many youth have been willing to work for the state for a comparatively low salary and would have been proud to do so, it now seems that the official bureaucracy will become even less able to grasp the opportunities that would connect Eritrea with the global economy. But frustration cannot only be felt on the part of young people. As a very committed member of the teaching staff at the University of Asmara said in a private conversation: "Why are we teaching here if there is no perspective for the future?"[15]

Ultimately, it could be a renewed war with Ethiopia that draws the population to rally behind the national project again, but such an outcome would be disastrous.

For the moment, the future of the Eritrean developmental project that started out so brightly looks bleak. As long as the only avenues for living resistance are inward migration or the increasingly difficult route into exile, the political leadership will lose more and more of its legitimacy, leading in turn to more oppressive politics. The Eritrean polity is at present experiencing a lesson history should have taught its leaders not least during the time of the Ethiopian occupation (see Rokkan 1975): you cannot reduce both the "exit" option and the option to "voice" opposition without endangering the balance of the whole political system.

Notes

1. While it has been argued that Eritrea lacked the resources to function in real terms as a developmental state, it had the aspirations to do so. And indeed, Eritrea did achieve a considerable amount of success in terms of "modernizing development." For further discussion see Bernal 2004; Fengler 2001; Luckham 2002.
2. For different conceptualizations of the developmental state, ranging from entities primarily concerned with national economic enhancement to facilitators of state-market synergies, see for example Pempel 1999; Wade 1990.
3. According to Minister of Defense General Sibhat Efrem speaking in various public appearances, National Service "means nurturing youths to be active and morally sound citizens." The National Service Proclamation came into force in 1994 and stipulates that all citizens and permanent residents of the State of Eritrea between the age of eighteen and forty are required to perform six months of military training and one year in other (reconstruction) activities. Usually, students are required to go to Sawa, the training camp, after they have sat for the matriculation exam or quit schooling. The first batch of national service recruits in July 1994 comprised 10,000 youth mainly from Asmara; accounts of their service were widely broadcast on radio and TV and made many young people register for the second batch. Eventually, 30,000 youth had registered, while Sawa could only accommodate a maximum number of 20,000 at any one time (see also Müller 2005).
4. The author has visited Eritrea on a regular basis since 1996. The academic year 2000–2001 she spent at the University of Asmara and during that time conducted in-depth interviews and a wider survey. She has returned for shorter research visits from November 2001 to January 2002, in December 2003, in May 2004, and in October/November 2006.
5. At the time UoA offered bachelor's degrees in the following areas: Agriculture and Aquatic Sciences, Arts and Social Sciences, Business and Economics, Science, Health Science, and Education.
6. The data presented here was collected as part of a wider research project on Eritrean elite women published in Müller (2005). All names were changed for reasons of confidentiality.
7. The latter was deeply unpopular for a combination of reasons, the most important being low salaries and continued direct interference by the government into their future professional lives. As shall be seen in more detail later, the vast majority of university graduates at the time aspired to work in the private sector.
8. It should be noted that Dr. Wolde-Ab has since left the country as a consequence of his own difficulties in working with the political leadership.
9. On state "hardness" see Forrest (1988).
10. The following account is based on field notes from conversations and observations from November 2001 to January 2002.
11. It should be pointed out here that as early as 1991 the first cautious attempts were made by different social actors to redefine the space for individual action. The reaction of the political leadership in all those cases followed a similar pattern: different degrees of repression, at times combined with measures to accommodate those demands that were deemed justified (for a more detailed discussion see Müller 2008). But it took the 1998–2000 war with Ethiopia to not only produce intensive political debate and open dissent within the higher echelons of the PFDJ, but to make an increasing number of ordinary citizens question the hegemonic project more generally.
12. The following is based on informal conversations with students in Mai Nefhi in October 2006.

13. The author had planned to readminister parts of the questionnaire on future aspirations she used in 2001 to the current students at Mai Nefhi in 2006. She could not obtain permission to do so, as doing any kind of academic research in Eritrea was very difficult at the time of writing. Having said that, however, in contrast to experiences during previous visits in 2004 and 2005, when many people were afraid to talk openly, people now voiced their criticism of government policy openly and many did not care whether that might have consequences for their future. The level of frustration was simply too great.
14. Male professional, thirty-eight years of age, working in the education sector, field notes January 2002.
15. Interview January 2002.

— *Chapter Five* —

AVOIDING WASTAGE BY MAKING SOLDIERS
Technologies of the State and the Imagination
of the Educated Nation

℮ ᷄

Jennifer Riggan

Introduction

One morning in late October 2003, I sat outside the staff room at the Senior Secondary School in Assab with Teacher Samson, one of the school's
senior teachers. As we talked, we watched several students flitting in and
out of their classroom, and several leaning through the open windows and
heckling the students and teacher inside. Teachers such as Samson were
constantly complaining that students were chronically late and truant,
that their behavior was increasingly difficult to manage, that they were
not studying, and that there was a severe crisis of motivation among the
students.

In the fall of 2003 new promotion policies were implemented in Eritrean secondary schools that abruptly transformed the Eritrean education system from a highly competitive one in which few students were
promoted to one that prioritized mass promotion. This policy change was
explained as a means of avoiding wastage, with "wastage" referring to
a majority of students who repeated grades, were not able to complete
high school, or had no opportunity for higher education. Concurrent with
the change in promotion policies, it was announced that all grade twelve
students would complete their education in a boarding school in Sawa,
the nation's military training center, and would be required to undergo
military training prior to completing high school. This occurred during a

period in which national service, once an eighteen-month commitment, had been extended indefinitely and there was increasing popular disillusion with the national service program.

I asked Samson what his understanding of the reason for the policy changes was. His response was quite different from the Ministry of Education's official argument that the old curriculum was overly rigorous and competitive, leading to the failure of large numbers of students and a high degree of wastage. Instead he suggested that educational problems in the schools were caused by the extension of national service and the economic and political conditions in Eritrea resulting from the unresolved border war. "The curriculum is not the problem," he told me, "the curriculum has never been the problem."

In a similar conversation Teacher Fitwi linked the idea of avoiding wastage with the government's intention of forcibly recruiting more students into Sawa for military training, "This new policy says that there should be no wastage, so this makes the students not work hard. They are thinking that the government is going to take them to Sawa and, because the government wants to send them to Sawa, there is no chance for them to repeat grades." For students, the fact that they would now go directly into military training following grade eleven signaled to them that becoming a soldier was the inevitable outcome of being a student, regardless of how well or badly they did in school. Their inability to alter this outcome led to what teachers referred to as a lack of "vision" or "bright future." For teachers this explained students' poor behavior, chronic truancy, and poor academic performance.

The transformation of promotion policies and the accompanying linkage of military training and education provide an opportunity to explore the unraveling of what was previously a tightly bound relationship between national ideologies and the state apparatus in Eritrea. Arjun Appadurai argues that in many cases, "the nation and the state have become one another's projects" and that "the hyphen that links them is now less an icon of conjuncture than an index of disjuncture" (1996: 39). I argue that there are varied articulations and disjunctures between the Eritrean nation and the Eritrean state and that exploring teachers' local-level reactions to policy change is a means to explore these phenomena.

Drawing on two years of ethnographic fieldwork that explored teacher adaptations to educational reforms in the remote Eritrean town of Assab, I argue that, while schools had always channeled some students into military training and subsequent national service, the transformation of promotion policies exposed schools' function as a mechanism to transform students into soldiers by tightening the linkage between educating students and training soldiers. This mechanism had previously been masked by the idea that educated persons would somehow have a different life from other Eritreans. This shift in the mechanism through which the state processed its educated people resulted in ruptures to what I call the educational national imaginary—or the way that those with a stake in the education system imagined the role of educated people in defining and shaping the nation.

Schools in many ways are an ideal site in which to examine disjunctures between national imaginaries and biopolitical state projects. On one hand, schools are an important institution through which the national imaginary is formed, disseminated, and inscribed on the bodies and in the minds of students (Althusser 1971; Hobsbawm 1990; Wong and Apple 2002). This process occurs through the dissemination of the national narratives contained in history, civics, geography, and English texts and through national rituals (such as flag ceremonies and holiday celebrations). However, the production and inculcation of a national imaginary also occurs as students receive subtle messages from teachers and others about their future lives as educated people, the necessity of education in developing the country, and their role as educated elites in this development. In short, as students learn to be educated citizens, their means of imagining their nation becomes linked to an ideal imagined future for the development of the nation. Messages about the future of the nation and students' role in bringing about this future are conveyed to students not only through their relationships with teachers, but also through structures of school promotion and disciplinary processes in schools.

Schools are one of the few institutions in which the state directly socializes its young and produces educated citizens. Schools are noted for their capacity to discipline and regulate—ideally, transforming students into obedient citizens (Luykx 1999). Foucault (1995) has cited schools, along with prisons and other modern institutions, as functioning, through the regulation of space, time, and body, as processes of surveillance and observation. Examination and normalizing judgment, moreover, produce particular forms of individual subjectivity (Foucault 1995). In this way, the state participates directly in the production of the educated person (Levinson 2001). Disciplinary practices simultaneously co-create both individual identifications with a particular subject position, such as student, citizen, or soldier, and collective identifications with a larger whole (Trouillot 2001; Mitchell 1991; Corrigan and Sayer 1985). However, I argue that the collective identification with a larger whole produced through schooling links the subject position of student citizen with both the larger collective of the nation *and* with a larger collective of educated persons. The change in promotion policies revealed a clash between these two forms of identification—the educated citizen, as imagined by secondary teachers and students, and the national citizen, as promoted through national service programs and the linkage of the military with secondary schooling.

Another primary concern of the modern state is to make its population legible through technologies of record keeping, collecting statistics, and mapping (Scott 1998; Trouillot 2001; Das and Poole 2004). These practices impose a sense of uniformity and order on a population by categorizing individuals and groups, ordering space, and organizing social life such that the state is better able to monitor their population or implement large-scale social mobilizations such as resettlement plans or, it could be argued, mass recruitment into the military. Schools are an ideal institution to render the educated population legible as they generally provide thorough mechanisms of record keeping as well as the means to categorize and sort students based on academic performance or other criteria. The mechanism in place to promote students from grade to grade served to make students legible to the state; however, the change in promotion policies altered the underlying rationale for this legibility.

Teachers' roles vis-à-vis nation and state are riddled with contradictions: they are positioned as state functionaries within this apparatus of disciplining and making legible, but also bring their own ways of imaging the nation into the classroom and their relationships with students. In the case that I discuss here, these two roles came into conflict as teachers found themselves required to implement new educational policies that contradicted the ways in which they imagined the role of educated people in building the nation. Whereas previously teachers believed that their intensive efforts to sort students was geared towards separating students based on academic performance, the shift to mass promotion made it clear that schools functioned as an effective conduit to shuttle educated persons into the military. James Scott notes that "a project of legibility" is always undermined by, among other things, "the resistance of its subjects" (Scott 1998: 80). Through my exploration, I show the complex ways in which Eritrea's project of making educated students legible for the purposes of enlisting them in national service was undermined through complex and subtle resistances on the part of teachers and students on the basis of their understandings of the role of educated people in building the nation.

Below I provide an overview of Eritrea's policy reforms as a whole and situate new promotion policies within those policy reforms. In doing this, I explore the Eritrean government's rationale for these policy changes and suggest that, while this rationale is responsive to internationally circulating rhetoric about "efficiency" and wastage that, ultimately, new policies were quite expedient in accomplishing the government's militarizing project. The remainder of the chapter builds on the arguments made above to explore tensions between the way teachers and secondary students imagine the role of education in building the nation and the shifting function of promotion policies as a technology to shuttle students into the military.

The Rapid Transformation of Promotion Policies

Although rationalized as an effort to make the education system more efficient, the popular perception of the transformation of Eritrea's promotion policies was that it seemed more effectively geared towards shuttling students into the military than improving educational efficiency and quality. Promotion policies were changed as part of a comprehensive educational reform package initiated in 2003 and referred to as the "Rapid Transformation of the Eritrean Education System." Eritrea's plan for the rapid transformation of the education system had an impact on every level of education—primary, secondary, and tertiary. In order to meet new educational goals over the course of the coming fifteen years, Eritrea planned to build more schools, develop regional vocational colleges, and implement new curricula (Ministry of Education 2002). At the tertiary level it included plans to build six new colleges. The secondary level of the education system was charged with addressing the problem of wastage (repetitions) and better preparing students for the job market and the university by altering course offerings to provide opportunities for students to specialize in particular subjects through choice of courses. The main aims of Eritrea's reforms are outlined in the following quotation from a Ministry of Education policy brief:

1). All wastage of manpower, resources, effort and time in the educational system must be abolished in as much as it is humanly possible.

2). All doors and opportunities must be open to Eritreans of all ages to develop to their full potential both professionally and personally.

3). Education must be employment oriented such that at the end of any level of education any person can find gainful employment commensurate with the person's level of education or training.

4). The standards and quality of education and training in the educational system must be high enough such that products of the educational system would have a high degree of acceptability in the international arena of education and employment. (Ministry of Education 2002)

The focus on avoiding wastage to which I now turn was a key piece of these comprehensive reforms and radically and rapidly changed the education system. In the year 2000, only 9 percent of Eritrea's high-school-aged youth attended high school, only 55 percent of students who entered high school had the opportunity to sit for the matriculation exam, and only 10–15 percent of those had the chance to go on to some form of higher education (Ministry of Education 2002). Promotion both from grade to grade within secondary school and between secondary and tertiary levels of education was highly competitive. The fact that there were few slots available in the nation's sole university necessitated this highly competitive education system, and the logic of promoting secondary students was based on the understanding that a small number of top students would fill a small number of slots in the university while others who would not survive in a highly competitive and selective university system were weeded out. Those who did not advance to the tertiary level were provided with a credential that was generally believed to enable them to get a good job. Although students ran a high risk of failing out every year, the struggle to stay in school as long as possible had direct benefits as each additional year of secondary and tertiary education added social status and the prospect of better jobs and higher salaries.

By the end of the 2003–2004 school year, high school teachers understood that students should not fail. To ensure that students would not fail, in the spring of 2004 the Ministry of Education dropped the grade necessary to pass from 60 percent to 50 percent and again in the spring of 2005 from 50 percent to 40 percent, meaning that almost all students would pass. As I noted above, the move to mass promotion coincided with sending grade eleven students to a boarding school located in Sawa for grade twelve, following a summer of military training. This effectively channeled students into the national service program before completing high school, and, thus, the lowering of the promotion grade was interpreted by many teachers and students as a means to ensure that students would enter into military training. Additionally, starting from 2003, the government did not assign any new students to the university. The failure to admit new students to the university was generally believed to be the beginning of the end of the university and all that it represented.

A question immediately arises as to why the government would change a policy that appeared to be functional and was well adapted to the reality that there was space for only few students in the university. The official rationale and the popular perception of the reason for the policy change differ significantly. When new educational policies were instituted in 2003, the government declared that student grade repetition, failure to complete high school, and the overly academic and not "practical" learning they did in school amounted to wastage of potential manpower to develop the nation (Ministry of Education 2002). Goals of avoiding wastage spoke to the need to make the education system more efficient by passing more students more rapidly through the school system. This was in keeping with many international organizations' emphasis on educational efficiency and the subsequent contention that systems that retained large numbers of students were "inefficient." Although the term *wastage*, as used in the overall educational goals, may refer more generally to other issues of efficiency — teacher efficiency and efficient use of instructional time — it most commonly references this perceived problem of student repetitions.

This type of perceived efficiency problem resonates with concerns of international organizations and has been examined by scholars of international education. Human capital theories have always suggested that the school's primary focus should be preparing skilled individuals to participate in and develop a national economy; however, the needs of a global economy and the ideals of neoliberal economics have reshaped thinking about human capital development. Globalization has led to a shift in the role of the state from the "welfare state" to the "neoliberal" state (Morrow and Torres 2000; Samoff 1999). While both are concerned with using education to build the economy through the development of skilled manpower, the neoliberal state, it is argued, gives primacy to economic doctrines and pushes this agenda further. "Finance-driven" reforms, oriented towards economic efficiency and avoidance of excessive public spending, lead to an emphasis on school efficiency and measurable effects of educational outcomes (Carnoy 1995; Samoff 1999). This leads to policies oriented towards accountability and measurement and may also justify privatizing or reducing expenditures on educational programs that are not shown to directly contribute to economic development. The substantial reduction in the availability of international funds for university education and pressures to privatize university education can be seen as an example of a move to greater educational efficiency (Welch 2001; Samoff 1999). The following quotation from a World Bank report on Eritrea's policy reform seems to reflect these finance-driven priorities in its discussion of the costs of student class repetitions:

> Internal efficiency indicators are unacceptably low. The repetition rate stands at about 20 percent for elementary and middle levels and 27 percent for secondary school. Repetition is encouraged by highly stringent selection examinations and the limited spaces as the learners progress up the education ladder. In an attempt to improve their chances of qualifying for a place in the upper grades, learners repeat grades sometimes several times. … In addition to increasing the cost of education, high repetition rates deny other children an opportunity for schooling. It is estimated that at a ratio of 42 learners to a classroom, about 16,870 repeaters occupy 401 middle school classrooms and 11,627 repeaters take up 277 high school classrooms. (World Bank 2003)

The report argues that the overly competitive education system is at fault for the large percentage of repetitions and is thus "inefficient." These comments, made the same year that the new policies were implemented, might suggest that Eritrea's choice of reforms are informed by (or result from) direct pressure from foreign donors. However, while it has been noted in many other countries that developing nations may have to succumb to pressures of international donors in order to fund their education systems (Berman 1992), Eritrea has long shown itself to be highly resistant to any type of coercive relationship with international donors and has been willing to reject aid at the expense of accepting that which does not allow the government significant autonomy over its own policies. In an interview, the director general of general education described relationships with donors in the following way: "We share with our partners as long as they believe that we have the ownership and we have the program. They focus on what we are interested in and what we want to focus on." Another curriculum writer I interviewed went into more detail about what he thought the process of international influence might be, concluding that it was ultimately a national process:

> I am quite sure there must be some kind of influence [from donors]. They have some ideas. But the good thing about our educational transformation is it has been initiated exclusively internally. … We identified our objectives and our mission and vision of education for this country. Once we set up this policy document, this document was sent globally to the World Bank. They were asked to give their opinions and response. They had their own comments to give. … There were a lot of missions coming from the World Bank and meetings with the World Bank and our policy people. … But the good thing is that most of the process is internal. … Of course you have to compromise sometimes. All this transformation could not be realized with only the resource of Eritrea.

It is significant that Eritrea's new policies are considered to be Eritrean in origin and not the result of international pressures. Perhaps most interestingly, the most controversial and radical element of Eritrea's educational policy reforms—sending high school students to Sawa—did not reflect international influence but rather promoted a uniquely national agenda of training Eritreans to be soldiers.

While the official government rationale for changing promotion policies was to "avoid wastage" and the notion of avoiding wastage was rationalized as addressing concerns about educational efficiency, the mandate to make the education system more efficient articulated with a broader national trend towards militarization. Young people in national service were retained there and enlisted in various development projects. And government efforts to round up and penalize those trying to evade national service were common. In an effort to ensure that those who wished to continue their education completed national service, students were to complete the first phase of their military training prior to beginning grade twelve. Although students repeating grades, failing out of the education system, and not receiving useful skills were seen as costly and not producing a return on the national investment in education, the end result of promotion from grade to grade was no longer a university education, but military training. Thus avoiding wastage converged seamlessly with militarization in the popular imagination of the education system. It is to this process of imagining and reimagining the nation and the state that I now turn.

Competition, Progress and the National Educational Imaginary

Teachers in Eritrea had great faith in social progress through individual improvement, the value of knowledge, and the role of education in transmitting that knowledge. Their way of imagining the nation was figured through these notions of progress and individual improvement. However, for teachers in Eritrea, their belief in the potential to develop Eritrea through education was challenged by the new policies.

Teachers had a very different perspective on the perceived problems of efficiency and wastage than the government and international agencies did. In Eritrea, competition and repetition have historically had a pedagogical and social function within the school system. The "stringent selection examinations" that were maligned by the World Bank gave value to being educated in many ways. Teachers who themselves were educated in highly competitive education systems described competition as an inherently motivating force that would help shape all students and provide rigorous training for top students. Teachers believed that students who were assured of promotion under the new policies and did not have to struggle would not see the value in working hard and striving for educational success. In interviews many teachers discussed the importance of challenging students through competition. In the following quotation, Teacher Solomon explains how facing challenges in one's education was essential for learning to cope with life and the demands of development:

> Life itself is difficult. We are teaching students to cope with life. ... We need to give them challenges. If we forget the difficult things in life how are we thinking that students are going to develop the culture? If we make things simple, how are they going to solve their problems? For everything we have to fight. Even for grades. There is now a very big difference between ... [the new policies] and the real life.

For teachers it followed that this shift to mass promotion undermined the rigor of the education system and, by extension, the quality of educated manpower needed to lead and develop the nation. The University of Asmara played a key role in shaping educational and national imaginaries; therefore, the perceived closure of the university further challenged teachers' ability to understand the government's plan for Eritrea's educational development. As the only university in Eritrea, it was the pinnacle of the competitive education system. Secondary students strove to gain entrance into the university, and teachers aimed to rigorously prepare their top students to succeed in this goal. The presence of the university functioned symbolically to determine the aspirations and define the imagined future of educated Eritreans.

Historically, universities, such as Addis Ababa University and the University of Asmara, have been inherently elite, competitive institutions. One gained admittance to the university through successfully competing one's way through eleven or twelve years of education. A quotation from Emperor Haile Selassie's speech at the inauguration of Addis Ababa University in 1961 acknowledged the nature of this institution: "The educational process cannot be a narrow column; it must be in the shape of a pyramid and broadly based" (quoted in Cowan, O'Connell, and Scanlon 1965). While the implication is that universities were to sit at the top of this pyramid, they, in theory, relied on competition for their success—a broad base for the top of the pyramid to rest on—such that the university would house the best and brightest of all students.

In the early days of independence in many African nations, universities were charged not only with developing nations by creating skilled manpower, but with the social, cultural, or spiritual development of the nation as well. The presence of universities marked these new nations as modern, or, at least, modernizing. They embodied hopes for social, political, and economic development. Haile Selassie's speech also spoke to this highly nationalistic and profoundly symbolic role that the university plays: "A university taken in all its aspects is essentially a spiritual enterprise which, along with the knowledge it imparts, leads students into wiser living and a greater sensitivity to life's true values and rewards" (quoted in Cowan, O'Connell, and Scanlon 1965). The quality and existence of institutions of higher education, the enlightened nature of the educated person, and the future of the nation were tightly linked together. The university symbolized the potential for the nation to become developed and modern and provided a means for educated people to gain the skills and character to develop the nation.

Competition for the scarce opportunities for university education combined with the university's symbolic value as a marker of "modernity," "development," and "national culture" shaped the educational imaginary in Eritrea. This ideal of a pyramid in which the competitive, intellectual elite rise to the top was the model of education that underlay the vision that many teachers and students had for education. Differentiated educational outcomes, with the university symbolizing a highly desirable, if not attainable, pinnacle created the imagined futures that ideologically drove the education system and provided hope for the future of the nation.

Eritrean teachers held such ideas about the nation and education. Teacher Fitwi told me that students needed to be able to imagine a "bright future" in order to achieve top performance in school:

> The thing I always think is that the curriculum should make the students have a bright future. … It should encourage them. How do you encourage them? This national service, going to Sawa, in my opinion should be voluntary. We should not push all people to go there. Then the students would have bright futures. So the students would try to compete in the classroom for opportunities.

This bright future was contrasted with a military future, which was seen to have a demotivating effect on students. Sending students to Sawa signaled a merging of student and soldier identities; it did not produce an identification with being a student, nor did it signal to students that they had a unique role to play in the nation's development as members of the educated elite. Students were to be shuttled through high school from grade to grade, ending up in the same place regardless of ability or accomplishment—military training and then national service. They were to be treated with a degree of militarized sameness rather than cultivated as educated elites through competitive, rigorous promotion policies and their accompanying practices in the classroom. Educated persons were expected, according to the militarized view of the government, to serve the country in the same way as noneducated persons.

Students echoed the same sentiments as the teachers. They believed in their duty to serve their country; however, they were wary of unnecessarily harsh conditions and seemingly endless years in national service. They also questioned the appropriateness of doing military service while still in school. While teachers and students alike suggested that grade twelve students were too young to go into the military, what this claim suggests is that being a student and being a soldier should not be merged.

It was difficult for teachers to understand why the government would undermine what they saw as a functioning education system by simplifying the curriculum and promoting the majority of students. The fact that everyone was then sent to Sawa for military training rather than on to more education or work made teachers even more concerned about the government's underlying motivations in changing promotion policies.

Although some teachers understood and supported the logic of helping weaker students and avoiding wastage by making sure all students learned, most felt that this clashed with their educational values of rigor and competition and undermined their primary role of cultivating elite students for participation in the university. The fact that the university, effectively, was in the process of being closed, and, at the same time, students were being promoted into the military, meant that teachers became even more skeptical of the government's motivations. They questioned whether the government really cared about education, and suggested that it did not. The perception was that what motivated the government to avoid wastage and institute policies of mass promotion was their desire to enlist all educated people more efficiently in national service. Schooling had been reduced to a conduit for producing soldiers.

Transforming students into soldiers, symbolically and literally, contradicts the role that the educated elite are imagined (by the educated elite) to play in developing the nation. This new and uniform military future in national service directly contradicted the vision of a "bright future" as an educated person that teachers believed students should have in order to perform well as students. The new policies of mass promotion towards military service signified a new, and bleak, future as imagined by educated persons.

Troubled Technologies of the State

Promotion policies were effectively a sorting mechanism that made the educated population legible to the state, to borrow James Scott's term, thereby allowing the state better control of their educated population through the keeping of records on educational progress and funneling educated persons into other state institutions (such as the military). Under the old policies, promotion functioned as a technology of the state through which educated citizens were differentiated from noneducated citizens, categorized based on their level of education, and slotted into a particular course of work or study.

An argument could be made that schools had always functioned to channel students into the military. Beginning in 1995, every Eritrean under the age of forty was required to complete a course of national service, including military training. Students had to complete national service following high school or university, and mechanisms of promotion and record keeping in schools provided an effective means by which the state could monitor and sort their educated citizens. If students passed to higher education, they were required to participate in military training to be allowed to enroll in university. If students did not pass to higher education, the government still had records of students who failed out of school, making it easier for the government to track down former students who should be joining national service. Furthermore, former students would not be able to apply for civil service or other office jobs, which were available to educated people, without showing that they had completed national service.

Thus, sending students to Sawa for grade twelve was not so much a radical alteration of the state technology of sorting and moving students into the military, but a tightening of the mechanism by which the state ensured that students would enroll in military training and begin their national service. In the early years of the national service program, there was a good deal of support for the idea of young people completing eighteen months of national service and military training, and, while some did try to evade service, most did not. As national service was extended indefinitely there were increased attempts at evasion. The tightening of the mechanism of channeling students into the military was occurring at a time in which popularity for national service was waning and attempts to avoid it increasing. Although there were many mechanisms through which the Eritrean government attempted to enlist all Eritreans into national service, it became almost impossible for those who wished to pursue a course of higher education to avoid it. By virtue of schools providing a comprehensive mechanism of record keeping and a channel for students into the military via their education, educated Eritreans were far more legible to the state than uneducated citizens.

The functionality of this technology of sorting students through promotion, whether it was one of mass promotion into the military or one of selective promotion into the university relied on the actions of teachers. Although the alteration of promotion policies effectively represented a tightening of state technologies of control rather than an introduction of new technologies, it is significant that teachers and students experienced this as a radical change. The change in promotion policy was perceived by teachers as a transformation from a technology of differentiation intended to sort, categorize, and ascribe different positions to differently educated persons to a technology of homogenization intended to channel all educated persons into a military institution that would provide students with the same military training as all others in the nation, regardless of their educational successes. This transformation was discontinuous with the ways in which teachers had traditionally imagined educated persons as comprising a national elite with a special and important role in developing the nation. In this way the transformation of promotion policies clashed with teachers' national educational imaginary.

In a remarkably short time, as I noted above, the Eritrean education system was transformed from one which was highly competitive to one in which almost all grade eleven students were promoted to the tertiary level. How could such a change be accomplished so rapidly and what were the side effects of such a rapid change? To begin, the curriculum was simplified and the role of teachers, who previously set highly competitive examinations and rigorous conditions in the classroom designed to weed out a certain number of students, was radically altered. Subtle and not-so-subtle messages made it clear to teachers that they were to ensure that their students were promoted before the end of the school year arrived. According to the new policies there were to be limited failures among students; however, initially there was a great deal of confusion as to how this was to be accomplished. Prior to 2003, students who failed a grade would be required to repeat the grade the following year. If they failed a grade two years in a row, they were forced to withdraw from school. Following the policy changes, initially teachers and students were told that students who failed would be required to take a summer makeup class (for which students would pay) and to pass a "re-sit" exam before being promoted to the next grade. However, during the two years of my fieldwork there was no makeup class given to students, few students wound up taking the re-sit exam, and all of them passed.

Teachers were also charged with the duty of following up with and helping "at-risk" students. Whereas previously a teacher's job was to set competitive conditions to weed these students out, their job now was to set conditions that it made it possible for them to succeed. Following the change in promotion policies, the term *at-risk* was heard for the first time in Eritrean schools. In fact, prior to 2003, failing students were clearly in the majority. They were not considered at-risk, but, rather, it was normal for a very large number of students to fail each year. Starting from 2003, these same students were abruptly labeled as at-risk of failure.

It was suggested that teachers take several measures to help students pass. For example, teachers were to contact students' families if students were doing poorly and to offer extra help to these students. Teachers were also mandated to "continuously assess" their students, by giving students more assignments and tests, a practice that most teachers believed made it easier for students to pass. Trainings pressured teachers to continuously assess students and laid out the rationale for doing so. A series of assessment "frequencies" mandated precisely the number of homework and classwork assignments, tests, quizzes, and projects teachers were to assign each semester for each subject. Although continuous assessment was not a new practice, following the change in promotion policy it took on a new weight.

From the time that new promotion policies were announced in fall of 2003, the director in the senior secondary school where I conducted my fieldwork pressured his teachers to provide more support for the at-risk students. He often reminded teachers that they would have to give makeup classes to failing students during the semester break and asked if they were assessing their students frequently in order to ensure they were passing. As early as December 2003, in meetings he told teachers, "If we hurt students by allowing them to fail we will cause social and economical problems to the family." The director explained that according to the "new system" it was the teachers' responsibility to pass the students. Teachers responded by raising concerns about students who weren't trying to help themselves. They noted that many students were cutting class even when they knew they would have a test or assignment due and they often failed to come to class prepared with books and pens. The director responded, "Our responsibility as a teacher is to try to help the victim because he is killing himself. That is the mentality of the new curriculum. According to the new curriculum, the maximum number of students should pass."

In effect, the director was suggesting that the role of the teacher was radically altered from one in which the teacher functioned as gatekeeper, largely responsible for determining students' future life trajectory by deciding who would pass and fail, to one in which the teacher was to monitor students' ongoing progress and ensure that they would pass and, thus, remain locked into the state's mechanisms of militarizing students. What the director categorized as "helping the victim," or managing students' lives by facilitating their promotion (even if the student resisted this intervention), teachers understood as efficiently feeding students into national service. Many teachers took this commentary as a mandate to pass all or almost all of their students regardless of student performance. Other teachers were uncomfortable passing students who were not coming to class regularly, believing that passing students who were not learning would undermine the value of education even more thoroughly. Furthermore, most teachers had a great deal of sympathy for students who were cutting school, hoping to fail and thus avoid the military. But many teachers also found it unfair that the brightest and most obedient students, who were dedicated to their education, came to school regularly, did their schoolwork, and passed tests, would be sent to Sawa, while students who lacked motivation might manage to avoid Sawa. While teachers' national educational imaginary, as I described in the section above, revolved around validating a competitive system to prepare the elite for special roles in developing the nation, teachers who both valorized and validated a system of competitiveness in the classroom suddenly found themselves charged with "facilitating student learning," which was tantamount to facilitating student promotion.

Despite the insistence of the school director and other Ministry of Education officials that teachers change their approach, the change in promotion policies was riddled with problems, largely due to student behavior. Problems with student motivation thoroughly influenced behavior in the classroom. Many students expressed sentiments that education had no worth anymore. Others tried to fail, and, when they realized they could not fail, tried to find other ways to delay completing eleventh grade. Teachers, who were now mandated to help students to pass, encountered students who, in many cases, were *trying* to fail. This meant that teachers' ability to enact the new promotion policy was highly problematic. The new mechanism of sorting was not working as smoothly as intended.

The technology of sorting became a highly troubled one as teachers struggled with varied and shifting educational values, pressures to help students pass, and the complex realities of dealing with unmotivated students. The problem of "incomplete" students reflected the situation in which teachers were mandated to promote students while students did whatever they could to attempt to avoid being promoted. Previously students who failed to do their work, come to class prepared, or show up for tests would have failed. Teachers were not responsible for reaching out to such students. While many teachers traditionally had provided support to students who requested extra help and had taught extra classes if the whole class needed support, in general the responsibility to help failing students reflected a new and very different role for teachers. Furthermore, starting from the 2003–2004 school year, the sheer numbers of students failing to complete tests and assignments presented logistical difficulties for teachers now charged with monitoring and improving student performance. Teachers felt that they were not allowed to fail these students, but were not comfortable passing them. As a result, they labeled these students "incomplete." This meant that, by the end of the school year, many teachers had an inordinate and unprecedented number of incomplete students, which raised substantial logistical problems.

The following description of a staff meeting, which occurred in February 2004, a year and a half after the new policies had been implemented, shows tensions that continued to emerge as efforts to transform students into soldiers tightened and teachers' national educational imaginaries were undone. The debate over the issue of incomplete students that I recount below illuminated the ways in which different teachers struggled to cope with changes in educational priorities and policies.

In this meeting, Henok, a new teacher who had been teaching for less than a semester and had a desire to be an effective teacher, asked earnestly what to do about incomplete students. The director answered that, first, Henok should try to "make the student understand his problem." The director then said that homeroom teachers should have a record from all classes and asked if Henok had such a record for his own homeroom class. Henok, growing frustrated, said he did. The director then asked if Henok had given these students "moral advice" to which Henok replied that he did not even know the students because they had never come to his class.

The assumption of the director was that Henok was not using the tools at his disposal to appropriately monitor and promote his students, while Henok pointed out that the new mechanisms by which students were to be educationally monitored were ineffective as there were too many students who were simply not showing up for class. However, because of new policies of mass promotion, these students could not be considered "school leavers," a category that no longer existed. In effect, Henok recognized that due to large numbers of students resisting the new policies, these students had rendered themselves illegible to the school and the state. The mechanisms of sorting and categorizing no longer functioned, making it impossible to distinguish who passed, who failed, and who had dropped out.

The director's response was to give Henok advice on how to better monitor the situation. Essentially he blamed the teacher individually for his inability to effectively implement new policies rather than acknowledging the larger issue of student resistance and the subsequent failure of the new technologies of state control. The director's comments also failed to acknowledge that teachers had very mixed feelings about the new form of promotion and the fact that most did not support it.

As the discussion continued, other teachers became involved in the conversation. A more senior teacher, Kessete, supported Henok by noting that there were a lot of students who were not attending classes. Another teacher, Shankar, argued with him, outlining his own techniques for making sure his students came to class and saying, "You are telling us that it is not a matter of the teacher." Kessete replied that he was not blaming anyone, just commenting on a bigger problem. Another teacher, Suresh, jumped into the debate, taking Shankar's side, and challenged Kessete to compare the different classes to see if the teacher makes a difference.

Another teacher then added that it was "not a teacher's work to do all of these things," meaning that it was not the teachers' responsibility to monitor students who refused to show up for classes.

To this the director responded with frustration that there was a common problem throughout the nation about the students' future, but the school was still charged with a particular responsibility. He said, "So what shall we do? Kick them out of school? Or try to help them?"

Shankar argued, "Students will not come to the teacher. The teacher should come to the students. When the student gets the results from the test you have to pick him out immediately if he isn't doing well. We have given them liberal chance. We have given them too much space because we are not monitoring. So where lies the fault?"

Kessete retorted, saying, "I'm not saying that we are not [partly] to blame, but we didn't do this."

Alem joined the discussion at this point and argued that while teachers could better take measures to monitor students, they could not resolve this problem: "In my four sections, all of the teachers are doing this kind of counseling. The attending students didn't fail. But some students had to sign a disciplinary warning for absences and still they are absent. If they are doing that to me, what are they doing to the new teacher?"

Mahendra said, "They should fail."

The debate continued in this way with a handful of teachers arguing that teachers needed to adapt to new policies and enforce new measures in order to better control unmotivated students, other teachers arguing that "this is not teachers' work," and other teachers arguing that the teacher could make a difference, but only in a limited way in light of these larger problems facing the nation. The director, charged with the responsibility of making sure the school ran smoothly and making sure that students came to school and were promoted, attempted to advise the teachers on how to monitor students in light of new policies. However, the teachers varied in terms of their perspective on the situation. Some were overtly resistant to their new role and were of the opinion that they were not responsible for taking new measures to monitor students. Others believed that teachers should comply with new policies and adapt their teaching methods accordingly. Yet another group believed that they had to acknowledge new conditions created by widespread resistance on the part of the students.

I would like to suggest that Suresh and Shankar's perspectives reflected the idea that teachers' new role of ensuring student promotion viewed teachers as an instrument of state policy—if the teacher took the right measures, the mechanism of mass promotion would work effectively and all students would be appropriately monitored, educated, and promoted. The other teachers' comments reflected a tacit understanding that the problem was much larger than teachers' failure to perform their function effectively and showed an awareness that the combined change in promotion policies and merging of education and the military had a deep impact on students' motivation and behaviors as well as on teachers' ability to monitor and regulate them.

Conclusion

In the first section of this chapter, I argued that, despite the rationale of increasing efficiency and avoiding wastage, it seemed apparent to most educated Eritreans that the government intentionally merged the implementation of a policy of mass promotion, the undoing of the university, and sending students to grade twelve in a military camp. In the second section, I argued that this awareness showed up in the unraveling of teachers' and students' national educational imaginary. Their beliefs about the potential of education to create bright futures for individuals and the nation was undermined by the understanding that the final destination on the educational pathway was now Sawa. In the last section, I looked at how the new state mechanism of promotion was deeply troubled by both students' resistance and teachers' sense that the new role they were being asked to play was impossible given what most of them took to be quite understandable conditions of mass student resistance to going to Sawa. Students rendered themselves illegible to the state by failing to come to school regularly; thus, teachers were unable to enact their new role of monitoring, sorting, and categorizing students in preparation for Sawa/grade twelve. The conversation in the staff room showed the ways in which mechanisms intended to make students legible to the state were rendered ineffective. Thus disjunctures emerged between state technologies intended to make the population legible and the educational-national imaginaries of students and teachers in secondary schools.

Prior to the change in promotion policies, the function of promotion to transform students into soldiers was thoroughly masked by the idea that those who were educationally successful would have a different and somewhat privileged course in life. However, rather than being marked as different at the completion of high school and channeled into university, students were now marked as soldiers. Previously, those who were promoted into university were identified as students and their time in national service seen as merely a hiatus, a parenthesis, in their existence as educated people. The new policies and structures of education now indicated that they were to identify with being soldiers, and that being a student was simply another form of being a soldier.

A couple of questions remain. First, what is lost, in terms of national development, if an elite, educated stratum is not produced? Most teachers would argue that national development cannot occur without the presence of an educated elite possessed of superior academic expertise and a sense of responsibility to lead the nation. Second, what threat does this educated stratum potentially hold for the Eritrean government's program of educational and military massification? The government would argue that, on one hand, they are attempting to create a more egalitarian society by creating educational opportunities for all *and* at the same time responding to the very real threats that constantly lurk at the borders by creating a large military force. Revealed in this clash of beliefs about educational promotion are very different notions of what it means to develop the Eritrean nation. For the government, education is intended to educate the entire population—the masses. Thus, education does not need to be differentiated from the process of militarizing the masses, which has long been part of the Eritrean government's strategy of shaping national (military) subjects and using military force to develop and defend Eritrea. In contrast, teachers recognize that Eritrea does not have the resources needed to educate all Eritreans to the highest standards possible and believe in the necessity of creating an elite, educated stratum endowed with academic expertise and critical thinking skills.

These different visions for national development each entail rather different biopolitical strategies for managing the population. For the government, schools are subsumed into mechanisms of military discipline intended to simultaneously create soldiers and docile minds and bodies, respectful of authority and willing to defend the nation. For teachers, schools are institutions that also produce obedient, docile subjects, and, in fact, teachers were troubled by students' increasing disobedience; however, schools prepare students to play a role in developing the nation as educated citizens. Although both involve forms of discipline and the creation of obedient subjects with loyalties to the nation, these different approaches to the governance and management of the population—one designed to stratify and one designed to homogenize—are largely incompatible, leading to ongoing tensions played out every day in Eritrean schools.

I would like to thank the Social Science Research Council International Dissertation Fieldwork Fellowship Program and Fulbright IIE for providing funding for this research. I would also like to acknowledge the teachers and administrators in the South Red Sea Zone, staff and officials in the Ministry of Education, and the Faculty of Education at the University of Asmara for the support they provided to make this project possible.

Chapter Six

TRAPPED IN ADOLESCENCE
The Postwar Urban Generation

ℰ⤳

Magnus Treiber

Mesfin, Andom, and Biniam: At the Edge of Existence

Mesfin, a young man in his late twenties, could usually be found sitting in the back room of Bar Hilton, a small local bar outside the Asmara city center. It was as dirty as it was comfortable, its name an ironic duplicate of a well-known and luxurious hotel company. During 2002 and 2003, when Bar Hilton was an ill-reputed but well-frequented bar, Mesfin could be found there from the early afternoon on, emptying a bottle of local gin, when he could pay for it, or when he had been invited to share a drink in the company of friends. Mesfin was a calm, decent, and clever young man, especially when sober. Given the limited range of possibilities available to him, however, he had chosen to become a nihilist drunkard, ignoring even the common urban prerequisites for attaining social respect, such as donning clean clothes and maintaining basic bodily hygiene.

Often enough he also ignored the state and its agents, fully aware of what could happen to a draft dodger like him. At least—and to the relief of his friend and age-mate Biniam—he would leave his table and disappear into the bar's hidden backyard when the guest next to the entrance door, assigned to watch out, signaled the approach of military police. As there is not a lot to talk about when you sit down every afternoon with the same friends, Mesfin lacked entertainment as well as the money and prestige that would gain the affection of the young women frequenting Bar Hilton. So he never missed an occasion to tell his own life story.

Before the Ethio-Eritrean border war (1998–2000) Mesfin lived in Djibouti, a "non-place" in his view, leading to his decision to return to Eritrea.

Somehow he managed to sneak onto a vessel anchored in Djibouti's harbor and was not found until the vessel had left. He was pulled out of his hiding place and nearly thrown overboard, but Korean crew members finally saved his life, insisting on bringing him back safely to Eritrea. From this adventure, supported by local gin, he developed the notion that he might be able to alter his life's course radically, and someday leave again for a more promising environment.

In contemporary Eritrea, and the urban environment of Asmara in particular, dancing in nightclubs, drinking in bars, playing soccer, or becoming entranced with gospel songs have become strategies for controlling one's own body amid heavily circumscribed demands on time, leisure, and personal agency. Mesfin, who chose intoxication as his method of personal control, left the Eritrean government no chance to claim and use his body. He died in winter 2004 in Halibet Hospital, abandoned by most of his former companions and friends.

I met Andom in another small, dark local bar near Meskerem Square in May 2005, when I paid my friend Biniam, who then ran the bar, an evening visit. Andom, who was about thirty years old, with an athletic figure and bald head, sat silently on one of the few bar stools at the cash desk near the door, keeping his long leather jacket on as if he would leave any minute. The small room was packed with loud and drunken guests, who debated, gesticulated, and hugged each other, clinking bottles and glasses while shouting or singing to Biniam's jukebox repertoire. Andom smiled timidly from time to time but seemed neither interested in taking part in the scene, nor getting involved with me, the stranger. Nevertheless he stayed until Biniam closed the bar around midnight and accompanied us, tight-lipped, on our way downtown before departing for home.

Biniam then explained his friend's introverted behavior: Andom, whom he described as once fun loving and open minded, had just recently been released from Nokra Island prison, housed in the ruins of an ancient Italian colonial prison and later used by the Soviets and the Ethiopian navy. Andom had used a piece of a plank as a "computer keyboard" to write a simulated prison diary on the inhuman cruelty he and others experienced.

Biniam, in contrast, had always managed to muddle through. He enjoyed the prestige and relative security of being a student of the now closed University of Asmara, successfully extending his studies as often as possible in order to keep an official student ID, which allowed him to move relatively freely within and outside the capital. His girlfriend, with whom he had one child, constantly quarreled with him about his former girlfriend, with whom he had another child, but in 2005 he at least was no longer suffering from poverty and hunger as in his early student years.

While dependent on his current girlfriend, who in fact rented the bar on her own account, he was able to feed himself as well as his children and to sleep in a proper room. He also successfully avoided re-entering the military, from which many young people have tried to flee only to be executed on the spot or imprisoned, like Andom, when caught. Andom was a living reminder to Biniam of what might easily happen to him, making his daily life, often experienced as frustrating and hopeless, look quite attractive.

From a local point of view, the very different hairstyles of these two friends hinted at how different their recent lives had been. Biniam enjoyed the freedom of sporting provocative long dreadlocks, turning him into a known public figure in the relatively small Eritrean capital of 500,000 inhabitants. Dreadlocks were popular among the Eritrean freedom fighters as so-called *jebjeb*, signifying an antibourgeois and rebellious guerrilla lifestyle. Biniam, however, personally referred to Bob Marley's music and, worse, to the romanticized "golden years" of the Haile Selassie era. Thus he expressed open opposition to the Eritrean myth of national liberation, but by using the *jebjeb*'s ambivalence and double meaning he was usually just frowned upon by the conservative middle class, who could never be sure he was not an explicit government loyalist. Andom was bald, which at his young age and within local contexts signified unusual hard times and made him look sick, old, and unattractive, further entrenching his social isolation. Neither a former prisoner nor a physically and/ or mentally sick individual was thought to bring good luck in such an environment.

Alcohol sometimes turned Andom all of a sudden into an aggressive thug, attacking friends as well as strangers, even those paying for his beer. Biniam reported that Andom on the one hand always felt sorry later for breaking the basic social rules of bars (where there are not many), but scared on the other by how antisocial he had become. Biniam added the following personal observation as evidence. One night, he observed from inside his bar Andom being approached by one of the feared military police patrols, asking for his *menkesakesy*, or military ID. Andom, Biniam reported, suddenly attacked them. He pushed them away violently and "ran away like a wild animal," defending his freedom at any cost.

As for Biniam, he learned from these two friends' experiences and sought to pursue a better path. He daily understood how the security authorities' permanent threat and Eritrea's increasing poverty, which had finally arrived in the capital and affected literally everyone, corrupted people's minds and actions, creating doubt, mistrust, and envy between generations, age-mates, and even close friends. He did not care much for his two "wives," as they—in his eyes—had never hesitated to pursue their own personal interests, but he felt responsible for his children's well-being.

Therefore, he eventually cut his beloved hair to keep a lower profile, and took up working in the country's administration as a *warsay*, an "heir to the struggle." Concluding that one ultimately must fend for oneself, he silently planned his flight into exile, from where he hoped to better support his children and live a life of security and peace. In an email sent to me in January 2007 he wrote:

> hopefully we might meet in addis [ababa] in august, this could be my last mail from asm[ara]. i will have plan to leave asm[ara]. so on. it seems much more difficult than before because a lot [more] soldiers are in this area than before as the result of war between ethiopia and somalia. there is no free zone nowadays around [the town of] adi quala [next to the Ethiopian border]. please pray for me even if you don't believe in it.

The Warsay Generation: Involuntary Heirs of the Nationalist Revolution

When Eritrea's leadership, evolving from the victorious Eritrean People's Liberation Front, introduced the *agelgulot* or the compulsory national service in 1994, it faced considerable opposition from urban youth.[1] Officially consisting of six months of military training and twelve months of work in the country's administration or developmental projects, the national service was meant to train men and women between the ages of eighteen and forty in several areas: the defense of hard-won independence and sovereignty, national development, and the asceticism and resilience of the EPLF's guerrilla lifestyle (Killion 1998: 324–25).

The national service program was promoted as an educational mission, teaching the young generation the EPLF's values and duties, which had been developed and cultivated in mountainous Sahel province known as "the field." Above all, they were to learn to place the national collective above the individual's needs and life. The young generation, growing up in the last years of the Eritrean independence struggle and after, was then called *warsay*, meaning "my heir(s)" or "my follower(s)" in the dominant Tigrinya language. They were thus the successor generation to the aging EPLF freedom fighters, the so-called *yikealo*, the "all powerful."[2] At first, the central military training center to be built at Sawa was no more than an empty open field, situated somewhere northwest from Agurdat in the Eritrean lowlands. The succeeding rounds of conscripts, however, were promised not only interpersonal and interethnic comradeship, but also a passage to maturity and adulthood, as described in a poem by Major Afwerki "Aklel" Iyassu who addressed young urbanites during the Ethio-Eritrean border war in the official newspaper:

This poem will tell you/where I'm going/a place/where you learn/the war game./a lion's den/where you/make/a big name./the talk/is always tough./you learn/to play it rough./the sissy/a play thing/to laugh./hero worship,/all,/that military stuff./the talk is/army lingo/forget the movies,/amigo./Forget those dancing,/the tango,/the icy beer/the mango./You sleep under stars,/moon lit/ venus and mars/forget those/sign of bars/the fancy clothes and cars./Ciaao Bar Diana/ciaao Hotel Savannah/and ciaao Red Sea Massawa/for now/I'm on my way/to Sawa.[3]

After some early resistance and draft dodging most urban youth accepted more or less voluntarily their conscription to Sawa as a hard but educational—and character building—complement to urban life and leisure. When the Ethio-Eritrean border war broke out all of a sudden, completely surprising the Eritrean public in 1998 and lasting until the end of 2000, the government managed quite well to convince young urban citizens to fulfill their national duties.[4] But this soon changed when the *warsay*—and parts of the not-yet-demobilized *yikealo*—asked for peacetime normalization and demobilization. In 2001 Eritrea's leading clique around Issayas Afeworki not only decided to crack down on internal "dissidents" and the private press, but also to silence student protests—imprisoning the elected members of the university's students' union for its president's critical speech on graduation day and exporting some 2,500 students to the coastal desert for forced labor. As a consequence, two students, Yemane Tekie and Yirga Yosief, died from heat stroke. Unlike today, when hundreds of draftees silently disappear in military camps and prisons or are even executed after unsuccessful desertion, these sad events became subject to public debate and were commented on by the official press as well as the then still-existing private papers.[5] Less known is an armed, spontaneous, and thus insufficiently organized upheaval of *warsay* soldiers in Sawa itself. According to then thirty-year-old Hussein, who learned about the incident only when he was reconscripted to Sawa in 2002, the rebellion's leading figures were immediately executed after the loyalist *yikealo* finally won back the upper hand.

Thus, widespread disillusionment among the young Eritrean generation prevails. Being assigned to the state's bureaucracy, mainly situated in Asmara, is a privilege of the relatively few who have enjoyed academic achievement. All others are permanently relegated to rural army camps throughout the country, where they suffer from boredom, lawlessness, and arbitrariness. Women are reportedly subject to sexual harassment.[6] Since 2004 only a small group of educated women, reaching the age of twenty-seven, and men between thirty-five and forty, have been officially demobilized. To my knowledge, however, the men have not yet been allowed to leave their office assignments and earn a regular salary instead of their monthly *warsay* pay of 500 nakfa, or their prewar salary in the case of demobilization, which is usually around 1,000 nakfa. Growing numbers of *warsay* in the field as well as in the capital or provincial administrations in fact simply desert their posts, becoming so-called *koblilom*, "erratics." From time to time the military police organizes raids during the day or at nighttime, so-called *gffa*, to arrest and punish the ones who illegally pour back into the capital, seeking to regain the possibilities of urban life, helping and supporting their families, and sometimes securing financial support from those families as well.

Whoever is assigned to the Asmara region or was accepted as a student of the now largely defunct University of Asmara is relatively privileged and safe from military service, at least in the short term. Those who fulfill their national service in the capital's bureaucracy are mostly academics who have finished their studies or even worked as experts for regular salaries before their (re)conscription into the army from 1998 onwards. But even having an official *menkesakesy*, a military ID, which allows one to stay in Asmara, does not guarantee permanent freedom of movement. Hiding for a couple of days from public places to avoid arrest is common among deserters during a *gffa*, which usually takes a day or two, until the provisional prisons—police stations, cinemas, backyards, and sometimes the stadium—are crowded.

When Mekonnen[7] did not show up in his office for several days in summer 2001, I started to get worried. While the common morale of administrative *warsay* is usually low and every occasion is used not to appear at work, Mekonnen enjoyed working as a historian and was known as very reliable and dedicated. So I asked the office's secretary if Mekonnen was sick. No, she smiled, he was doing fine, he was just being prevented from coming to the office for a few days. Mekonnen later explained his absence in a bit more detail. His *menkesakesy* had expired and in order to stay in Asmara safely he had to extend it at his local army representative's office, which had run out of the official paper for military IDs, so he was sent home and ordered to come back in a few days. He could not risk to be caught without valid papers: "Even if your office is asking for your release, you will have already been brought to Sawa and it will take them two or three months to get you back to Asmara again." Indeed, the military police, armed with Kalashnikovs, wooden sticks, straps, or cut hosepipes, and controlled by uncompromising ex-fighters, are not known for long discussions. Two events illustrate this explicitly.

On 5 November 2004, in what is now known as the "Adi Abeito incident," young urbanites were rounded up at several military road blocks in the city; even a valid *menkesakesy* did not provide protection. A young man reported how he was arrested and brought to Adi Abeito, a little village just outside of Asmara, where a huge prison is situated. Gathered together in the open-air prison, the mass of young people finally managed to push one wall down. The military forces present reacted with an assault on the panicking prisoners. The young man's account was published on an oppositional news website, and is worth quoting at length:

> We joined around three thousand youngsters with the same lot as ours. STUDENTS, WORKERS, OFFICERS, FIGHTERS AND GUYS FROM THE NATIONAL SERVICE...but no body expecting the 11 o'clock [p.m.] tragedy. As darkness started to take its hold, a state of chaos were emerging. Our camp or cell was as big as two foot ball fields surrounded by a 3 meter high wall and with two big doors. A terrible cold and darkness. And four young soldiers were guarding, mounted at top of every corner but they were collaborating with the prisoners by supplying cigarettes and other things. Then the soldiers left that position for fear being stoned in the darkness.
>
> A small group of about twenty people started a fire fuelled by car tyres. And that same group opened one door. And the soldier's attempt to close the door from outside was met by stones. THEN FIRING TO THE SKY FROM THE GUYS NEARBY THE DOOR IN THE OUT SIDE, DRAWING THE ATTENTION OF shaebia commanders [high-ranking military commanders and former EPLF-fighters] like wutchu [General Gebrezgheir "Wutchu" Andemariam, dreaded and influential military commander of the Asmara region] who I guess was following the situation through contact radios. And a push from inside stumbled the wall towards the fire point on the outside, which hurt the gunners, followed by 2 similar pushes and falls. AND FIRRING [sic] INTENSIFIED [...]. AFTER FEW MINUTES A FLOOD OF SOLDIERS STORMED THROUGH THE OTHER GATE. A REAL HUJUM [Tigrinya for "assault"] COMPACTING INDISCRMINATELY THE WHOLE PEOPLE INTO ONE CORNER ACAMPANIED [sic] BY HEAVY FIRE POWER AND STICKS. People running on the head of other people, which followed dying from overcrowding. only few people died of bullets. from that what i witnessed was a NIGHTMARE.[8]

This eyewitness report appeared on the popular website asmarino.com just one day after this tragedy, which cost dozens of lives, including five military guards, and was later confirmed by my own informants, one of whom was a prisoner for two months himself. The reports were also inadvertently confirmed by Information Minister Ali Abdu, who, after the reports leaked outside of the country, was forced to admit the use of "routine controls" and later the death of a couple of "gangsters."[9] As if to confirm that such horrors might take place regularly in Eritrea, one year later the Italian daily *Corriere della Sera* published three photographs under the title "Eritrea: Fotografie di morte," which show the shooting of a young man who tried to escape his arrest but was hit by Kalashnikov fusillades. Already lying on the ground, he was then executed by a military officer. The pictures were covertly taken from inside a diplomatic car in summer 2004 in Asmara's city center.[10]

In today's Eritrea, 10 percent of the population is presently conscripted into the army and held in remote camps in the countryside, from where many subsequently escape, or attempt to escape. Amnesty International estimates thousands to be in jail because of desertion, forbidden minority religious faith, and political opposition.[11] What in the government's view is a legitimate control and use of its citizens' bodies, minds, and workforce—even necessary due to the permanent Ethiopian aggression—urban *warsay* (often from the educated middle classes, and to an significant extent, supported by their families) increasingly take advantage of this relative privilege by deserting, hiding out, or fleeing abroad. Being subject to the constant threat of arrest, torture, and death plants the seeds of subversion deep in young urbanites' minds. The Eritrean government is seen as the main obstacle to an intellectually creative and economically prosperous society, as well as a successful individual life career, attractive to and acceptable for educated urbanites.[12] Unlike in the mid-1990s, young urbanites no longer positively identify with Eritrea's national development project. Politics, on a national level as well as in general, is seen as a sphere of corrupt and immoral power, endangering those who come too close. "It's just politics. …" is a common resigned comment. Those who have tried to take part, express prudent critique, initiate changes, or just pursue a political career, have usually failed. Political issues cannot be discussed in public, nor even in private anymore.[13] Usually government spies, or *seleyti*, are easy to identify. They are poorly trained, behave in an obvious manner, and are often commonly known. But one can never be sure. After his release from three months in prison, Mesgenna, a member of the independent students' union crushed in 2001, expressed his surprise that close friends at university had actually been sent by the authorities to "sound him out." Hence, mistrust is increasingly widespread.

However, despite feeling incapacitated and trapped in prolonged adolescence where impecunious urban youth are completely dependent on pocket money from irregular and mostly illegal jobs or funding from relatives, they remain creative actors with a certain agency in their urban environment (cf. Nageeb 2004). Professional careers as well as family planning require a certain bricolage approach, but cannot be fully blocked by Eritrea's generational policy of material and social homogenization. Despite the consistency with which their life situations are structured and the shared generational habitus (Bourdieu 1993) of young urbanites, the diversity of individual and collective life-concepts, outwardly expressed in differing modes of being (Schulze 2000; Giddens 1991), and the flexibility of social statuses, are all striking.

Throughout my fieldwork, conducted over several periods of varying length from 2001 to 2005, the young urban generation was spread over a limited range of more or less formal social statuses. These included students (a status which has likely changed with the current transfer of academic education from the capital's only university to several military-led colleges in the countryside), *warsay* (those in active service), deserters or *koblilom*, and demobilized soldiers. These four formal categories are more dynamic than they might seem and do not necessarily follow a linear development: a regular *warsay* can turn into a *koblilu* and vice versa, for example, after imprisonment. In few cases university graduates could pursue further postgraduate studies after temporary *warsay* periods, while those who were demobilized were not safe from future remobilization. Those permanently assigned to military service outside the capital could not become direct subjects of my research, however.

Despite my initial plans to document and analyze a postrevolutionary country's political discourse, urban youth introduced me into their daily lives and problems, thus transforming my questions and research inquiry. Data has mainly been gathered through participant observation in a political period quite unfavorable for social research. Thus the results of this study do not claim any statistical certainty, but document certain empirical tendencies. My approach has largely focused on discerning and describing social space and place, individual and collective identities, and strategies for action in daily life among urban youth. Bourdieu's terminology of field, habitus, and capital have proved analytically useful (Bourdieu 2005, 1997, 1993, 1989), from which I have developed further propositions regarding the construction of physical and social space and shared social identities, or "milieus," from the ethnographic observation of young urbanites.

Forced Homogeneity and Collective Habitus among the Warsay Generation

> Liberalism stems from petty-bourgeois selfishness, it places personal interests first and the interests of the revolution second, and this gives rise to ideological, political and organizational liberalism. (Mao Tse-Tung: "Combat Liberalism" [1937] in 1967: 32)

In Eritrea's official national myth, the EPLF freedom fighters, the *yikealo*, appear as heroes who developed a democratic program of nationalist liberation and social development "in the field." To disguise the fact that the country today is ruled by a relatively small clique around President Issayas Afeworki,[14] and to invoke a close relationship between the masses and the leadership (Pool 2001: 164), the *yikealo* (or less officially, the *tegadelti*) are presented as the preceding generation that sacrificed its youth in the distant mountains of Sahel[15] to bequeath an independent nation to the next.[16] Thus the younger *warsay* generation is morally obligated to its predecessors.

In the country's physical and geographical center, however, Asmara's *warsay* emphasize their urban identity, which has provided them, in their view, with education, civilization, and esprit. A bitter wit,[17] constant and often offensive gossip about the leaders' private lives, and a sense of detachment from both nationalist development projects and daily politics, reveal the shared contempt towards the ruling clique. These shared hidden transcripts (Scott 1990) with respect to the lives and identities of former *yikealo*, however, who have managed to pursue a professional career in different levels of the military, or the PFDJ's administrative hierarchy, must be restricted to special occasions due to mutual mistrust and, since its foundation in 1998, the Internal Security agency's omnipresent spies. "Weapons of the weak" seem better applied in public, while facing the powerful, and are based on the privilege of formal education and on socialization into an urban—"civilized"—lifestyle, creating ambivalent situations that are meaningful to "insiders," but misleading or irrelevant to the powerful and their agents (cf. Scott 1990; Goffman 1969). The following examples illustrate what I mean by this public ambivalence as a form of resistance.

Jersilem, then twenty-five years old, was assigned to an army office in Asmara in 2002. During her coffee break we went together to a café, mainly frequented by *yikealo*, government officials, and supporters. To demonstrate her disdainful perception of "them," or *shaebia* (Arabic for "popular"), a term that grouped together the former EPLF; the current government; and government-controlled "mass unions" of women, youths, and workers, she blustered, in English: "We are all living in jail. Look at them, they are so stupid, they cannot even understand what I am saying. You can say about them whatever you like as long as you say it in English." To my relief, people continued to chat and sip their tea without paying attention to us.

Similarly, Hussein reported another strategy of resistance arising from the punitive campaign against the students in 2001. In the coastal desert in August of that year, General Wutchu held a moralizing speech in front of the gathered crowd comprised of students whose independent union had resisted participation in a nearly unpaid summer work program. In an unforeseeable moment, the crowd suddenly started cheering the general's speech in a demonstrative and exaggerated way, such that continuing applause finally forced Wutchu to stop after each sentence. While the arrested students amused themselves by making fun of the powerful amid their own powerlessness, the vain general seemed to enjoy what he understood as respect and approval. One has to add that Wutchu, who is nowadays one of the most influential military leaders besides President Issayas Afeworki, has become for urbanites the cliché of an uneducated, backward, antimodern, and anti-intellectual *yikealo*, ruling (and damaging) postindependence Eritrea.[18]

Choosing Heterogeneity through Urban Milieus

Given their forced conscription into the government's ideological and military project, the *warsay-yikealo* campaign, young urbanites react with fundamental subversion, which can be described, in Bourdieu's terms (1993), as a kind of habitus. Their belonging to an extrinsically constructed generation, whose common day-to-day experiences as military conscripts during and after the war has prevented the achievement-oriented pursuit of happiness and created a shared class situation or "Klassenlage," in Karl Mannheim's terms (1978), wherein potential capital advantages (such as differences in material and social support) are eclipsed. However the common class situation neither produces an all-embracing and solidly unifying class consciousness, nor does it explain the obvious differentiation into mutually exclusive social groups, or what I call "milieus."

In analyzing this phenomenon, a focus on re-creation, or describing, contextualizing, and analyzing how physical and social space is occupied by young urbanites in their leisure time proved useful. *Warsay* work is considered to be forced labor, while family life is most often shaped by dependence, constraints, and strict control. So leisure time provides the only creative space in which "to express oneself," as thirty-year-old Mussa put it. In other words, young urbanites used this limited time to behave like mature and responsible individuals and to seek respect as such. Commenting on youth lifestyles in Brazzaville, Jonathan Friedman notes a similar dynamic (1994: 163): "It is a state of total insecurity, the anguish of non-existence, that can only be solved by capturing the gaze of the other who can affirm one's own being. By contrast it might be said that, for the holistic subject, the 'gaze of the other' is always upon one." Policies of homogenization, in effect, do not allow more than "role play" and so the simulation of social status in certain defined social contexts express what youth would like to put into reality, if only the means to do so were available.

In my different fieldwork visits between 2001 and 2005, three milieus (among possible others, of course) could be identified in participant observation, showing clearly differing, partially exclusive lifestyles. These included the evangelical or *pente* religious milieu, the milieu of the chic bars, and the milieu of the ill-reputed bars. All three represented differ-ent, seemingly apolitical collective lifestyles, pursuing different ways of self-constitution: assimilation in the *pente* milieu, exclusion in the milieu of the chic bars, and integration in the milieu of the ill-reputed bars. To il-lustrate the methodologies of choice and the ethnographic findings of my approach, three respective actors will be introduced: Hagos (35), Jersilem (25), and Biniam (25).

A Study in Three Milieus: Hagos, Jersilem, and Biniam

Hagos was born and raised in Asmara, making him a true "son of the city," or *wedi Asmara*. He is the son of an old, established, middle-class family, with whom he lived in Gedjeret, a middle-class quarter. Two years ago he formally married a woman from his neighborhood, who now lives in the diaspora. In daily life, Hagos acts in a double role as his parents' child as well as an independent bachelor. Jersilem comes from similar family back-ground: her parents are teachers. The family moved from Ethiopia soon af-ter Eritrean independence and now lives in Godaif, a semirural area in the city's outskirts. Jersilem is single and does not think about marriage yet. She gave up her mother tongue, Amharic, and now speaks Tigrinya flu-ently. Biniam also moved from Ethiopia in 1993. He left his family in Addis Ababa and joined distant relatives, but soon left their household to start an independent life. In contrast to Jersilem he calls himself *AMCE* (pro-nounced as "amitche"), a commonly used term for sons and daughters of former Eritrean migrants to Ethiopia. Tens of thousands moved to Eritrea either voluntarily after independence or were forcibly deported during the war of 1998–2000. AMCE originally is an acronym for Automotive Man-ufacturing Company of Ethiopia, a bus and truck factory in Gerji/Addis Ababa, which assembled imported components from Italy, thus alluding to the contested identity of those Eritreans born and raised in Ethiopia, still perceived as foreign there as well as in Eritrea. Biniam speaks Amharic with other AMCE, and he has two little children with different mothers.

Besides being part of the *warsay* generation, Hagos, Jersilem, and Biniam all possess academic educations and favor the possibilities and choices of urban life—despite the given limits—and value the notion of the pursuit of happiness. Genuine and attractive options, or "blueprints" in Beck's (2002) terms, for career and life development can neither be pro-vided by the *yikealo* nor by their own parents and relatives (cf. Beck 2002; Schulze 2000).

Although they are all Tigrinya speakers, only Hagos claims Tigrinya as his mother tongue. Jersilem and Biniam had to adjust from being primarily Amharic speakers. For his part, Biniam maintained his specific identity as AMCE. Hagos, Jersilem, and Biniam all enjoy the support of their family or more distant relatives, although they experience a different balance of individual autonomy versus social control through their relationships with their parents (in the case of Hagos), their children (in the case of Biniam), or wider gender norms and gendered morality (in the case of Jersilem). Hagos had worked as a *warsay* accountant in the capital's bureaucracy, but later left his assigned post illegally to work for the United Nations—now for a reasonable pay. Biniam helped his girlfriend to run a local bar while remaining a student for as long as possible until he was assigned to work as a teacher near the Ethiopian border, reducing his time in Asmara to only the weekends. Jersilem finished her studies in literature and fine arts and was then working as a secretary in a military department until she finally managed to leave Eritrea.

Of capital importance, however, are the differing recreational activities pursued by each of these young people. Hagos is a regular guest in Asmara's chic bars; Biniam in ill-reputed bars (temporarily managing his girlfriend's property, Bar Hilton), while Jersilem is a *pente*, a follower of a banned evangelical congregation. Our exemplary actors barely know each other and do not desire closer personal relationships, meeting each other instead with disinterest and, if pressed, disaffirmation of the others' preferred social spaces. It is interesting to consider some of their views on other milieus. Of the ill-reputed Bar Diana, Hagos says, "This is not a place where a man with manners should be seen." Meanwhile, Biniam, says of the guests in Mask Place, a chic bar, "These people would consider me dirty." Jersilem, for her part, comments on guests in chic bars, "They try to act as somebody else, they don't feel good with themselves." She adds about ill-reputed bars, "I don't feel at home in bars, men are there, drunken all the time, it is noisy and there is a lot of smoke." On religion, Biniam says, "I am only thinking about the next day, for me it is only important how to survive the next day."

While the social and material differences between Hagos, Biniam, and Jersilem provide some context for their views, dynamic changing of individuals between milieus is possible. So we find impecunious Tesfai, of the same age as Hagos, in chic bars, while younger Abraham changed from frequenting ill-reputed to chic bars as he tried to increase his social prestige. Classically understood ethnic similarities or differences, or those based on class and gender, do not help explain differences among our actors and their views and would require significant conceptual revision to be helpful here (for example, AMCE, who fit no clear ethnic designation, can be found in both bar types as well as among the *pentes*.) The concept of milieu instead proves fruitful here, for it is the openness of milieus that

allows adequate closeness to field and field data, emanating from participant observation (cf. Fuest 1996; Werthmann 1997). In contrast to socio-
logical mass milieus, there is no need to allocate every field actor into an
ethnographically identified milieu.[19] Thus, competing milieus of a similar
character obtain relatively precise limits, and the spatial bonds of individuals acting with high profile in such milieus provide clear information.
While professional milieus and milieus of social and local provenance may
overlap in Asmara, milieu affiliations in recreational milieus are mutually
exclusive, with symbolic differences expressing moral oppositions.[20]

Recreational Milieus and Life-concepts in Asmara

What constitutes and identifies social and physical space as "chic," "ill-
reputed," or *"pente"* in the local context (cf. Bourdieu 1997: 160–63)? Chic
bars are those that are understood to be "clean" (e.g., new or renovated)
and located in relatively expensive parts of the city. These include The
Mask Place, Cocktailbar Zara, or Sunshine Hotel Bar. Their distinguished
interior design, underscored by soft and unobtrusive easy-listening music and exclusive prices for drinks and hamburgers, allow well-dressed
young men and women to feel a bit more socially distinct considering the
general restrictions of youth life in Eritrea. The common motto is "to see
and to be seen," so an adequate look and behavior is required. Drinking
might also be restricted due to the exclusive prices, but it is also subject to
the stricter rules of behavior: drinking is considered inadequate in the chic
bar, morally as well as aesthetically (cf. Douglas 1981: 106–12).

Ill-reputed bars, in contrast, are simple, run-down, smoky, and often
out-of-the-way places like Bar Diana or Bar Hilton. Loud Eritrean or imported music and cheap prices for beer and drinks promote collective
intoxication and contribute to a common feeling of unselfconscious relaxation, temporary refuge, and security from the outside world. The environment also provides a relatively self-determined alternative to cramped
living conditions, family demands or obligations, and the daily incapaci-
tation of *warsay* assignments.

Finally, the religious *pente* milieu is comprised of a dozen or more different evangelical congregations, which have become illegal since 2002.
Prior to that, the *pente* congregations were extremely successful and held
worship services in many of the city's numerous small church buildings,
reminders of American missionary activities in the 1960s. Open windows,
loud praying, and gospel singing were meant to invite worshippers to
join. Social activities, collective solidarity, and the emphasis on education
and social advancement attracted far more young urbanites than the offi-

106 | *Magnus Treiber*

cial National Union of Eritrean Youth and Students (NUEYS). Today, congregation members have to meet secretly, praying in a member's living room—always in danger of being arrested after denunciation by neighbors, who are paid with extra food rations.[21]

All three of these milieus reveal their respective actors' individual agency and choices (Treiber 2007b). Despite the government's generational policy of forced homogenization, creative social heterogeneity exists and evolves. Recreational time and space have to be seen as countering the time and space of forced labor, of cramped habitation under tight social control, and of military assignment in the rural areas. Different recreational milieus and their typical lifestyles provide information on respectively shared concepts and understandings of the content and quality of one's life. This is revealed in the very conceptualization of time and space, in which, if extremely unstable as well as uneventful, boredom prevails (cf. Jahoda, Lazarsfeld, and Zeisel 1975). Dead time has to be transformed into meaningful time. In contemporary Asmara, this means "having a good time" in the ill-reputed bars, simulating a desirable future in the chic bar, and retreating into collective prayer and trance in the *pentes'* now-illegal, secret meeting rooms. Physical space is arranged accordingly, becoming "our space" through appropriation by the respective milieus (cf. Bourdieu 1997: 163–66). In Bar Diana this means joining one of the groups sitting together for the night and enjoying the collectively preferred music, while being hidden from public view. The Mask Place, with its vast windows facing the street, is transformed into a stage that displays the physical division of inside and outside, and allows the guests to present themselves to the public. *Pente* prayer groups, who have lost their churches, withdraw completely from public physical space and such are able to turn simple living rooms into ad hoc churches. Further, strategies of action and body—commitment or protest to assigned gender roles; bodily self-control in the nightclub, on the football field, or in trance—provide different answers to military order (cf. Foucault 1976).

Thus, the movement of bodies, styles of clothing, and social performance play an important role as social symbols and evidence of agency in these different milieus (cf. Reischer and Koo 2004; Tranberg Hansen 2004; Bourdieu 1982). Young urbanites in general invest in fashionable clothes—the sine qua non for entering Asmara's downtown boulevard, Godena Harnet (Liberation Avenue), and the central space for the public performance of self and social networks. Caring for one's outfit, which probably refers back to the days of Italian colonialism, nowadays signifies efforts to avoid military combat dress and reassert the values and experiences of urban life. Beyond that, explicitly decent clothes are chosen by guests of the chic bars, allowing them to pass the guard at the entrance door and providing a mutual feeling of exclusiveness. So Mesfin, the drunkard, was usually stopped at the door when he wanted to enter Mocambo nightclub, another chic location where such markers of social identity are prerequisite.

Identified concepts of purity and impurity as well as inclusion or exclusion can even be read as possibilities for an alternative society and social order, often implicitly expressed, and only rarely so in a more explicit manner (cf. Douglas 1969, 1981; Girtler 1995). While achievement orientation is a common phenomenon—conflicting with the generation-wide standstill ordered from above—different models for a desirable society evolve from still different collective ideas of social respect and prestige, which in Bourdieu's terminology can be described as fields requiring differing forms of capital (1993). These models for an alternative society can be characterized as integration (for the ill-reputed bar milieu), exclusion (for the chic bar milieu), and assimilation (for the *pente* milieu). Moreover, typical future visions of social and professional success, which are widely gender transgressing among the academically educated, can be identified in these different milieus. Those within the chic milieu dream of leaving the transitional space of the bar itself, where the candidates for social success meet, and of being recognized in the Mask Place's adjacent restaurant section, and finally even holding a European or North American passport after successful migration. However, most bar patrons in this milieu still cannot afford to order a meal in the chic restaurant. Those within the milieu of the ill-reputed bars would like to combine prosperity and a head for business with generosity and reliable solidarity, thus remaining an always welcomed guest within the bar scene itself. The *pente* milieu aims at pursuing prosperity and at the same time a morally impeccable life, returning open admiration with generosity towards the respective congregation.

Order, Ambivalence, and Modernity

The significance of these different milieus and the possibilities they represent to urban youth for an alternative society are best understood in the context of the Eritrean revolution and its conceptualizations of liberation and development among both Eritreans and foreign sympathizers. During the liberation struggle foreign intellectuals played an important role as promoters of Eritrean independence and sources of support, including generating an (often romanticized) sympathy among Western pressure groups and politicians (see Connell 1997; Papstein 1991; Gottesman 1998; Firebrace and Holland 1985). Roy Pateman, a scholar of political science, illustrates the EPLF's organization and efforts, the struggle's daily hardship as well as its emancipatory and developmental aims, in his famous and well-informed book *Eritrea: Even the Stones are Burning*. In its second edition (1998: 244) he adds in an afterword:

> Wage levels in Eritrea are among the lowest in the world, and although there is Labor Law, there are few effective government regulations to protect the work force, in particular, women workers. As the labor unions are small, and were, for a long time, largely an arm of the ruling party, Eritrea is a particularly favorable area for businessmen interested in a disciplined, stable, cheap and willing labor force.

This statement, expressed by an ardent—and seemingly not-too-critical—admirer of the Eritrean liberation struggle at the eve of the Ethio-Eritrean border war, shows the Eritrean national project's transformation after victory and independence. A revolutionary struggle, declared and perceived as anticolonial and attuned to an emancipating world-revolutionary process, which won sympathy and credit among the Western left because it was both anticapitalist and anti-Soviet,[22] thus turned into a state capitalist project controlled by a totalitarian dictatorship. Once a genuine mass movement to which its committed followers dedicated their lives, the regime has since become an oppressive, hated, and isolated ruling clique, which is nowadays put on a similar level with the Ethiopian Derg, the military dictatorship that ruled both Eritrea and Ethiopia until 1991.

This phenomenon is not unprecedented; in the period of African decolonization in the 1950s and 1960s, anticolonial and nationalist struggle was seen as a class struggle against foreign colonizers, before the respective elites could place themselves at the top of a claimed "imagined community" (Anderson 1991; cf. Grohs 2004) that usurped the colonizers' power and infrastructure. These public means then could be used to bring the country's resources as well as its internal critical tendencies under factional control in the name of the nation's collective fate, precipitating a form of postcolonial state violence not restricted to Africa (cf. Chabal and Daloz 1999; Escobar 1995; Patel and McMichael 2004; Rigi 2003). Within Africa, however, notable examples include the suppression of the Sudanese workers' movement by General Nimeiri and the Muslim Brothers in the 1970s, and Robert Mugabe's double role as hero of Zimbabwe's anticolonial struggle as well as the country's current dictator (cf. Schmidinger 2004; Engel 2004).

In Eritrea, a popular movement of workers and intellectuals was crushed by Haile Selassie's regime after the 1958 general strike (Killion 1997), leading to militant resistance dominated by more conservative groups (Pool 2001: 36–58, Treiber 2007a).[23] Rendering the liberation struggle more efficient, as demanded by young ELF dissidents in the 1970s who would soon form the EPLF, also aimed at suppressing critical voices and establishing centralized control through loyal chains of command in the evolving EPLF (Pool 2001: 76–87). David Pool (2001) emphasizes the role of Issayas Afeworki's military and political training in China, which strongly influenced the EPLF's organization, propaganda, and identity-formation as well as decision-making up to the current day.[24]

As in China, Maoism proved to be a very successful concept for Eritrea's guerrilla warfare. It absorbed its fighters (coming from various ethnic, religious, and class backgrounds) into a communitarian collective, while claiming to represent a whole nation in an anticolonial class struggle. Under the pressures of war against an external enemy, the individual guerrilla had to put the collective aims above individual rights, and indeed, the individual and the collective needs and objectives were defined as one and the same. Internal enemies—or more colloquially, "traitors"—were not only punished but actively expunged, whenever they put the project of national revolution at risk. By assuming that the guerrilla leadership embodied the will of all the fighters, the idea of democracy could be realized without time-consuming debates and decision-making (Oppenheimer 1971: 70–71). The concept of nationalist and anticolonial class struggle was thus as simple as it was flexible. Once the war was won, there would be no more classes, just free homogeneous masses. And as there is no exploitation in a classless society—just national solidarity to protect and develop the liberated society—questions of socialism or capitalism do not really matter, an idea that Eritrea seems at least in principal to share with today's China (see Mao 1967; Pool 2001; Kipnis 2003).

Another compelling example of collective social development, whose influence might be less concrete and obvious, can be found earlier in Eritrean history. Benito Mussolini's fascist Italy contributed decisively to ideas of nation and modernity in the small and poor Red Sea colony. The fascist years in Eritrea are usually remembered as racist and exclusive, but also central to processes of modernization. For Italy, this was largely aimed at preparing for the "Abyssinian campaign" of 1935–1936, a period that might be called "a great leap forward." Italian engineers and Eritrean workers built paved streets throughout the dry and mountainous country, an impressive railway, and a transport ropeway, which also connected the coastal plains to the plateau of Asmara at a height of 2,300 meters.[25] Agricultural plantations were introduced, industry was established, Massawa's port was improved, and last but not least, a genuine capital city was designed and realized in modernist architecture, symbolizing the idea and power of modernization and development under Italian rule (Denison, Ren, and Naigzy Gebremedhin 2003a, 2003b). While Eritreans themselves were little more to the fascist ideologues than useful human resources (Andall 2005; Locatelli 2003; Yemane Mesghenna 1989), they not only continued to use the infrastructure after World War II and under the British Military Administration's extractive compensation policy, but they also adopted a powerful notion of modernity that seems to have contributed to nationalist resistance against the feudal arrogance of Haile Selassie's officials who subsequently poured into the capital (Smidt 2003).

Ironically, Mussolini, who promoted the assault on feudal Ethiopia as a campaign of Italian workers who would internationalize modernist fascism and bring development and liberation to the suppressed masses of Abyssinia, shared quite a similar idea of permanent revolution for the sake of a collective development as Mao and Issayas Afeworki (Scheuer 1996: 104–5). As modernity always involves conceptualizations of the future, it is not surprising that youth faced enormous demands in all three settings: colonial Eritrea, transitioning Ethiopia, and postindependence Eritrea.[26] Today, however, the political desire to realize a future utopia with the help of youth requires both technological capacities and biopolitical modes of social engineering such as militarized discipline and forced labor.

In *Modernity and Ambivalence*, Zygmunt Bauman (1992) illustrates how the modern longing for order and unequivocal classification by inclusion and exclusion, as a prerequisite for social development, inevitably creates confusing and disturbing ambivalence. Total order remains an ideal, impossible to realize; Bauman thus calls order and chaos "modern twins" (1992: 16). This, however, did not prevent visionaries of "development" (Foucault 1976: 207), "cultural 'modernization'" (Donham 1999) or "high modernism" (Scott 1998: 4) from pursuing the realization and materialization of their ideological dreams by inscribing them into a collective body, whether the city (cf. Harvey 2003), the modern nation-state, the guerrilla movement, or the individual bodies of the citizenry (Farquhar and Zhang 2005; Foucault 1976: 212–16; B. Turner 2004). Education towards asceticism, discipline, and specific assignments is, according to Foucault, provided, enforced, and inscribed into the individual through schools and military training, two institutions that are closely interconnected in today's Eritrea in order to prevent youth from draft dodging. Eritrea has become a country of educational, training, and penal camps, trying to enforce order and fight ambivalence.

Brutality, a daily experience during the liberation struggle, and now the contemporary moment, reveals anxieties about the inability to succeed at such a project. It is tempting to speculate as to whether any inside Eritrea's leading clique still believes in such developmental modernity or if the frustration of an unwilling, uncooperative, and stubborn population, especially the youth, is prevailing. Certainly Eritrea's leadership seems to be failing at delivering on its own claims, unable to grasp the hidden as well as public resistance of the next generation, and especially of *warsay* from the urban middle classes who transfer their critique into the sphere of the ambivalent by pursuing personal control in the various milieus identified here. Only those who are hunted down, punished, or forever removed from the drawing board of an Eritrean utopia have left the ambivalent and entered the explicit. Deserters cannot count on mercy, nor can the evangelical *pentes*. They explicitly object to the "wrong Messiah," the EPLF's former secretary-general and current president Issayas Afeworki, while embracing an alternative and uncompromising moral ideology perceived as "foreign" to Eritrea national culture but central to their realization of a community of mutual respect, solidarity, and trust amid the government's unfulfilled promises. In response to their clear and alternative ideas of modernity and social advancement, the regime confines them in metal shipping containers that serve as makeshift prisons.

Since the end of the Ethio-Eritrean border war, living conditions and personal security have become worse and more uncertain. "Eritrea," Biniam says, thoughtfully shaking his head, "is the saddest place of all." For him, leaving the country is just a matter of time, a dream that expresses an agency he will not surrender in the pursuit of "a good life."

Notes

1. There is conflicting evidence about this, but see Daniel Mebrahtu, "National Service — the facts," *Eritrea Profile*, 4 June 1994.
2. The word is derived from the Tigrinya verb *me'khal*, "to be able to." The popular singer Wedi Tukhul sings *"yikealo kulu zekalo, nebry jhka zeyblu gedelo,"* meaning "the freedom fighter does not give up and is experienced and strong as a tiger."
3. Afewerki Iyassu, "Pack my things," *Eritrea Profile*, 7 August 1999.
4. Later efforts to analyze and understand the outbreak of the so-called border war explain it as a political option, chosen by both countries after a year-long history of failed cooperation, to win political hegemony in the region, and thus define the bilateral relationship and stabilize political power internally, cf. Tekeste Negash and Tronvoll 2001; Bakonyi 2001: 82–83; Reid 2003; Gilkes and Plaut 1999. See also prewar publications like Alemseged Abbay 1998: 221–32; J. Young 1996: 105–20.
5. "University Students Return to Capital, New School Year to Start October 8," *Eritrea Profile*, 29 September 2001; "Ab hospital k'ele ztsenhe tmaharay yuniversiti 'arifu," *Admas*, 20 August 2001; see also "Student's daring jailbreak in Eritrea," *BBC News*, 9 August 2002; "Students die in Eritrea detention camp," *BBC News*, 20 August 2001.
6. UK Home Office, *Immigration and Nationality Directorate: Fact finding Missions: Eritrea.* See 8.3.3, where Patrick Gilkes is quoted as follows: "There is no doubt whatever that there have been cases of rape and sexual abuse at the Sawa national service camp, and while these have certainly been talked up by the opposition, the evidence suggests the numbers are considerable. ... I think I am right in saying that the figure for HIV/AIDS in the general population is around 3–4%, whereas it is 22% in the armed forces. It has been suggested this is one reason why the government is reluctant to demobilise."

(http://www.ind.homeoffice.gov.uk/ind/en/home/0/country_information/fact_finding_ missions/eritrea/military_service.html. Accessed 28 July 2004. See also Hussein's report on Sawa in Treiber 2005: 241–42, 243.

7. To be correct, thirty-five-year-old Mekonnen was no *warsay*, but still a *yikealo*. He joined the EPLF in late 1980s and was never formally released. He worked as a teacher before the outbreak of the Ethio-Eritrean border war in 1998 and was then remobilized. In fact he was treated like his *warsay* age-mates (who had never been EPLF members) and officially demobilized in 2004—but was not allowed to leave his assignment as a historian, which at least was considered better than most other posts.

8. Wedi Asmara, "I was there," www.news.asmarino.com, 6 November 2004.

9. "21 Wounded At Adi Abeito Die At Halibet," *Gedab News*, 17 November 2004 (www .awate.com); *Eritrea. Fear of torture / Incommunicado detention/Arbitrary killings. Thousands of people held at Adi Abeto army prison*, Amnesty International, (AFR 64/008/2004) 9 November 2004; "Eritrean authorities deny reports 20 died in prison 'incidents,'" *Agence France-Presse*, 7 November 2004.

10. Massimo A. Alberizzi, "Eritrea: Fotografie di morte," *Corriere della Sera*, 13 September 2005, http://www.corriere.it/Primo_Piano/Esteri/2005/09_Settembre/11/speciale_eritrea .shtml. See also: "Eritrea: Photographs of Death," *www.asmarino.com*, 12 September 2005, http://news9.asmarino.com/content/view/551/86/.

11. Amnesty International, *Rundbrief Eritrea*, Herausgegeben von der ai-Äthiopien/Eritrea-Koordinationsgruppe, September 2005; Amnesty International, "ERITREA. 'You have no right to ask'—Government resists scrutiny on human rights," AFR 64/003/2004, May 2004; Cf. Amnesty International, 'ERITREA. Religious Persecution', AFR 64/013/2005, 7 December 2005.

12 . In theory, all youth, urban as well as rural, have to complete the *agelgulot*, the national service. While there is little data available about rural *warsay*, the Eritrean Defense Forces seem to recruit less rigorously from rural Muslim populations. The reason is probably mistrust of the rural Muslims' political loyalty. Also, the leadership tries to prevent rural Muslims, who object to the draft of their daughters, from supporting oppositional and "jihadi" activities in the widely uncontrollable countryside. This contrasts with the official nationalist and supraethnic ideology the leaders profess, wherein they are training and educating the government's successors on an ethnically and religiously blind basis. Rural *warsay* nevertheless play an important role in controlling the Eritrean towns and the country's capital, as they form the core of the military police conducting the raids. During the day they are usually kept in military camps outside Asmara and enter the city in the evenings. Deep mistrust towards the city's diversity and perceived amorality surely helps encourage them to commit violence against agemates. But in such a small country as Eritrea, friends and relatives often find themselves on both the side of the prisoners and the side of the guards, which sometimes leads to a joint escape.

13. Political programs developed by the exiled opposition in the diaspora are not seen as useful alternatives. First of all, they cannot be discussed openly. Moreover, most suspect that politicians only pursue their particular individual or group interests, whatever their programs might say. And finally, their programs are viewed as quite irrelevant in the current daily life and suffering inside Eritrea.

14. To speak of "the government" is problematic; power is actually constituted by the president, a few formal officials, representatives of the military, the police, the secret services, and leading members of the People's Front for Democracy and Justice (PFDJ) party, founded after the formal dissolution of the EPLF in Naqfa in 1994. EPLF's former secretary general and the current president, Issayas Afeworki, has vested himself with the incontestable right to appoint and dismiss political staff, a tool that has allowed his evolution into a genuine dictator, while internal rivals have successively lost power

and influence. Those who survived the cleansing of the last years strongly depend on maintaining Issayas's goodwill (see Pool 2001:171–75).

15. Concerning the role of the remote Sahelian town Naqfa for the EPLF and Eritrean nationalism, see the entry "Naqfa" in the Encyclopaedia Aethiopica (Abdela and Treiber 2007). Interestingly the EPLF's nationalism mainly evolved from the country's periphery, before taking over its center.

16. In fact, the EPLF is now officially dissolved, and many former *tegadelti* or *yikealo* have become disillusioned, turning their backs on the now ruling clique, inside and outside the country. Even during the victorious last years of the liberation struggle, 1988–1991, the EPLF, claiming full national representation, always faced more or less explicit political opposition from various social and political groups (Gilkes 1991; Hepner 2005; Mesfin Araya 1997).

17. One example is cited as having actually happened in the mid-1990s. In the early morning the recruits lined up for military training and work in Sawa Military Training Center. Different recruits claimed to be sick and asked for exemption. The officer, a rural *yikealo*, asked for the reasons, already suspecting them to be shirking. The first one reported influenza. His request was rejected and he was sent back into the line. When the second suffered from heavy back pains, the *yikealo* would not even listen. Finally the third one stepped forward and said, "I have *lekaleka*." The *yikealo* hesitated, as he had never before heard of that, and excused the recruit. Whereupon, several others claimed to also have *lekaleka*. Fearing a possible epidemic, the officer sent them all for a medical checkup, not knowing that *lekaleka* means lollipop, a common gift on a child's birthday in Asmara.

18. While the EPLF included many committed intellectuals, Issayas Afeworki always restricted their influence before and after independence. Today, many have gone into exile or have withdrawn into themselves. An extreme example is found in the formative years of the EPLF, during the so-called *manka'a* crisis, in which Issayas Afeworki revealed his Maoist understanding of how to build up and guide a guerrilla organization, when he successfully banned and later executed a group of fighters who demanded more democratic rights for rank-and-file members (Pool 2001: 76–87). See also the satiric letter of an Eritrean singer to Issayas Afeworki in which he makes fun of General Wutchu's technological backwardness (Ahmed Abdulrahaim: *Salamat Aya Isaias, Wasup?* 20 May 2006, www.awate.com).

19. Hussein, one of my most important field informants and a close personal friend, did not participate in any of these three recreational milieus. While he would have liked to go out for a drink from time to time, he had to respect Halima's wishes, who—as his wife—strongly objected to drinking and smoking. Another example was Mesgenna, son of a renowned *yikealo*, who felt he had to protect the family's good reputation. Additionally he lived in a newly established suburban area far from the city center, so that public transport to his neighborhood was still very rudimentary. He preferred to frequent Asmara's street cafés alongside the central boulevard Godena Harnet after work or on weekends. In these busy cafés, people who would otherwise choose different bars mix up and often share tables.

20. Anthony Giddens speaks of "milieux of action" in which typical lifestyles occur: "A life-style can be defined as a more or less integrated set of practices which an individual embraces, not only because such practices fulfil utilitarian needs, but because they give material form to a particular narrative of self-identity." (Giddens 1991: 83, 81). *Lebensstil* or "lifestyle" is understood here as constantly (re-)constructed identity through daily decisions and actions. Markers of "lifestyles" can be hairstyles, clothing, the music one prefers, and of course the physical space one chooses to spend one's spare time—in an environment of quite restricted possibilities to choose from. Recreational milieus evolve when individuals share space, time, and lifestyle markers, which

makes their individual lifestyle symbolic, typical, and collective as well as exclusive towards possible alternatives. Giddens and Bourdieu emphasized the role of daily social practice, leading to Bourdieu's notion of "habitus." But also in the academic tradition of the German-speaking countries ideas of milieu and lifestyle (*Lebensstil*) have been discussed in classical as well as more recent publications: see Hartmann 2002, Schulze 2000, Meyer 1997, Hildenbrand et al. 1984 concerning the field of current sociology, Girtler 2004, Werthmann 1997, and Fuest 1996 in the field of social anthropology. Simmel (2001) and Weber also used the term *Lebensstil*, the latter to describe Protestant ethics (1947), while Husserl (1986) and Schütz and Luckmann (1975) developed a notion of "*Lebenswelt*"(life-world).

21. "Evangelicals face Neighborhood 'Spying'. More Arrests," *Compass Direct*, 13 February 2004. This information has been confirmed by Hussein, who remembered similar "techniques" from his time in the EPLF.

22. Eritrean People's Liberation Front. 1982. "The Eritrean Revolution and the World Revolution." *Vanguard*, January 1973. In *Selected Articles From EPLF Publications (1973–1980)*, 30–35. Rome: Eritrean People's Liberation Front; "Banality of Soviet Propaganda," *Eritrea Now*, October 1979, ibid. 162–68.

23. Hamid Idris Awate, whose group attacked an Ethiopian police unit at Amba Adal in September 1961, thus "started" the armed struggle and led to the formation of the Eritrean Liberation Front and became Eritrea's "national hero," but is better described as the local leader of armed bandits, fighting and looting in his own interest (cf. Treiber 2007a). The early ELF predominantly fought the urban and clandestine Eritrean Liberation Movement (*mahber shewate*, "cell of the seven"), formed by radical members of the educated urban middle class (cf. Pool 2001: 36–58).

24. One of the most contested, but also most famous decisions of the EPLF's leadership, finally proving successful, was the strategic retreat to the mountains of Sahel around Naqfa, which is often referred to as the Eritrean long march, leading to the isolated formation and specific nationalist-communitarian socialization of the *yikealo* generation (cf. Tekeste Fekadu 2002; Pool 2001: 98–101; Selahadin Abdela and Treiber 2007). See also Issayas Afeworki 1998.

25. Eritrea's railway was rebuilt between the mid-1990s and 2003 and was promoted as a postindependence symbol of Eritrean steadfastness and the commitment to develop the country. In order to run and maintain the railway, retired staff in their seventies and eighties, who were trained under Italian rule, were reactivated. See J. Fisher, "A ride in the clouds of Eritrea," *BBC News*, 9 July 2003. See also Kolonialwissenschaftliche Neuigkeiten, "Eine Seilbahn für Eritrea," *Koloniale Rundschau*, ed. C. Troll, Leipzig, 1937, 443–44.

26. See for example Filippo Tommaso Marinetti, "Manifest des Futurismus," 1909, in *Handbuch literarischer Fachbegriffe*, ed. Otto F. Best, Frankfurt/M., 1989: 167–68; Vanguard, "Reportage: Youth are the bearers of the revolutionary torch," June 1977, in *Selected Articles from EPLF Publications*, ed. The Eritrean People's Liberation Front, Rome, Brussels, 1982: 97–102; Mao Tse-Tung, "The Organization of the Youth Movement," in *Selected Works of Mao Tse-Tung*, ed. Foreign Languages Press, Peking, 1967: 241–49.

— *Chapter Seven* —

SEEKING ASYLUM IN A TRANSNATIONAL SOCIAL FIELD
New Refugees and Struggles
for Autonomy and Human Rights

℮↜

Tricia Redeker Hepner

Contemporary Eritrea is comprised not only of the diverse populations living within the territory of the nation-state but also a diasporic citizenry that makes up an estimated one-quarter to one-third of the total population of the country. While census data has not been recorded for independent Eritrea, and while no reliable figures indicating the actual size or regional breakdown of Eritrean populations worldwide are yet available, an estimated one million people settled outside of Eritrea permanently during the struggle for independence (see Hepner and Conrad 2005). Despite efforts to repatriate several hundred thousand refugees in Sudan back to their home regions in Eritrea following independence (Assefaw Bariagaber 2006a: 135–52), the numbers of those remaining abroad, or seeking safe haven and better living conditions, has not necessarily declined. New waves of refugees have emerged since the 1998–2000 border war with Ethiopia, after which political repression, economic hardship, and the exigencies of militarization described in rich detail throughout this book reached unbearable proportions for younger, educated urbanites in particular. Eritrea's crisis of human rights, well-documented in humanitarian reports, news media, and by Eritreans themselves, is closely related to the government's strategies of development through militarization. In pursuing its agenda largely through coercion, and disproportionately targeting the most skilled and educated sectors of society for ideological and physical discipline, the government has precipitated nothing short of a hemorrhage of human capital in recent years.

From 2000 to 2004, almost 15,000 applications for asylum were filed by Eritreans worldwide, with more than half of the total in Germany and the United States (see Table 7.1). Recent news reports indicate another 15,000–16,000 people have registered in the Shimelba refugee camp across the Ethiopian border, many of them reportedly young men and women who have fled the *warsay-yikealo* campaign, political repression, and lack of educational and employment opportunities beyond those controlled by the government and military (Heinlein 2007; Malone 2007; McClure 2007; Mongalvy 2007). Additionally, the United Nations High Commissioner for Refugees (UNHCR) reported a 57 percent increase in asylum applications filed in industrialized countries by Eritreans between 2005 and 2006 alone.[1] These astonishing figures likely represent but a percentage of the total number of Eritreans not only "yearning to join the diaspora" (Gaim Kibreab 2005) but at various stages of risking their lives, and possibly those of their family members left behind, to actually do so. An Eritrean woman in her forties who fled to Sudan after authorities in Eritrea detained her repeatedly due to her employment with an international NGO described the situation in our ongoing email correspondence:

> Here in ——, Sudan, there are so many engineers and contractors who were forced out of Eritrea by the government taking over buildings and projects and arresting them. The flow is continuous, especially in the labor force, like skilled and ordinary masons, plumbers, electricians etc. There are also others with various other professions like water drillers, auto-mechanics etc. ... It is now getting crowded by Eritreans and Ethiopians who either come from Sudan, Uganda as well as from Ethiopia through the border. ... Before few weeks, we heard in a rumor that the government has a plan also to round up all Eritreans in the area. We were shocked, on what the government of Eritrea is doing, always running after us, when they could have worked for the well-being of their own citizens inside the country, to avoid running from them. ... In general the Eritrean populace [in Sudan] is in a very bad state. Their morale is down, even if they are working. They always think of their family back home. Everybody says if I ever collect small money, I will just move to Europe somehow, and if the worst comes to South Africa. And some of them are with the hope that America will pick them from here. Many of them are in Sudan for the second time; when Ethiopia was pillaging and burning villages in the lowlands of Eritrea before 30 years or so and now for second time. I don't know what is to be done.

Like tens or even hundreds of thousands of others, this woman struggles and waits, building connections with those who might somehow help, hoping to find a way to come to the US or Europe. However, those who successfully leave Eritrea and eventually declare asylum in places like the

United States find themselves contending with unanticipated challenges as well as opportunities. These challenges are related to the ways that new Eritrean refugees arrive into a sociopolitical field defined at once by the prevailing transnational relationships problematically binding the diaspora to the Eritrean party-state, and the exigencies of the asylum process itself in the post–September 11 world. New opportunities are also available within this field, however, as the observable growth in recent years of Eritrean organizations with agendas based on international human rights, as well as nationalist political opposition, attest.

This chapter addresses the ongoing trajectory of Eritrean political struggle as it plays out transnationally between Eritrea proper and its growing and restive diaspora, amid the pressures of asylum policy and procedure, the institutions and strategies of transnational governance and repression first established by the EPLF in the 1970s, and dramatic new contestations over party-state hegemony, popular autonomy, and the substantive meanings of freedom, liberation, and rights. Based on historical and ethnographic research conducted in 2000 and 2001 in both Eritrea and the United States (Hepner 2003, 2005, 2008), as well as current ethnographic work with recent asylum seekers and emergent transnational human rights initiatives in the US, Germany, and South Africa (see Hepner 2007), the chapter suggests that forced migration as a result of militarism and human rights abuses have begun shifting political consciousness away from the exclusivist nationalism promoted, and enforced, by the EPLF/PFDJ. This shift has reinvigorated struggles for sociopolitical autonomy vis-à-vis the totalizing power pursued by the party-state both at home and abroad. It also illuminates the ways in which the EPLF/PFDJ have long pursued a program of "enforced transnationalism" (al-Ali, Black, and Koser 2001) that has made the Eritrean diaspora a key location for the production of centralized state power as well as the site of public contestation and sociopolitical mobilization all but excised from Eritrea proper.

Eritrea as a Transnational Nation-State

Like many developing and postcolonial societies around the world coming to terms with the political-economic, cultural, and technological changes of the global era, the Eritrean nation-state can be described as transnational (see Basch, Glick Schiller, and Szanton Blanc 1994). As such, it is emblematic of the "reconstitution of the concept of the state so that both the nation and the authority of the government it represents extend beyond the state's territorial boundaries and incorporate dispersed populations" (Glick Schiller and Fouron 2001: 20). However, Eritrea remains somewhat unique in that the transnational dynamic has been present since prior to the state's formation; indeed, the nationalist revolution was waged, and independence secured, at least partly by transnational means.

Beginning in the 1960s, refugee and exile populations scattered across the Northeast African region, the Middle East, Europe, and North America played a crucial role in articulating nationalism and garnering resources for both the Eritrean Liberation Front (ELF) and the Eritrean Peoples Liberation Front (EPLF). As the percentage of Eritrea's population outside the country increased throughout the 1970s and 1980s due to refugee flows and UNHCR-assisted resettlement of tens of thousands of people to North America, Europe, Australia, and elsewhere (see Koehn 1991; Tekle Woldemikael 1998), the EPLF developed formal strategies to effectively channel the energies and financial resources of exiles into the front. These included establishing institutions such as chapters of mass organizations and of the EPLF itself, and later included community associations and wings of the front's relief, development, and research organizations. Additionally, policies intended to mirror and strengthen the EPLF's nationalist orientation, as well as its particular structure of command and authority, were propagated among diaspora communities (see Hepner 2005).

Following independence, these institutions were maintained, and new policies introduced, as important components of governance and mechanisms for the management of long-distance nationalism and citizenship. The 1992 Citizenship and Nationality Proclamation, for example, recognized any person born to one Eritrean parent anywhere in the world as a citizen of Eritrea, with the requisite obligations and rights, and the introduction of a 2 percent flat tax on the annual income of adult citizens abroad assured steady financial support directly to the government. Managed by members of PFDJ chapters, embassies, and consulates, these measures and others, such as formal encouragement for other kinds of financial investments like bonds and property sales, have several important implications. First, they have contributed greatly to Eritrea's incipient economy: an estimated 34.4 percent of GDP was comprised of diaspora remittances and investments in 2004 (see Tekie Fessehatzion 2005) Second, they have enabled the government to monitor the degree of compliance with official nationalism and state-led development by keeping tabs on those who express political loyalty through such contributions versus those who do not. Finally, they increase the centralized power of the party-state by establishing leverage over, and often instilling fear in, potentially noncompliant exiles.

Perhaps most importantly, however, the transnational social field forged by the EPLF and its supporters abroad has been a key location for the reproduction of the front's, and now the party-state's, exclusive control over diasporic identities, organizations, and activities. That is, since the 1970s, the EPLF (and later the PFDJ) pursued a program of transnational governance that actively repressed or destroyed efforts of Eritreans abroad to formulate and sustain autonomous organizations or agendas. Part of this trend was related to the fact that, after 1980, a significant portion of diaspora communities in the United States were comprised of former ELF fighters and civilians who had been pushed into Sudan during the intermittent civil war between ELF and EPLF (1972–1980). Many former ELF affiliates and others who were critical of EPLF's nationalist configuration, its political practice, and/or its economic demands struggled to forge organizations that were independent of the front's administration (including ones that could address their needs as refugees in North America), but were actively thwarted by the front. By relying upon EPLF activists in diaspora who helped extend its ideological authority and carry out its policies abroad, and by sending cadres into diaspora locations to bring exiles in line with proper revolutionary ideology and praxis, the EPLF reproduced its own hegemony over the nationalist movement to retain exclusive claims over the resources and identities of Eritreans abroad. Those who resisted EPLF's administrative authority and continued to pursue autonomous institutions, including those who otherwise supported EPLF's efforts towards independence, found themselves subject to isolation within the nationalist movement and accused of betraying or undermining the liberation struggle.

Thus, Eritrea itself was imagined and forged by complex networks of cross-border relationships and material exchanges, as well as through governance institutions and ideological commitments not unlike what EPLF practiced in Eritrea. By the time independence was achieved, the vast majority of Eritrean organizations throughout the world were directly affiliated with EPLF and subject to its policies and control. Few to no Eritrean groups existed that could genuinely claim autonomy from the front, and those that did were often ephemeral and isolated at best within the wider transnational environment. Because EPLF's particular form of homogenizing nationalism mitigated strongly against the development of ties with non-Eritrean groups, or to agendas linked to either supranational or subnational subjectivities, diasporic associational life was exclusively geared towards Eritrea, with communities exhibiting insularism and disintegration vis-à-vis their societies of settlement. Moreover, these communities themselves were marked by dramatic conflicts and power struggles among those who acted as agents of the front and new party-state, versus those who advocated autonomous or opposition organizations and alternative visions of nationalism or nation building. These conflicts were often expressed in a bewildering mix of revolutionary-era language, postrevolutionary calls for "reconciliation," and debates over democratization.[2]

The ongoing presence of the party-state among diaspora communities in the US and elsewhere has also meant that the current repression experienced by those in Eritrea continues to be felt by those who have left the territory behind. It is not uncommon for organizations and individuals who articulate a critical political stance to receive threats from the government or to find themselves being photographed, videotaped, or otherwise surveilled by PFDJ party members (Conrad 2005, 2006; Hepner 2007, 2008). Thus, one of the party-state's objectives appears to be preventing the formation of an effective transnational civil society that may challenge its ideological and administrative power, and which represents, among other things, a conduit for the pressures of globalization (Hepner 2007, 2008). Relatedly, the characteristics of those seeking asylum in the US suggest that it is precisely those individuals whose identities, opinions, and beliefs are most challenging to the party-state's hegemony and that represent "foreign or external agendas" that are subject to abuses and forced into exile.

"Bare Life" in Eritrea and Exile:
Situating the New Refugees

In what is now a nearly classic observation on the refugee under conditions of modernity, Hannah Arendt noted that the plight of those forced outside their territories of origin signaled at once the global triumph of the sovereign nation-state form while highlighting the reduced humanity of those cut adrift from "their" states (Gibney 2004: 2–3; Arendt 1973). Conceiving of refugees as representing "bare life," or those for whom statelessness entailed rightlessness, Arendt critically evoked the Hegelian notion that,

Table 7.1 | Eritrean Asylum Applications, 2000–2004

Year	Worldwide*	USA	Germany
2000	1,244	253	251
2001	2,241	220	299
2002	3,884	246	378
2003	4,400	196	556
2004	3,124	193	453

Data source: Migration Policy Institute, http://www.migrationinformation.org/datahub/asylum.cfm

* 39 industrialized countries

under conditions of modernity, it is the nation-state that confers human worth and likewise holds the power to reduce humanity to little more than flesh, bones, and breath. Agamben (1998), Harrington (2005), and others have since drawn upon this notion to show how refugees (and asylum seekers as a specific type of refugee) are subject to further biopolitical management by receiving states. Indeed, Agamben observes that "the refugee … has now become the decisive factor of the modern nation-state by breaking the nexus between human being and citizen" (quoted in Harrington 2005: 442).

In other words, in a world physically divided among nation-states as the most "natural" form of political organization and collectively imagined as such (Malkki 1995b; Wimmer and Glick Schiller 2002), humanity is derived from legal placement or citizenship. When a person's citizenship comes into question as a result of displacement from the nation-state territory, his or her humanity likewise comes into question. Further, when one's own government violates one's humanity through violence, repression, inhumane or unlawful incarceration, disenfranchisement, torture, exile, and so on, the meaningfulness of citizenship vis-à-vis that state falls away. Those who flee such conditions to stake new claims on human rights or citizenship in another state do so not as full, rights-bearing subjects—despite this presupposition in international human rights instruments—but as those already reduced to bare life, the nexus between citizenship and humanity broken (see Gibney 2004).

Thus, the status of "bare life" begins and ends not with the refugee experience itself, but extends both prior to it and after it as well. Abuse and dehumanization by state authorities that occur prior to flight and exile are necessary to make legitimate claims to refugee status under national and international policies and laws, which likewise manage "the refugee" not as a whole person grappling with enormously painful experiences, but as a technical problem to managed and controlled (Malkki 1995; Thieman-Dino and Schecter 2005). The adoption of the 1951 Convention and 1967 Protocol Relating to the Status of Refugees essentially placed states in a position (indeed, obligated them) to reconfer humanity on people dehumanized due to persecution or exile on the basis of nationality, race, religion, political opinion or membership in a social group. It is the biopolitical experience of being rendered "bare life" in one's own nation-state, and then proving as much through the technical, depersonalized asylum process in another, that refugees are in essence *rehumanized* by another nation-state's affirmation of their rights to life and to legal residence or citizenship. New Eritrean refugees and asylum seekers are therefore enmeshed in a complicated and painful cultural, political, and legal situation wherein abuses suffered in Eritrea, rationalized by the party-state as necessary for the preservation of sovereignty and security—to wit, a "free Eritrea"—are a prerequisite for justifying one's humanity, and thus one's right to reside, in another "free" country.

These issues, and how changes in asylum policy in the US and elsewhere in recent years prolong and intensify the biopolitical experience of being rendered "bare life," as well as shape people's consciousness about legality and rights, will be addressed further in later sections of this chapter. At present, it is necessary to examine the patterned experiences in Eritrea that underpin the reasons for seeking asylum, and the ways in which the Eritrean party-state's deterritorialized, transnational power continues to render asylum seekers vulnerable, as well as inspires their resistance, long after they have departed Eritrea proper.

Bound, Beaten, and Spit Upon: Patterns of Abuse

I was serving as a teacher in Sawa. ... I told my commander that some of the kids were too young to be serving in the military. My commander told me that my statements were anti-government and anti-Eritrean, and he accused me of being anti-Eritrean. ... A few weeks later I was arrested by military police. They tied my arms and legs behind me and left me in the sun for six or seven hours... I was then placed with ten people in a solid metal box. ... We were only allowed to leave the box twice a day, early in the morning and in the evening. — "Abdu," age twenty-eight

* * * *

One of the guards led me to a room inside the building. The room was eerily dark and the guard led me into a corner using a flashlight. The smell of urine and stench was unbearable but it took me few minutes to see the silhouette of many inmates sleeping on the floor. I couldn't close my eyes the whole night. At dawn, I could see that room was so crowded and there was a big container at the entrance of the room; apparently it was used as a toilet for inmates. ... The next morning my name was called and I was taken and was kept in solitude for sometime after which two persons in military attire came in. For several hours, I was interrogated and beaten by these two soldiers. I was asked if I was delivering a message to any church or group. I was also asked of any involvement in opposition groups in Europe. ... I was informed to keep everything I went through to myself, and I was made to sign an apology letter addressed "to the government of Eritrea" stating that I was engaged in unlawful acts against my motherland. The officer informed me that the letter I signed is a binding agreement not to talk about politics or take part in any activities not organized by the government. He warned me that he will keep a close eye on me and that breaking the agreement will have serious repercussions on me and my family. He advised me that I was expected to use my knowledge and position to motivate the youth to advance the goals of the government rather than engaging myself in unlawful defamatory campaigns against the government. —"Girmai," age thirty-three

* * * *

The detention center was a high security military prison called Track C. The prison cell was about four meters by four meters and I was held there with 14 other prisoners. It was very dirty. There was a hole in the ground that used as a bathroom. We were not given any blankets and fed a small amount of bread with sauce twice a day. The food was given to us in dirty buckets. One of the other prisoners was about 30 years old and a Jehovah's Witness. Most of the other prisoners told me they had been army officers, and many were in their 30s or 40s. Many had requested to be released from the army or had opposed their superiors and were consequently facing punishment. ... While I was held in this prison, I was tortured about twice a week. For these sessions, I was escorted from the cell by two guards into a separate room that looked like an old kitchen. In this room, two younger guards were armed with wooden sticks. One older officer would ask me questions such as, "Do you know the rules of the military?" Even if I replied "Yes," the guards would beat me with their sticks. They told me over and over again that I had to do anything the government told me to do and that the government did not need educated people. ... Later, I was taken to a military detention camp. ... I also had to go to political education training session for two hours every day with other detained recruits. During these sessions, the military officers told us we had to respect the government and the military. The officers also told us the opposition was evil. —"Philemon," age thirty-one

The statements of recent asylum seekers in the US reveal in wrenching detail the systematic and patterned nature of abuses in Eritrea.[3] Such abuses appear to be common within the context of military service, where they are more easily hidden from public or international view, and under the guise of routine military discipline. Abuses are also closely linked to the party-state's project of self-reliant development through militarization, and its antipathy towards sociocultural or political-economic tendencies that the government views as emblematic of internal social divisions or external political-economic pressures. Internal divisions, including those related to religion, class and educational status, ethnicity or nationality, and political opinion are threatening to official nationalist ideology and authoritarian claims to power. Relatedly, citizens' linkages to "external" or "foreign" agendas or institutions are perceived as compromising independence and national security. Any expression of dissidence—cultural, political, or economic—is not tolerated, especially within the military. Indeed, it is through human rights abuses and other forms of repression that the government seeks to reassert totalizing sovereignty over the whole Eritrean terrain, from the minds and bodies of people themselves to the diasporic locations to which many have gone.

Analyses of a sample of asylum claims filed in the US in recent years suggest a possible correlation between repression by state authorities and a simultaneous shift in social and political consciousness away from the party-state's exclusivist nationalism and militarized approach to development. The government tends to target those individuals and groups who represent not only political opposition, but who also show propensities for identities, values, and relationships oriented towards the "world outside." However, repression by the government, and especially the experiences of forced conscription and labor, detention, and torture, are unsuccessful tools for consolidating national identity and assuring political acquiescence. Rather, repression encourages people to leave the country by any means necessary, and for some, becomes a basis for sociopolitical action once they have joined the diaspora. This may be especially the case for educated urbanites.

Patterns of abuses, and the responses of asylum seekers, are significant for their comprehensive and compounded quality. For example, people who have been persecuted due to their beliefs, practices, and institutional affiliation with "foreign religions" like Pentecostal Christianity may make their religious affiliation the primary basis of their asylum claim, but often indicate that in the process of being imprisoned, beaten, tortured, and/or induced to recant their faith, they developed a political consciousness that ultimately led them to join an opposition group after departure or secretly while still in Eritrea. Similarly, those who claimed to have been abused as a result of speaking out from within the ranks of EPLF/PFDJ tended to become real political dissidents as a result of the government's imputing and punishing of suspected opposition. Finally, most cases in which political opinion is the primary claim suggest that the *warsay-yikealo* program in particular, and especially military service and the harsh forms of "discipline" exacted there, are a trigger for critical consciousness and the search for new ways of defining what national liberation and independence might mean. As the authorities punish conscripts harshly for offenses ranging from owning a contraband Bible to questioning the authority of a superior officer or government official, political critique intensifies and sharpens rather than dissipates. Moreover, political activism in diaspora itself forms an additional dimension of many asylum claims due to the transnational presence of the party-state described earlier. Asylum seekers and others who become active within the transnational public sphere are often personally threatened, but more commonly they are told that their family members in Eritrea will be arrested, forced to pay exorbitant fines, or lose their jobs due to their activism abroad. And indeed this does happen.

Table 7.2 | Categorical Breakdown of 58 Asylum Claims Filed
in the US, 2001–2007

Religion Only	Political Opinion Only	Nationality Only (part Ethiopian)	Religion and Political Opinion	Religion and Nationality	Political Opinion and Nationality
7	25	6	13	2	5

Source: T.R. Hepner, data files

Table 7.2 shows a very simple breakdown of fifty-eight asylum claims in terms of the primary basis on which the claim was filed. However, the table does not reflect the complexity of most people's situations, in whose lives multiple characteristics and histories converge, and through which repression is experienced as a multidimensional assault on one's whole personhood. For instance, the category "political opinion" actually contains many different elements that evoke varied historical moments and lines of fracture in Eritrean history and society. In addition to claims filed by people whose families have long been affiliated with ELF and have maintained an underground allegiance to it over several generations, claims also appear by those who were members of EPLF/PFDJ until targeted for imputed dissidence, usually in the wake of the arrest of the G-15 reformers in 2001, as well as those of the *warsay* generation, who have responded to militarization and repression by joining one of many proliferating opposition or rights-based groups abroad. Other cases are filed by people who worked for international NGOs, foreign embassies, private companies, or the United Nations, and were later targeted by the government for their linkages to "foreign agendas and/or capital."

Similarly, while most religious claims are due to membership in one of the minority faiths banned by the Eritrean government in 2002, and for which people have been harshly punished in both the military and society at large, others continue to be filed by Jehovah's Witnesses (JWs). The small JW religious community was historically persecuted throughout the liberation struggle for adherents' refusal to take up arms according to principles of conscientious objectorship. Today, JWs continue to refuse military service, and as a result experience not only social and political discrimination but deliberate efforts on the part of the government to strip them of both substantive and legal citizenship, effectively rendering them non-persons from the state's perspective.[4] Religious persecution for most Eritreans is difficult to separate from politically motivated abuses, as the government makes little or no distinction between religious and political dissidence. Maintaining foreign-originated religious beliefs is as much a violation of national security and sovereignty, in the view of authorities, as belonging to a clandestine opposition movement. Indeed, one does often lead to the other, but not because of an inherent link between foreign belief systems and political dissidence, as the party-state would have it. Rather, it is the harsh response of authorities to anything deemed "un-Eritrean" that pushes people to question, and redefine, what national identity, belonging, and governance is all about.

Finally, the category of nationality includes former citizens of Ethiopia or people of mixed Ethiopian-Eritrean heritage who were deported, or whose families were deported, during the border war, and who fear returning to both countries. It also includes Eritreans who lost their Ethiopian citizenship while residing abroad following the border war and may have obtained passports from Eritrea, but whose political opinions, religious beliefs, or cultural attributes make them fearful of returning there. This particular group of asylum seekers faces an especially difficult situation as they are often rendered stateless twice over: first by Ethiopia due to their Eritrean background, and then by Eritrea as a result of their perceived Ethiopianness or other religious, political, and cultural characteristics that suggest that they may not be authentic Eritreans, but rather potential spies for Ethiopia. The propensity of the party-state to charge all imputed dissidents with loyalty or ties to Ethiopia is especially acute when those in question have lived in Ethiopia and held citizenship there, sometimes for generations.

Departing Eritrea proper, however, does not mean that one is beyond either the national terrain or the reach of the government. All Eritreans who migrate abroad are inserted into the transnational social field that conjoins the diaspora and the party-state into a single, if differentiated, entity. Thus, when asylum seekers arrive in the United States, they enter into a vast network of cross-border relationships, institutions, and policies that has long been controlled by EPLF/PFDJ. While marked by conflict since its founding in the 1970s largely due to the tensions among ELF and EPLF political identities and the struggle for popular sociopolitical autonomy vis-à-vis the EPLF/PFDJ, this transnational social field has intensified in recent years as the primary battleground where coercive state power across long distances meets the heightening struggle for democratic praxis and rights among citizens abroad. As the party-state in Eritrea eradicates all social institutions it cannot fully co-opt or control, and removes from the national community or territory people who represent oppositional views or unwelcome aspects of globalization, these re-emerge in the transnational social field that has long comprised part and parcel of Eritrea. Recent asylum seekers play an important role in this development.

Experiencing Asylum: Policy, Law, and Rights as Constraint and Consciousness

Seeking asylum is no easy task; it requires ingenuity, courage, resources, emotional and psychological strength, resilience, and patience (see Leach and Mansouri 2004). Anecdotal evidence gathered by new US-based organizations such as the Eritrean Community for Human Rights and Refugee Protection indicate that asylum seekers often traverse a dozen or more countries and must raise more than US$10,000 to shoulder the costs (Yonas Mehari 2007). This suggests that most asylum seekers who make it to the United States are privileged by local standards and/or well connected to friends and relatives abroad who can help support their dangerous journeys. Others who declare asylum do so after they have already been able to come to the US by other means, such as on student visas. The alternatives for their less privileged or unlucky compatriots include languishing in refugee camps across international borders, hoping to be registered and resettled by the UNHCR; fleeing to nearby countries such as Egypt, Sudan, Kenya, or Uganda and living there illegally; and attempting to cross the Red Sea or move northwest through Libya, where a boat to Malta may be taken as a way-station to Europe. Many who try do not make it (see Plaut 2007).

The right of asylum, and the obligation of countries not to return asylum seekers to countries where they will be persecuted (*non-refoulement*) has been an important component of international human rights guidelines for refugees since the 1951 Convention and 1967 Protocol. In Germany, the right of asylum was written into Basic Law in 1949; as a result, Germany has accepted more asylum seekers than any other Western industrialized country (Bosswick 2000; Gibney 2004). However, national migration policy changes have steadily eroded guarantees to refugee and asylee rights in countries like Germany and the United States over the past several decades and since 9/11 in particular (Hansen and Gibney 2003; Gibney 2004). Some of these policy changes in the US include a one-year filing deadline and expedited removal practices (HIAS 2005); the increasing incidence of detention and forced deportation of unprocessed or failed asylum seekers (Frelick 2005), often by private firms contracted with the US government; and rendering those who have fought in armed, nonstate (e.g., "terrorist") movements potentially ineligible for asylum (see Mahmood 1992).

Even those who successfully move through the asylum process can find their cases dragging on for months and years. They struggle to find ways to live "normally" while their lives are on hold, feeling vulnerable not only vis-à-vis the US legal system but the transnational Eritrean environment as well. Asylum seekers live in paralyzing fear that compatriots loyal to the PFDJ—perhaps even their own relatives—may discover and report that they are filing for asylum, and that loved ones back in Eritrea may suffer the consequences for their "betrayal." Meanwhile, many people must confront the legacies of the abuses they suffered at home, at the hands of a government once idolized for its heroic liberation of the nation. Scarred bodies, deeply injured psyches, loneliness, guilt, and recurring nightmares haunt the survivors of human rights abuses, sometimes for a lifetime (Ortiz 2001). The constant worry about whether the party-state will arrest or levy exorbitant fines on parents, capture and abuse siblings in their stead, or take away employment or property from struggling relatives, is a profoundly heavy weight to shoulder.

In addition to these many constraints, however, seeking asylum may also be a consciousness-raising process that leads to changes in the way Eritreans think of themselves as political and legal subjects. This, in turn, may lead to changes in political behavior within the Eritrean transnational social field. Asylum seekers must articulate their experiences and the social and historical context to American immigration authorities in ways that simultaneously align with international human rights definitions (e.g., that of a refugee), current national migration policy, and the political and cultural predispositions embedded in law and judicial practice. They often do so with the help of attorneys and other advocates who both inform them of their rights and demonstrate how they are defended within a (reasonably) coherent legal framework. This is a striking departure from the Eritrean reality, in which the constitution remains unimplemented and citizens are unable to know and access their rights, and where any appeals to either national law or international human rights norms are either dismissed or manipulated to serve the interests of state power. And while ongoing research and analysis will bring these dynamics into clearer focus, initial findings suggest that asylum procedures require and encourage Eritreans to think of themselves as rights-bearing individuals, often for the first time.[5] Moreover, they enrich the understanding of many Eritreans that human rights principles and laws exist above and beyond national laws, and can provide a means of critiquing and circumventing the hardships introduced by the absence of a legal and judicial system in Eritrea distinct from either government or military and thus capable of defending citizens' rights against the excesses of the state. As a result, people are encouraged to reflect critically on issues of politics, law, and rights not only "back home," but also vis-à-vis the treatment of refugees and asylum seekers in countries like the US, and the behavior of the Eritrean party-state within the transnational social field.

The party-state has not been blind to the exigencies of forced migration policy in countries where Eritreans have sought safe haven, and in some cases has tried to manipulate these to punish people who resist the government's transnational authority. The clearest example of this comes from the experiences of Eritrean postgraduate students in South Africa (see Hepner 2008; Daniel Mekonnen and Samuel Abraha 2004). Initially sent to South Africa in 2001 for further study and training by the government of Eritrea under a World Bank-funded program, many of the young people developed critical, activist positions once they were safely abroad. From cities all over South Africa and facilitated by the Internet, they developed a highly sophisticated organization known as the Eritrean Movement for Democratic and Human Rights (EMDHR). EMDHR has criticized the *warsay-yikealo* project, agitated for advances in human and democratic rights in Eritrea, and educated compatriots about principles of nonviolent struggle and political change. In response to EMDHR's formation, the government arranged a visit by President Issayas Afeworki himself and posted an ambassador to South Africa who was made responsible for overseeing the World Bank-funded program as well as monitoring the activities of the students.

As in other countries where Eritrean embassies and consulates have played similar roles, the embassy in South Africa initiated a series of actions intended to crush the autonomous student movement there and silence dissent. In addition to making threatening phone calls and pulling some students' tuition, stipends, and health benefits, the embassy also revoked the passports of at least eight students. It then notified the South African Department of Home Affairs that these Eritreans were in the country illegally (Daniel Mekonnen and Samuel Abraha 2004). Exploiting the already volatile situation facing all immigrants and refugees in South Africa (Handmaker 2001; Klaaren and Ramji 2001; Landau 2004; Nyamnjoh 2006), the Eritrean government essentially asked the Department of Home Affairs to begin deportation proceedings and force the students to return to Eritrea. However, the wider EMDHR organization, which included among its leadership Eritreans trained in human rights law under the auspices of the South African program, was able to intervene successfully on their colleagues' behalf and recast their situation in terms of the South African Bill of Rights and other human rights norms.

This example highlights not only the ways the Eritrean party-state operates transnationally to thwart political resistance and autonomous organizations in diaspora. It also reveals an attempt to wield the constraints of South African migration policy against its own citizens for purposes of repression. But perhaps most significantly, this example shows how Eritrean citizens abroad leveraged the greater power afforded to them by virtue of being outside Eritrea proper, and that of a more coherent and accountable national and international legal and policy environment, to resist the party-state's impunity and its transnational, authoritarian power.

Transnational Human Rights Initiatives: The Renewed Search for Autonomy and Accountability

Efforts to forge and retain popular autonomy from below, and to assert party-state hegemony from above, have been an important part of Eritrea's unfolding transnational story. Attempts by Eritreans of different persuasions to create organized groups with independent agendas date to the early 1970s, as does the capacity of EPLF/PFDJ to weaken, co-opt, and destroy such efforts (Hepner 2005; Tekle Woldemikael 2005a). And while this dynamic has persisted into the present, the sociopolitical ruptures in Eritrean society that largely coincided with the Ethio-Eritrean border war of 1998–2000 have engendered a structural and ideological shift of possibly great significance.

The increasing authoritarianism of the PFDJ at home; state policies that pursue sovereignty, security, and development through militarization; widespread repression and human rights abuses; and the concomitant spike in new waves of refugees have all converged to precipitate changes in the Eritrean transnational social field. Among these changes are the ways that Eritreans have begun adopting human rights concepts and strategies that connect their organizations and experiences to international institutions, discourses, and identities in new ways. Indeed, this development has little to no precedent in the Eritrean experience, which has long focused on, and fostered, isolationism and exceptionalism as key components of nationalism and sovereign power. Driven by the experience of abuse and asylum, recent refugees have picked up on the ways that human rights discourse and movements connect them to legal and political norms that present genuine possibilities for resistance beyond the nationalist and nation-state framework. In previous decades, the totalizing, transnational capacities of both nationalist ideology and EPLF/PFDJ governance discouraged—indeed, actively prevented—Eritreans from making such connections unless it was clearly in the service of nationalism and under the control of the Front or party-state. Today, Eritreans are exploiting the historic transnational social field, but in novel ways, and with the intention of subverting authoritarianism and redefining the national political environment.

Thus, emergent human rights initiatives signal a structural shift in the transnational social field from one that connects dispersed Eritreans only to one another and the party-state, to one that also connects Eritreans to international and global networks and discourses. As Eritreans "vernacularize" (Merry 2006) human rights concepts to the Eritrean experience, they also genuinely engage with supranational ideas and legal frameworks, inevitably expanding their sense of political subjectivity beyond the confines of a narrow nationalism. As this trajectory develops, moreover, we might expect that Eritreans develop critical new insights on the history of the independence struggle, including the ELF-EPLF civil war and relations with Ethiopia, in ways that help all parties move beyond conflict, alienation, and chronic violence. As anthropologists and others working in the field of human rights have observed in many contexts, specific engagements with international human rights concepts and instruments often precipitate important cultural and political shifts that ultimately help societies confront, and resolve, their legacies of violence (Afflitto 2000; An-Na'im 1992; Sanford 2003).

While the appearance of Eritrean rights-based initiatives and activism in the transnational social field is certainly cause for hope in an otherwise bleak landscape, there are reasons to be cautious as well. The historical evidence to date shows that Eritrean organizational life has been weak, fragmented, and compromised by both party-state interference as well as internal political struggles among contending opposition forces. Indeed, some of the most conscious and critical young Eritreans I have met in recent years have refused to join any organization, regardless of its platform, because of the near-impossibility of retaining autonomy from either the government or from the existing opposition parties. Attempting to develop a nonpartisan, postnationalist human rights platform in a well-established transnational social field is a radical departure from previous patterns of political behavior. Not only are organizations subject to interference, but Eritrean people themselves also continue to work out the legacies of a proud tradition of self-reliance developed over the course of the long struggle for independence. The ethic of self-reliance, at once a great strength and also a great liability (as the party-state's behavior has shown), tends to discourage Eritreans from making the kinds of connections to non-Eritrean institutions that might provide sustenance and insulation from the interference of the party-state or other political bodies and help rights-based initiatives to flourish. Even this may be in the process of changing, however, as emergent rights-based initiatives build new linkages with international rights organizations and humanitarian agencies that handle refugee issues. Thus, from seeking asylum to establishing rights-based initiatives in diaspora, new shifts are observable in both the individual subjectivities of men and women, as well as structurally within the transnational social field.

Conclusion

The experiences of new Eritrean refugees, whether they remain stranded in camps or declare asylum on foreign soil, are intensely biopolitical ones. From forced conscription and detention to dislocation and dehumanization in both Eritrea and exile, the lives of these men and women illustrate how state projects—from militarism to forced migration policy—are actively engaged in the breaking and remaking of humanity. These experiences are linked directly to the Eritrean party-state's quest for development and sovereignty locally and transnationally, and the national and international policies that structure the treatment of "people out of place." Each of these dimensions is also intensely biopolitical, overseeing the shifts that Eritrean people undergo from bare life and back again. However, amid the many ways that nation-states manage human life in ways beyond the control of individual men and women, we nonetheless glimpse striking examples of agency, determination, and resistance. The emergence of organized rights-based initiatives among transnational Eritreans is one such example, as are the critical reflections articulated by those who possess the courage to speak out against abuses suffered by themselves and their compatriots. These are genuine efforts, it seems, to reclaim liberation, freedom, and rights as long ago promised, but not yet delivered.

Notes

1. "Eritrea Exodus Gathers Speed." News24, 30 August 2007. http://www.news24.com/ News24/Africa/News/0,,2-11-1447_2174545,00.html. Accessed 30 August 2007.
2. My forthcoming monograph, *Soldiers, Martyrs, Traitors, and Exiles: Political Conflict in Eritrea and the Diaspora* (University of Pennsylvania Press), documents these developments from 1970 to the present.
3. Analysis in this section is based on the broad patterns exhibited in over one hundred asylum cases filed since 2001, fifty-eight of which have been analyzed for these purposes. The excerpts from asylum statements are drawn from actual cases with the informed consent of asylum seekers and their attorneys, if applicable.
4. A 1994 directive expelled Jehovah's Witnesses from government employment and excluded them from government services, including basic ones such as obtaining legal documents like birth or death certificates, visas, or passports, or denying them busi-

ness permits and the right to buy or sell property. In 1995 the Minister of Internal Affairs stated that JWs "lost their right to citizenship because they refused to accept the Government of Eritrea and the laws," and added that "they will not have the rights equivalent to any other citizens" (Amnesty International 2005: 7; Hepner and Hepner, forthcoming).

5. Connection e.V., a German NGO affiliated with both War Resisters International and the Frankfurt-based Eritrean Anti-militarism Initiative, which was founded by Eritrean asylum seekers, quoted one person thus: "It is a new experience for me that there are groups which are engaged with the issues of CO [conscientious objectorship] and advocate against war. ... As a soldier I would have never thought that this was possible. In Eritrea you cannot even talk about it. ... Here I learned that resistance is possible" (EAI/C.e.V. 2004, German edition; trans. by B. Conrad).

— *Chapter Eight* —

THE ERITREAN STATE IN COMPARATIVE PERSPECTIVE

Greg Cameron

Wey Gobo kun wey ab Gobo tetsegai.
Either be the mountain or lean on the mountain.
— Tigrinya saying

The Developmental State and Eritrea

When the Eritrean Peoples Liberation Army (EPLA) marched down As-mara's Godena Harnet (Liberation Avenue) and into history in 1991, this consummation of their struggle could rightly be seen as confirming the Eritrean revolution's reputation as one of the twentieth century's most successful national liberation movements. Yet postwar governance of the revolutionary state would prove to be far more complex a challenge than militarily removing the USSR-supported Ethiopian Derg (Provisional Military Advisory Committee) regime from Eritrean soil. The liberation "moment," (now undoubtedly remembered by many Eritreans as a kind of golden age, as in similar countries in Africa), was one in which the independent, nonaligned and isolationist Eritrean Peoples Liberation Front (EPLF) would now apparently have to march to the "end-of-history" drum-beat emanating from the wider global milieu.

Emergent Eritrea faced a world of corporate globalization, the pro-capital international financial institutions (IFIs), the Western bloc's "Third Wave" democracy agenda, an atrophied post–New International Economic Order (NIEO) United Nations, and a collapsed Eastern bloc. In the early 1990s, in a special issue of the journal *Political Studies* ambitiously entitled "Contemporary Crisis of the Nation State?" Geoffrey Hawthorn sought to conceptualize the developmental prospects for a generic bloc that he classified as "Southern states" (including Africa). Hawthorn argued that the broad crises facing the developmental projects (including in some cases even statehood itself) of the Southern states encompassed both the undertaking and sustaining of democratization, and the related crisis of accumulation (Hawthorn 1994: 131–32). That Eritrea's postrevolutionary trajectory has yet to either sustain some form of democracy, or to create a strong economy, is beyond a doubt.

From the revolutionary left to the leaders of Western governments, high expectations greeted Eritrean independence in 1993. Yet a second war with Ethiopia and deepening authoritarianism within Eritrea itself would lead to widespread disillusionment. The standoff with Ethiopia continues amid a deteriorating regional context. The chronic "no war, no peace" stalemate in turn infects all aspects of Eritrean polity, society, and economy, ranging from a growing securitization of public life to deepening poverty and disaffection. Caught between a rock (a faltering peace process with Ethiopia) and a hard place (the Eritrean regime), life in Eritrea has become acutely difficult: tightening military control and checkpoints, ration cards and shortages, endless conscription service, unemployment and swelling numbers of beggars and street children, housing shortages, deepening gender oppression in society, growing malnutrition in the villages, and a perpetual "state of exception" devoid of a functioning constitution. Mitigating factors that hold the situation together include the relative ascetic governance style of the political class, the generally efficient provision of social services such as electricity and water, an ongoing if strained relationship with donors and the Eritrean diaspora, and the common fear of Ethiopian resurgence.

Eritrea's image of being developmental, or as somehow different from the rest of Africa's development history—its perceived exceptionalism—in part stems from the massive social upheaval of a thirty-year national liberation movement that transformed large swathes of Eritrean society and forever altered the balance of power in the Horn of Africa. Useful in trying to situate this transformation is a simplified overview of Barrington Moore's "three routes to the modern world"—the liberal democratic route ("no bourgeoisie, no democracy"); the fascist/conservative modernization route ("revolution from above"); and the revolutionary communist route ("revolution from below")—each deriving from the timing of industrialization and the (agrarian) social structure at the time of transition (B. Moore Jr. 1966). The English, American, and French Revolutions are prototypical of the liberal democratic pathway. The Russian and Chinese Revolutions represent the peasant revolutionary path. Late nineteenth- and early twentieth-century Germany and Japan exemplified the conservative modernization path of state-led, feudal-supported modernization. Such a framework draws our attention to the titanic struggles waged between social classes in times of war and revolution. In the latter two pathways, the postrevolutionary state subsequently embarked on large-scale societal transformation, aligned to key groups of a ruling coalition, in a "big push" to economic power and self-reliance. External threat added impetus to this big push (e.g., Japan vis-à-vis predatory Western colonial powers in the nineteenth century, Stalin's USSR in the face of a resurgent Nazi Germany). The concept of developmental states within this wider macrohistorical framework allows both a closer examination of the state itself as a development actor, and further, situates the birth of a developmentally active state through revolution, wars, and national liberation movements — conditions that are germane to both East Asia and the African context.

Eritrea shares a pedigree of rural-based and Marxist-inspired national liberation movements such as those found in Zimbabwe, Tanzania, Namibia, South Africa, Mozambique, Angola, and Ethiopia and would thus appear to be of the revolutionary communist pathway. Yet the paradox of the Eritrean Revolution is that a Marxist movement upon seizing state power sought to emulate the capitalist East Asian developmental model whose origins resemble the conservative modernization path. If this is the case, then what references, structures, or experiences does Eritrea actually share with East Asia? First, the East Asian "tigers" were identified as models in the development discourse of the Peoples Front for Democracy and Justice (PFDJ, the successor to the EPLF) in the pre–border war period during a time when outside observers touted Eritrea as an example of the putative "African Renaissance." Second, concrete policy directions were charted based on export-led growth, a hallmark of the East Asian model. Third, post–border war Eritrea further shares attributes with Taiwan and South Korea in terms of a cohesive conservative nationalist model with a comparatively low degree of predatory corruption vis-à-vis the discharge of public goods. Finally, in both the post-1945 northeast Asian and African contexts there was/is an "existential threat" posed to the developmental state that both justifies rapid economic transformation and authoritarian political control (e.g., Red China and North Korea; apartheid in South Africa, Ethiopia). The usage of the concept of a "developmental state" in this chapter thus refers to issues around the macropolitical positioning of the state in the global economy, and not simply a Keynesian model of fiscal interventions by a large public sector that delivers high per capita growth and good governance norms, as argued to be the case in Botswana (Goldsmith 2004: 94).

To what extent did the Eritrean state actually follow the East Asian developmental state model? And what did the policies of the Eritrean state reveal about the nature of its relationship with society? In attempting to address these questions I will give only a schematic overview of the East Asian model as it pertains directly to the Eritrean case. Central to the achievements of the South Korean and Taiwanese (and Singaporean) developmental models were state capacity: executive dominance; a well trained, efficient, and relatively uncorrupt bureaucracy; a large pool of policy instruments; the political capacity to insulate economic decision making and implementation from contending political and social interests; and a state committed to economic growth for legitimization (Clark and Chan 1994: 360–64; Koo 1987: 174). Crucially, the northeast Asian states, South Korea and Taiwan, inherited a relatively integrated agrarian sector from Japanese colonialism. Primary production was not confined to some foreign enclaves, with only limited spillover into subsistence agriculture like in Africa and Latin America, but also encapsulated individual tenants and small farmers. Through the introduction of agronomic inputs like improved fertilizers, advanced irrigation, and new seed varieties, together with investment in railways and agro-industries, the colonial system laid the basis for the postcolonial South Korean and Taiwanese states to implement successful "land-to-the-tiller" policies for the smallholder sector, backed with efficient extension systems, and the buying out of the landlord class from the countryside (Haggard 1990: 82–83; Koo 1987: 166–67, 170).

Indeed, North Korea and communist China had already made South Korea and Taiwan taste the bitter fruit of rural communist insurgency. As a consequence of these land reforms, income and asset distribution became more egalitarian, another important lesson for African countries, like Eritrea, that are already facing the pressures of unequal access to land (Bräutigam 1994: 117–18). Backward and forward industrial linkages between the rural and urban sectors (i.e., locally manufactured goods found markets in rural communities) during the early import substitution period in the 1950s further deepened the modernization process in agriculture (e.g., fixed prices for fertilizer, diversifying from rice to higher-value crops) while providing the food surplus required for urban wage-earners. All of this helped to promote economic growth in the 1950s and 1960s, first through import substitution industrialization (ISI) and later export promotion (EP) (Bräutigam 1994: 121–22, 127). Though politically marginalized, the peasantry acquiesced to EP due in good part to the fact that the sector was protected from competitive imports, similar to the support farmers received in the West (Haggard 1999: 36). Low wages were maintained for the industrial working class through corporate control of labor unions or repression. The popular sector, therefore, was unable to block

EP as the developmental state embedded itself closely with key elements of the dominant business class who responded positively, with backing from the US (Koo 1987: 174; Evans 1995).

This model, many argue, weakened neoliberal claims that only the market can get the prices right. Strategic intervention by the government does not necessarily lead to failures: "getting the prices wrong," it is claimed, can promote greater industrial sophistication and depth, foreign exchange earnings, some political liberalization, and provide a pathway out of dependency (Clark and Chan 1994: 360–64; Hawthorn 1994: 130). In short, South Korea and Taiwan (and Singapore) managed the "dual transition" of economic and political liberalization in an often-hostile capitalist world economy in comparison to those Southern states still mired in the periphery.

In comparing Taiwan to Africa, Bräutigam cites comparable levels of development prior to Taiwan's take-off. These parallels included a difficult transition out of colonial rule, civil war, refugee resettlement, skyrocketing inflation, overvalued exchange rates, a large and inefficient public sector, and an economy dominated by agricultural commodity production (1994: 112). What is of comparative interest vis-à-vis Eritrea are the pre–take off transition(s) of the East Asian models out of primary agriculture, to ISI, and then to EP. Of less relevance to Eritrea is the literature on the East Asia model pertaining to the subsequent complex sequencing of product cycles, targeted government support, and other EP-deepening policy instruments. This is because an overly powerful Eritrean state never got beyond an aborted EP before the border war happened. Clark and Chan, writing on the Asian context, crucially note that strong is not necessarily better: "In fact, the strongest and most autonomous states may well be in the greatest danger of degeneration because they can resist pressures for change and can use their powers to become a 'predator' over society." (Clark and Chan 1994: 332). Evans (1995), applying his notion of "predatory" to Mobutu's Zaire, talks of the state as being captured by private interests in pursuit of public wealth.

But in the Eritrean case it was not so much predatory behavior by individual personnel of the EPLF/PFDJ, but rather the way in which a hard state imposed itself over an organizationally denuded society. After thirty years of conflict in the countryside, the EPLF emerged as the undisputed military victor over the Ethiopian Derg regime. Neither did the EPLF have to contend with a rival political force within Eritrea itself or defer to a foreign patron. Consequently, Eritrean policymakers pursued growth strategies bereft of control by domestic constituencies, not only of the popular sector such as labor and the peasantry, but also without even a national business class. Therefore from the beginning in 1991 the Eritrean state may be characterized as having a kind of "disembodied autonomy" based on its extreme insularity from external and domestic constituencies, an attribute that would limit its growth prospects and perhaps play a role in the economic, political, and military crises that were to follow.

The following is a structural analysis analyzing the systemic reasons for the current crisis of governance in Eritrea. The focus is less on the instruments of economic policy, contemporary national politics, or the social origins of the political leadership, but rather on the political economy of a strong but exclusionary state. I seek to explore the nature of this political exclusion as well as the economic policies that it spawned. This first section has juxtaposed the hard but embedded nature of the East Asian state with what I term the disembodied Eritrean state. The second section begins with an overview of the accumulation strategy of the pre–border war period (1991–1998) detailing the structural weaknesses of its export promotion strategies. It shows where Eritrea's experience converges/diverges from the classic East Asian state capitalist model by evaluating specific Eritrean policies and their national and international contexts. It further contrasts their different agrarian contexts and in doing so argues that the Eritrean state's macroeconomic strategy failed because it did not resolve the agrarian question. Section three outlines the relationship of the Eritrean state to outside powers and argues that the catastrophic reversion to war provided the Eritrean state the autonomy to "securitize" the accumulation process in the name of national sovereignty (1998–present). Section four examines some of the parallels with the failed radical nationalist projects once found in southeast Africa, arguing that Eritrea shares more in common with these now-discarded models than its leadership might perhaps wish to admit. Nonetheless the Eritrean state is more akin to an exclusionary nationalist conservative model than a socialist one. The conclusion assesses whether the Eritrean state's increasingly extreme regulatory control of its population can be sustained. It also sketches an alternative pathway by suggesting popular-based policies within a renewed coalitional alignment.

From "Open Door" to "Self-Reliance"

The Eritrean Revolution released immense state and social power, but it was power harnessed to a weak accumulation base. Unlike the earlier radical nationalist regimes of Ethiopia, Angola, and Mozambique, or the northeast Asian "tigers," Eritrea had no Eastern bloc or Western bloc patrons to provide military security guarantees or to support exceptional "national security" powers, investment funds, aid, or closed overseas markets (Hawthorn 1994). Foreign direct investment (FDI), remittances from the Eritrean diaspora, World Bank concessional lending, some bilateral aid, and regional integration strategies would be the primary cornerstones of an accumulation regime that had to generate the required social transformation on the back of the wreckage of the thirty-year liberation war. Eritrea's efforts to rebuild the war-shattered economy would prove to be further constrained by drought, and the general legacy of a disarticulated colonial economy that Ethiopian colonialism did little to transform.

In the East Asian cases, agriculture was the foundation, but the same cannot be said of Eritrea. Modern Eritrea entered the world system as an Italian colony. And thus the structural constraints facing Eritrean agriculture were framed by European colonization, especially around the introduction of cash crops and the concomitant neglect of peasant/pastoralist modes of economy. While Italian colonialism certainly did leave a centralized state, a modern educated class of Eritreans, and a light industrial base, the countryside suffered massive appropriation of land for Italian settlers, rural-urban migration, loss of biodiversity, and the military recruitment of rural Eritreans for colonial Italy's Africa campaigns (Murtaza 1998: 58). The subsequent British and Ethiopian occupations from 1942 to 1991 witnessed asset stripping, the granting of more land for commercial agriculture, and the forceful imposition of a flawed socialist model in those parts of the countryside under the Derg (Murtaza 1998: 67, 79). At independence, Eritrea's agricultural sector was in dire need of reconstruction and balanced development.

Going over some of the literature on Eritrea's economic strategy during the pre–border war years (1991–1998), there is little in the way of analysis situating agriculture within the wider macroeconomic framework. Tellingly, the thrust of these analyses centers on Eritrea emulating Taiwan and especially Singapore, an entrepôt without a rural hinterland.[1] Urban bias was further evident in the argument made that agriculture did not offer a significant source of growth; rather trade and industry would provide the comparative advantages to propel Eritrea from being a low-income agrarian country to a middle-income industrial society, all within three decades (Futur 1993: 177). And while the weak linkage between industry and agriculture is acknowledged (Gebremedhin 1998: 111, 113, 115; Habte-Giorgis 1993: 38), ISI models in sub-Saharan Africa, Eastern Europe, Latin America, and South Asia are criticized for their high tariffs and protectionism (Gebremedhin 1998: 118). Rather, similarities were noted between Taiwan and Eritrea prior to EP (Gebremedhin 1998: 113; Futur 1993: 181). Ignoring the repressive features of the East Asian models towards the popular sectors, Habte-Giorgis for instance, states: "Following the example of the newly industrialized countries of Southeast Asia, the free enterprise system, with government, union, and management working together is a proven method for creating a thriving economy" (1993: 38).

But there was nothing about how the highly vulnerable Eritrean peasant and pastoralist small-scale sectors would fit into this wider macroeconomic transformation as a prerequisite to EP, as was done in East Asia.[2] Moreover, the working class was at best demobilized and represented by a trade union confederation that seems to have had little say over wage policy, frozen from 1997, and which speaks to its structurally weak position. Further, the private sector was envisioned to be the engine of growth in vague and aspirational terms (Futur 1993: 183). Singapore-style "hubs" were to be based on the promotion of Eritrea's old industrial sector as well as on electronics, technology transfer, and technical services (Habte-Giorgis 1993: 42). It was also announced that small export-oriented firms would qualify for competitive exchange rates and loans under the Recovery and Rehabilitation Program. Yet the industrial sector consisted mainly of forty-five public enterprises geared toward the Ethiopian market, many of which had outdated machinery. Though this Italian industrial-era base in Asmara remained intact, there was no politically significant Eritrean capitalist grouping to speak of, at least one that had a say over policy directions. It was the Eritrean diaspora that provided crucial financing for the macroeconomic path charted in these early years, but which, due to its scattered offshore nature, had no direct influence on government policy despite private transfers averaging 37 percent of GDP over a ten-year period (IMF 2006). Left unspoken in this picture therefore was the reality of a "phantom private sector" behind which stood a behemoth lurking in the shadows—the PFDJ party-state.

The general public perspective on development in ruling circles fitted the Modernization Theory (MT) paradigm of a market society, guided by the state, reaching ever-higher levels of productivity and urbanization over a traditional subsistence-based economy, with the objective of eventual take-off into self-sustaining growth, modernity, and integration into the world economy. Liberal economic reforms announced in August 1994 slated investment, land tenure, monetary and fiscal policy, and trade. Eritrea's reform program represented a major change from a wartime command economy to a peacetime liberal market economy. The country's leadership made a clear commitment to a private-sector-led, outward-oriented development strategy, with a minimal regulatory role for the state around law and order, and sound macroeconomic policy. Eritrea also started with a clean slate (no external debt, no entrenched civilian bureaucracy, low inflation, and "zero tolerance" for corruption). Public finances were also on a sound footing. Early newspaper articles are replete with accounts of visiting USAID/EU delegations, ascension to multilateral agencies,[3] demobilization and resettlement programs, food security initiatives, warnings on the dangers of aid dependence, human capital concerns, the formulation of an FDI code,[4] road building, investor-friendly land tenure reform, commercial settlement schemes, constitution making, estimates on cereal production figures, and the brain drain of youth due to the US green card system. In early 1998, authorities developed the National Economic Policy Framework (for 1998–2000) to consolidate the above-noted trends and to further deepen structural reforms such as shifting spending to health and education, broadening the tax base, decontrolling interest rates, privatizing the banking system, and accelerating the privatization program (as of the end of 1997, eleven nonutility enterprises had been privatized out of forty-five) (IMF 2006).

While some progress was made towards these goals in the 1990s, many of these policies would be reversed. Common in the literature is that this reversal came about due to the border war, a position that has validity. It may also be the case, however, that economic growth between 1991 and 1997 was simply insufficient to more or less simultaneously transform the shattered agricultural and industrial sectors, satisfy the general societal expectation for "development," and financially maintain an overdeveloped party-state. The stresses and diminishing returns may have been too great in spite of the 7.9 percent growth average rates over this period quoted in the literature (World Bank 2006: 26).[5] What in fact was actually happening in the real economy requires closer scrutiny and research. But by all appearances these growth rates were insufficient for sustainable macrolevel stability let alone a more ambitious transformation that would have qualitatively altered Eritrea's political economy along the lines of an "African Singapore." Dan Connell noted at the time that "apart from food aid, the Eritreans are finding development capital hard to come by, though some FDI began to appear in 1996 for joint ventures in a few key areas, such as oil and gold exploration" (Connell 1997a: 138). He further observed that capital investment, from the diaspora and foreigners alike, was lagging far behind expectations in a private sector still dominated by PFDJ enterprises (Connell 1997a: 157).

At the same time, the Ethiopian People's Revolutionary Democratic Front (EPRDF) regime in Ethiopia was facing formidable economic challenges of its own. The EPRDF eschewed comprehensive planning, but it did have a loose, medium-term economic framework for federal and regional economic development. This "agricultural development-led industrialization" strategy aimed to promote medium-scale industries based on agricultural processing in larger regional capitals, including in Tigray province, the EPRDF's regional bastion. Certainly it is difficult to trace causalities of the ways in which political economy affects policy prefer-ence and political processes. But there may have been competition over inadequate amounts of FDI between Ethiopia's ISI model and Eritrea's EP model. This is not to claim that the slide to war stemmed solely from structural factors, but merely to suggest that declining economic performance on both sides of the then-hardening border (i.e., when the naqfa replaced the Ethiopian birr as Eritrea's currency) may have channeled intergovernmental relations in an antagonistic direction. From the ashes of this calamitous reversion to war, there arose a *dirigiste* state.

The border war between Ethiopia and Eritrea was a catalyst for the Eritrean state's assumption of greater regulatory power over all aspects of its wartime economy. War saw the collapse of GDP growth; massive disruption of agricultural production and infrastructure (for a second time); the displacement of 1 million people; the acceleration of inflation fueled by massive central bank borrowing to finance the expanding deficit; the loss of port fees with Ethiopia; the draining of international reserves; the damage of the external account due to the virtual cessation of trade with Ethiopia, which had previously accounted for two-thirds of Eritrean exports; and the massive defense expenditure which became equivalent to 25 percent of GDP. Further, the mobilization of an estimated 300,000 soldiers and national service draftees (about 15 percent of the labor force) reduced labor for the public administration and the private sector (IMF 2006).

The limitations of the pre–border war macroeconomic strategy exacerbated the new wartime economy. The economy had few dynamic export sectors: exports were estimated at US$12 million in 2005 and imports at US$463 million (IMF 2006). Crucially, however, remittances from the diaspora reportedly reached US$447 million in 2005. Development strategy remained based on the MT paradigm, however, but one hitched to an ever-widening and deepening securitization of the accumulation process. The paradigm adopted in Eritrea thus fits with Patel and McMichael's observation that "Third Worldism" leaves intact the mechanisms of capital accumulation, and thus shares a similar set of assumptions as the West, even if economic nationalism can frequently clash with US hegemony (Patel and McMichael 2004). Increasingly the MT perspective on development became a process without agents and a technocratic fix soldered to economic securitization: regional autarky from Ethiopia, the mistrust (often justified) of international NGOs and multilateral food agencies, neomercantilist export policies, increasingly stringent controls on foreign exchange and foodstuffs, and a nationalist-cum-modernist narrative on infrastructural investment in agriculture.

Similarly, Bundegaard aptly notes that developing new approaches different from that of the battlefield would prove the weakness of the PFDJ government—that the perceived necessity of market-based economic policies and good governance would clash with the ideological preconceptions of the PFDJ leadership, especially in the post–border war period. Bundegaard argues that the PFDJ was unable to transform the basis of its legitimacy in a civic or governmental direction; the revolution became institutionalized and bureaucratized, memorialized as the system to end all systems. The priorities therefore became security first, democracy last, and development somewhere in between (Bundegaard 2004: 40, 59, 62, 63). I would concur that the differences in the governance of the PFDJ pre– and post–border war were more apparent than real. And that the economic problems facing Eritrea were inevitable anyhow, with the border war perhaps only accelerating the economic crisis.

Nowhere is the MT worldview more evident than in Eritrean agriculture, the sector in which up to 80 percent of the population is occupied. Agriculture remains the "Achilles Heel" of Eritrea's modernization ambitions. The agrarian question concerns the issue of attaining food self-sufficiency in agriculture, together with the ability to generate surplus for industrialization and to feed the cities. Yet Eritrea suffers from chronic underproduction even by sub-Saharan Africa standards. Coupled with this structural underdevelopment is the manner in which the Eritrean state approaches the countryside as if it was another "front," a campaign waged in the government press and marked by the state slowly but successfully occupying a rural terrain through the mapping and installation of the ever-expanding girders of modernity (microdams, roads, electricity grids, health clinics, commercial farm start-ups, vaccination stations, and so on), with the national conscripts of the *warsay-yikealo* campaign being the main agents in an otherwise citizenless rural terrain without history or social fabric.[6] Certainly some of these campaigns have been successful on their own terms, in particular the excellent road-building programs, food-for-work campaigns to prevent hillside erosion, and rural electrification. This in a context where aid agencies and NGOs are ever more restricted from operating in the countryside, as the government seeks cereal production self-sufficiency. The years since independence have been marked by erratic fluctuations in food grain production (e.g., teff, sorghum, millet, barley, and wheat). In good years the harvest can meet up to two-thirds of domestic demand (roughly 650,000 metric tons of cereal), while in bad years less than one-third. The deficit must be met by either aid donations, or commercial imports purchased with scarce foreign exchange. The state challenges can be summed up in an old popular saying: "We don't care whether it rains or not, as long as it rains in Canada."

Thus with the increasing imperative to securitize accumulation on the vital agricultural front, the Eritrean state has pressed for self-reliance and the elimination of food aid dependency even though sustainable food security is far from guaranteed and malnutrition still prevalent. A case in point was the expulsion of USAID, and reference in the government press to bilateral donors as being "neo-colonialist" and *"Wazungu"* (Swahili for "white men," which can also be pejorative for "overbearing" and "domineering"). More recently, a PFDJ press release talked of practical action, not "empty theories," as the only way to eradicate rural poverty in a world of "muscle-flexing bullies," "exploiters," and "discredited governments," so that the Eritrean nation may attain economic emancipation and thus national security (shabait.com 2007). Despite such measures, the picture remains bleak even from the security lens of the Eritrean state. Government allocations of land concessions to investors have not made a significant contribution to the country's food security status. Demobilization, when it happens, will present even more daunting challenges to the country's already fragile economy. Many soldiers have become urbanized in the army and face limited economic prospects in impoverished villages. Until full demobilization occurs, labor shortages will continue to have a negative affect on the rural labor supplies such as the ability of families to plow and harvest crops.

Agricultural policy since independence points to the peasantry's weak voice. Select trends in key sectors of agriculture will highlight the state's MT perception of village transformation. While data is difficult to interpret, current expenditures for agriculture in Eritrea have shown a relative constant share of state expenditure since 2000, with a marked decline in capital expenditure of 167 million naqfa to a low of 30 million naqfa in 2003 followed by a slight rise in 2005 (IMF 2006). This, on the back of pre– border war public sector retrenchments (1995–1997) amounting to 10,000 from 30,000 employees, which reduced critical services to the rural areas including health, education, inputs, and rural extensionists (Murtaza 1998: 105; Soeters and Tessema 2004: 629). Similarly the power of local government institutions is not defined nor is there devolution of control over local resources to traditional village councils (Murtaza 1998: 99). Village-level government and regional administration are firmly under centralized control. Land tenure reform legislation was promulgated in 1994, under which the Eritrean state would maintain ownership of all land, while farmers would be allowed lifelong leases on currently held land in their home village. The implications of this land tenure reform for pastoralist communities are unclear especially as the policy is one of sedentarization.

To compound this uncertainty, the land act allows the government to lease land for resettlement and commercial purposes, a grave threat to pastoral grazing lands and a potentially serious schism between Muslim and Christian communities (Murtaza 1998: 105). Preliminary evidence indicates little land tenure change in the highland peasant communities. The land tenure reform to which the state continues to aspire remains controversial vis-à-vis the traditional peasant communal form (*diessa*).[7] Whether *diessa* holds back national productivity, as claimed by urban-based modernizers in the Eritrean ministries, will remain a moot point until substantial investments are made, especially in human capital. An appropriate understanding of the extent to which profit-maximizing behavior trumps a more communitarian, moral economic ethos in the different rural regions is also essential. Moreover, the Ministry of Agriculture continues to lack sufficient capacity in areas such as extension, regulation, and information provision. Co-operative legislation, backed by technical support from the International Labor Organization (ILO) in the late 1990s, remains in hiatus. Without an independent cooperative movement there are few channels for village-level input in areas such as government technical assistance, management training, and pricing policy. There is little in the way of local-level capacity even among the few government-sponsored farmers' associations. A series of recommendations by agricultural professionals in March 2006 recognized the need for a more "farmer-centered" approach, but it remains to be seen if these recommendations will be incorporated into the state's food security framework. Technical perspectives are in part derived from the fact that most if not all Ministry of Agriculture department heads are trained in technical fields, and perhaps can also be explained in terms of the administrative culture in the bureaucracy. But fifteen years of independence is more than enough time for the political center to learn from mistaken technocratic approaches. This dualist approach towards agriculture was in part underwritten by the Eritrean diaspora, a constituency that would have little to say about rural development, generally speaking, due to its having been socialized in Western industrialism (Murtaza 1998: 184).

Global Actors and the World System

In the wake of the border war, both the EPRDF and PFDJ governments, erstwhile Marxist fronts (though of different ideological tendencies), turned to militant nationalism(s) and the internationalization of their interstate conflict. The end of the Cold War would have appeared to offer Southern states the space to reduce military expenditures in a new post–Cold War context, but there was always the possibility of what Hawthorn terms "local conflicts," and whether the West and/or the UN would have the will to intervene to solve them (Hawthorn 1994: 141–42). But in the post–border war period it is unclear what the United Nations Mission in Ethiopia and Eritrea (UNMEE) and its Western backers' "will to intervene" actually represents: simple peacekeeping and border demarcation; or a new security terrain to contain, but never really structurally resolve, "local conflicts." The lugubrious "Great Game" endures in the Horn of Africa, as elsewhere. Given the bleak possibilities for FDI-driven industrialization for most Southern states and Africa (except perhaps South Africa), Hawthorn crucially argues:

> Where the possibility presents itself, their most rational hope is to enter an alliance with a stronger economy. In this way they can protect themselves against the worst of the increasing international competition for trade and investment, and once they have overcome the more immediate political consequences, in making an economic alliance, of dislocation and adjustment, insure themselves against the turbulence that comes from declining advantage and increasing despair (Hawthorn 1994: 144).

In pursuit of such an alliance, and in time-honored tradition, the regional superpower, EPRDF Ethiopia, opted to "lean on the mountain." This is Ethiopia's "Faustian Bargain."[8] For Eritrea, after perhaps similar and tentative overtures to Imperial America, including joining the "Coalition of the Willing" in the Iraq debacle, the PFDJ regime realized the US terminally favors its larger so-called "linchpin" neighbor, including around the border standoff, and thus opted to "be the mountain," revving up a rewarmed anti-imperialism that only further heightened the sense of siege that Eritrea was under and affirming the leadership's telos of a second betrayal of Eritrean statehood by the UN, US, and Ethiopia. In turn, this hostile disposition towards the US deepened the imperative to securitize development and accumulation against external threat. The leadership has also sought to forge economic alliances with the apparently up-and-coming hegemon, China, which also maintains good relations with Ethiopia.[9] Nonetheless the question of revenue remains crucial to state capacity (Hawthorn 1994: 142).

The economic realities become grimmer when the conundrum presented by the IFIs is taken into consideration. The IMF maintains that Eritrea, one of the world's poorest countries, must extricate its peasant economy from the border conflict as much as possible, and move ahead with needed reforms: demobilization, reducing military expenditure, poverty alleviation, curbing high inflation, reducing fiscal deficits and national debt, addressing declining international reserves and export levels, instituting transparent policymaking, and removing unnecessary regulatory and exchange rate controls. According to the IMF, Eritrea's growth prospects remain bleak. While its growth rate during 2000–2004 was 3.6 percent (World Bank 2006: 44), the IMF estimates that growth for 2005–2010 will be only 1.2 percent, and 0.9 percent over the long run, below the projected population growth rate of 2.4 percent, as structural imbalances, stifled private investment, and persistent foreign exchange shortages impede economic recovery (IMF 2006). Aid per capita in 2004 stood at US$61.3, placing Eritrea among the top ten countries out of forty-eight in sub-Saharan Africa (World Bank Africa 2006: 89). These sobering economic trends could be offset to some extent by higher aid flows, an increase in diaspora remittances, and the coming onto stream of mineral exports (including gold) (IMF 2006). More than half of Eritrea's population lives on less than US$1 per day. The country is ranked 157 on the United Nations' Human Development Index of 177 countries, and shifts slightly upwards annually in relation to some of the advances made in the social sector in reducing illiteracy and infant mortality, and the opening of new regional hospitals (IMF 2006).

Regardless, systematically moving up the rankings of the development index, let alone the core/semiperiphery/periphery, becomes ever more of a chimera. And where would market reforms take the Eritrean economy? For while the argument is that deflation and devaluation, the deregulation of investment and trade, and the denationalization of enterprises would both make economies more efficient via the world economy, and create a more "democratic" society (Hawthorn 1994: 136), the actual results of such policies in Africa are at best mixed. For example, after over twelve years of neoliberal reform in Mozambique, and growth rates of 8.9 percent over 2000–2004, and 6.3 percent over the previous decade, 70 percent of Mozambicans still live below the poverty line, even with integration of portions of the national economy with South African capital (Taylor 2003: 320–23; World Bank 2006: 26). Rajeev Patel and Philip McMichael correctly identify the IFIs with neoliberalism (2004: 234), though they undoubtedly exaggerate, as history warns us, by labeling such global social forces "fascistic" without elucidating their social content. Bundegaard also notes that the PFDJ resists "good governance" from the well-known experience of other African countries (presumably he means phenomena like corruption, genocide, and foreign interference), but opines that such a "style" hurts an aid relationship that the regime must maintain if it is to access the required investment funds (2004: 55–57). It is possible that the Eritrean state believes it can hold at bay being "adjusted" as it seeks alternative FDI strategies to securely recalibrate its accumulation strategies.

Such a possibility may lie with the World Trade Organization (WTO). Eritrea is an observer but not a full member of the WTO. Eritrea's status allows it to pursue a neomercantilist strategy, to restart its EP approach, and without the reciprocal opening of its crucial service sector. Eritrean officials are hopeful that Eritrea's Economic Processing Zones (EPZs), particularly Massawa, will attract significant investment since it has special preferential access to overseas markets due to its low per capita gross national income of less than US$1,000. Production in the EPZs requires 40 percent local input. Potentially this could provide the surplus required for a service sector dominated by Party Owned Enterprises (POEs) to secure the national economy (roads, electricity, airports, decentralized locales for colleges, military installations, etc). Relatively little is known about the wide range of ventures owned wholly or in part by the POEs, but they include businesses in the construction, information technology, publishing, and tourism sectors (e.g., Red Sea Corporation). For the PFDJ, the state has a basic moral responsibility for social service provision—an economic covenant—and thus must resist IFI dictates or domestic forces that are perceived to threaten its proclaimed principles of self-reliance and social justice. Whether talk on preferential access to Northern markets in the current Doha[10] round will allow Southern states to exploit their comparative advantages of labor intensive industries in EPZs is by no means evident, even assuming the elimination of new forms of Western protectionism (Hawthorn 1994: 142).[11]

Turning once again to East Asia for comparative insight, Taiwan established one of the world's first export processing zones (EPZs) in Kaosiung in 1965 in order to encourage technological advance and to expand exports. The Kaosiung EPZ successfully attracted FDI. However the Kaosiung EPZ never accounted for more than 10 percent of Taiwan's exports because export activity occurred throughout the Taiwan economy (Bräutigam 1994: 131). This stands in contrast to the dualistic nature of the Eritrean economy raised above. Historical timing is also important. EPZs have been around since the 1970s, starting with Malaysia, and are now a general sight in Southern states. Even autarkic North Korea has its own EPZ, the Kaesong Industrial Complex, which has had mixed success due to its international pariah status. Hart-Landsberg and Berkett note that the Association of Southeast Asian Nations (ASEAN) themselves have not met with successful ISI outcomes, and their EPZs, dominated by foreign multinational corporations (MNCs), have few linkages to local national firms (1998: 100–101). Even the East Asian "tigers," South Korea and Taiwan, face challenges, for despite considerable progress in aggregate growth terms and social well-being, recent developments call into question the ability of their domestic growth strategies to survive a regionalized accumulation process that incorporates Japan and the ASEAN countries. For example, South Korea's technological capacity is inferior to that of Japan's; at the same time, South Korean firms face ever-deeper trade deficits and overproduction due to competition from ASEAN countries for export markets. Both South Korea and Taiwan also face pressure from the US to open up their domestic markets to US exports. There are many other similar examples of which the PFDJ regime could take note before fully embracing the EP model.

Ideological Ground Shifts

Eritrea, a war zone during Africa's "lost decade" of the 1980s, missed the massive counterattack of the IFIs against the development projects and "transitions to socialism(s)" of Africa's radical nationalist regimes. Examples include, in Mozambique, the Front for the Liberation of Mozambique (FRELIMO) Fourth Congress of 1983, a Soviet-style New Economic Program (NEP) made en route to the capitalist restoration of the Fifth Party Congress in 1989; in Tanzania, the Chama cha Mapinduzi (CCM, an acronym in Swahili that means "The Revolutionary Party") and its Zanzibar Declaration of 1991, which undid the Arusha Declaration of 1967; and in Ethiopia, the belated right turn of the Derg when the revolutions in Eastern Europe precipitated a collapse of Ethiopia's overseas alliances and financial support. By the early 1990s, state-led left-wing developmentalism in Africa had shot its bolt.

The fate of these African monoparty developmental states, and their deeply fractured "dual transitions," is probably more instructive in assessing the prospects for the contemporary Eritrean state than reference to East Asia.[12] The common denominator underpinning these failures roughly cover the areas of antipeasant policies; a financially overdeveloped state; low tolerance of domestic internal, interparty or intraparty reform challenges; and external interventions/interference by Western powers. What of Eritrea? It certainly appears to have all of these qualities. One observer has noted, "One might be inclined to perceive the country as one of the last instances of the 'vanguard politics' of the revolutionary projects of the 20th century, with the Eritrean nation-building process seemingly suffering from one of the state's common 'child diseases': democratic deficiency." (Bundegaard 2004: 65).

But it goes deeper than a simple democratic vacuum. Certainly the collapse of the Eastern bloc may have narrowed policy options in regards to a noncapitalist pathway out of underdevelopment at the time. But what went into the historic dustbin was authoritarian "actually-existing socialism," not the ideal of socialism per se, especially in a plural world resisting corporate globalization (Kellner 1995: 25–26). Though the fighting qualities, political mobilization, and commitment of the Eritrean liberation fronts were beyond a doubt, there was no real doctrinal innovation by the leaderships in terms of forging an organic Eritrean socialism. The northeastern Eritrean town of Naqfa was the redoubt to which the EPLF withdrew after its "long march" in 1979, but, unlike the Yen'an of the Chinese Communist Party, there appeared to be little in the way of original theoretical work produced in this liberated zone. Rather, the leadership aptly applied already tried and tested Marxian tenets to the mobilizational, organizational, and bureaucratic collectivist structures of the EPLF (e.g., the Maoist "people's war," Leninist "democratic" centralism, etc.). Like elsewhere in radical Africana, however, the socialist content of the Front's politics was abandoned by the late 1980s: "Indicative of EPLF pragmatism, the programmatic shift from Marxist-Leninist-Maoist policies in favor of democracy, pluralism and the market at its 1987 congress facilitated sympathetic U.S. mediation" (Pool 1995: 33). With victory in the air, and perhaps seeing the writing on the (Berlin?) wall, the EPLF made its own right turn by formally abandoning Marxism, and even a modified Eritrean socialism with a "human face."

The mass mobilization/party centralist models of the liberation war were to endure into the postindependence period, but with very little socialist content. This aversion to socialism cannot be explained solely by the international climate at the time, which was by no means static as the 1990s progressed, as Latin America's contemporary left-wing populist resurgence demonstrates. Remarkably, unlike the other radical nationalist regimes in Africa, there was not even lip service paid to empowering popular economic organs like cooperatives and trade unions.[13] An antitheory predisposition appears to be the norm in PFDJ ruling circles, which in turn infects its relationship to intelligentsia, university students, party publications, national planning priorities, and postsocialist theory building. Certainly front-sanctioned periodicals containing foreign-written articles on the concept of popular democracy by Marxist Africanists circulate among PFDJ cadres from party headquarters and the wider public. But there are no signs of any official sanctioning of autonomous organizations. As an opposition website correctly notes: "The PFDJ prides itself on being 'pragmatic' but the problem with pragmatism is that there is no underlying principle, only what 'works' or appears to work at any given time. It is this pragmatism that took the PFDJ from embracing Maoism in 1971 to liberal democracy in 1987 and back to Maoism in 2002."[14] It is on the assertion that 2002 was some kind of "left" turn that the analysis errs. Rather, more akin to Taiwan's Kuomintang (KMT)—the Chinese nationalists, originally a Leninist party—the PFDJ morphed into a nationalist party-state as it sought supervision in all spheres of state, economic, and social life. This had little to do with socialism. Such a process has been termed a "monolithic regime" (Kong 2004: 351), and indeed there are general parallels worth examining between the KMT and the PFDJ, while of course keeping the differing contexts in mind.[15]

Like KMT, the PFDJ is a fusion of military and political administration. EPLF/PFDJ is a highly disciplined and centralized political and military organization. As Kong notes, monolithic regimes are led by parties committed to permanent rule, where political control extends beyond political deactivation and instead takes the form of intense politicization of the state and social spheres. Intense politicization in turn ensures that the party presence is ubiquitous, while pre-empting alternative regime options. In reference to South Korea and Taiwan, Koo states:

> Political division in both countries and continuing confrontation with the Communists provided the state with a permanent excuse for violence and repression. They also led to hyper-militarization and the maintenance of an extensive security system of police and intelligence. ... Because administrative and coercive organizations are the most important bases of state power, this hyper-militarization of society inevitably enhanced the power of the state over society (1987: 172).

To some extent this power was checked by security dependence on the US and therefore the South Korea and Taiwan regimes could not repudiate liberal democratic standards altogether. Moreover, KMT authoritarianism had to be accommodated within the context of capitalism, and therefore Kong terms the KMT "quasi-monolithic" (2004: 348). I would argue that the PFDJ is more politically monolithic than the KMT since it does not (nor never did) have a Great Power patron that could influence its policies. While the Organization of Africa Unity (OAU), through its liberation committee, supported the southern Africa national liberation movements with material, bases, and publicity against settler and white colonialism, Eritrea's liberation fronts (also opposed by the superpowers) received only opprobrium from an Addis Ababa-based OAU that viewed the Eritrean question as "secessionist." After thirty years of protracted warfare, followed by massive conventional warfare during 1998–2000, the PFDJ was grimly determined to dominate the new nation-state of Eritrea after having carved and forged it through the struggle. Strong internal cohesion was aided by the absence of political rivals who came to be based outside the country from earlier struggles. The state was very cohesive, with most key ministries being held by former EPLF political bureau members and secondary ones held by central committee members (Pool 2001: 172–73).

More than any other liberation movement on the African continent, the EPLF was very isolated from the fractured society that spawned it (Pool 2001). Due to the war and other transformations there were few local-level modern or traditional elites with which to necessitate the courting of political alliances, meaning that in the Eritrean case the PFDJ had asymmetrical political power in favor of a centralized executive. Related to this, the PFDJ, like the KMT, was anti–big business, perhaps for ideological reasons, but more likely because it opposed the emergence of an autonomous national bourgeoisie independent of the Eritrean state and its allied business and party enterprises. This is similar to Zimbabwe under the Zimbabwe African National Union-Patriotic Front (ZANU-PF) (Dashwood 2000: 93–94), except that civil society is much more evident there. The Eritrean state did not, as a consequence, have to make political coalitions with any particular nonparty social grouping. There in fact appears to be a widening chasm between the fighter-political bloc and the mass of Eritrean society, a form of "disembodied" autonomy as distinct from Evan's "embedded" concept. Or to put it in the words of one *Asmarino*'s dour utterance, "Fighters and the people mix like oil and water."

Politically speaking, therefore, the PFDJ state is beholden to no one for its self-legitimization. As Haggard states, "The plausibility of ideological arguments for policy choice increases with the degree of autonomy of political elites from societal or international constraints" (1999: 47). This is both its strength and its weakness: it has significant political autonomy but diminishing state capacity, economic decline, and no contemporary Great Power patron to underwrite its postrevolutionary rule. Governmental structures such as the legislature, judiciary, civil service, and even the executive branch have been corroded by this extreme concentration of power. The National Assembly is somnolent. The judiciary has failed to enforce the constitution. The civil service, aside from its top apexes, suffers from low pay, politicization of appointments, lack of skilled staff, and tension between university graduates and the less-educated ex-fighters who administer them (Soeters and Tessema 2004). Increasing numbers of younger civil servants are in fact fleeing Eritrea, which only further erodes administrative capacity. Even the cabinet appears to have been eclipsed by the increasingly centralized president's office, especially in the spheres of internal security, military zonal commands, expenditures, and economic policy. Economically the Eritrean state can only stay the course on an ever-deteriorating plain of tight budgets, anti-inflation and exchange control measures, food rationing, wage freezes, and so forth. Whether it aspires to be developmental or not is a moot point as there is now little room for the Eritrean state to maneuver.

While the East Asian states eventually confronted the dilemmas of economic prowess—the development of a middle class less tolerant of authoritarianism, new emergent coalitions, policy shifts, and a more complex economy to manage (Hawthorn 1994: 140; Koo 1987: 17; Panayiotopoulos 1995: 17)—the Eritrean state maintains control through deepening securitization bereft of societal transformation. A moving war memoir written by a medical surgeon tells the story of the moment crestfallen EPLF fighters received the news of the Soviet intervention on the side of the Derg, but, equally, retained hope of ultimate victory because Marxism had taught them that internal factors determine the "development of a matter" (Fekadu 2002: 126). For an erstwhile Marxist movement that once claimed the internal dialectic as primary, the contemporary Eritrean state perceives the external as primary. Here the narrative of nationalism, sovereignty, economic securitization, and forms of superregulatory control of human beings co-alesces. The extreme autonomy of the Eritrean state and its perception of external and internal threats therefore requires coercive governance, and economic centralism. It is a forced march through history on behalf of those who died in the struggle. The walled martyrs' cemeteries erected throughout the countryside, some painted with the images of the *tegadalti* (fighters), are a reminder of those who never experienced the dream of independent nationhood, as well as those yet born—as Benedict Anderson reminded a gathering in Asmara in the summer of 2006—both emotive if voiceless constituencies. The current generation is like a passenger in this journey and must play their subordinate part in the back seat of an increasingly aging vehicle. Media exhortations and portrayals of Eritrea as a "neo-Sparta," its martial golden age being shown on *EriTV*, reminds its middle class audience that the "enemy may be at the gates" and thus the "hoplite" nation-state needs unity, undivided loyalty, military expertise, self-discipline, adversity to pain, bravery, and ever-readiness to meet the next "Thermopylae."[16] As Bundegaard aptly notes, the postinsurgency state becomes detached from society to become an end in itself: the curse of revolutionary legitimacy means maintaining heroic commitment (Bundegaard 2004).

Hence national liberation movements, in contrast to governments coming to power through election or power transfer, must satisfy more people with ever greater expectations. And without constitutional rule, the PFDJ confronts the formidable challenge of governing based upon the nationalist narrative itself (Bundegaard 2004: 55–57). Perhaps the greatest paradox from the early 1993 period is that Eritrea resembles another northeast Asia model—North Korea. Like the North Korean army poised along the 38th parallel of the Korean peninsula, the Eritrean Defense Forces (EDF) face another pro-US regime's army across the border to its south. With an endless border standoff, growing xenophobia, mass repression, collective punishment, anti-US sentiment, extreme food insecurity, technological and trade stagnation (Eberstadt 2000), the wasting of human development potential, and ever persistent shortages in Asmara that some have equated to Pyongyang, the EDF remains the state's only strategic asset. The two armies hang over the region like metaphorical wrecking balls. Through both circumstance and will the Eritrean state lies suspended in the political economy of conflict in a race to the bottom with its neighbors.

Imagining a Developmental State in Eritrea

As argued in this chapter, the lack of a coalition to lobby for alternative policies, a cohesive yet totally insular political leadership, a *dirigiste* MT, weak governmental capacity, external threat, and nationalist ideology all radically enhanced the Eritrean state's autonomy but incapacitated its accumulation capabilities. Caught between the devil and the deep blue sea, the Eritrean state stares at two dangerous alternatives: the status quo nationalist paradigm or the completion of the neoliberal transition under severe macroeconomic instability. With the only "take-off" in sight being the hemorrhaging of its citizens, the PFDJ's nation-building model is mired in a crisis of unmet expectations: it is a Leviathan on clay legs. Aside from select bilateral aid and the World Bank, the Eritrean state remains dependent on remittances from an Eritrean diaspora that is no longer willing to remit its money so uncritically to the homeland. Youth migration is the closest thing to a social movement in Eritrea (and for that matter in the other Horn countries). The option of choice for increasing numbers is neither "voice" nor "loyalty" but "exit," as youth vote with their feet to the unknowns of the great trek north, into alien countries, over deserts, across seas, and into the arms of Fortress Europe/North America to become exploited informals, if fortunate enough. Once beyond the Eritrean borderline, Eritrean youth are no longer desired by their motherland, and in fact are not even remarked upon in passing by the government press, even when deaths on the high seas are reported in the international media. Their broken dreams can be summed up by one youth who remarked, "Singapore—I don't know you."

Short of an outright regional conflagration, the PDFJ state will most likely not exit the historical stage anytime soon. Whether Eritrea has its "Thermidor" is difficult to predict (i.e., when power slips from the hands of an original revolutionary leadership and reverts to some kind of conservative regime). In the Eritrean case, what would follow would most likely be a kind of political thaw to a less monolithic regime, but with further integration into the world economy from a position of economic weakness. Short of this, there is clearly no will to democratize among the leadership. The PFDJ regime itself never felt any great allurement for the bourgeois path, which the tepid 1991–1997 economic experience only reinforced. Müller argues that pre-1998 "governance and state building in Eritrea could rightly be seen as a quite successful counter-narrative to the global agenda of 'good governance' as a prerequisite for African development." But subsequent reversion to an outdated model of a one-party state has unleashed the forces of modernity with "their own dynamics and cannot be easily be subdued again under authoritarian control" (Müller 2006b:

520). This is a very important point, but one that leaves unspecified the precise identity of these forces and their dynamic given the arguments made in this chapter about the disembodied nature of the Eritrean state. The liberal democratic path of political pluralism, open markets, civil society, NGOs, and so forth does not have a historical agent. After over a century of multiple authoritarianisms—Italian colonialism, British Military Administration (BMA), Feudal and Derg Ethiopia (though the Federation may be an important qualifier here)—there is no organic groundswell for liberal democracy in Eritrean society. There remains much hard work to do in Eritrean society to build the critical mass required to peacefully establish a new political dispensation and the required opening up of state and society, and this without certain opposition elements making their own "Faustian bargains" with outside powers. "Good governance" in the Eritrean political tradition, at least generally speaking for the urban areas, would mostly likely revolve around a developmentally efficient state—with strong regulation and some government ownership—that catalyzes steady material advances in the standards of living for all citizens, along with a functioning constitution that would prevent arbitrary state behavior.

What does the Eritrean case study reveal about the economic challenges facing Southern states? Like other scholars influenced by Clive Thomas's seminal work (1974), including myself, Hart-Landsberg and Berkett passionately argue that only popular struggles from below (of trade unions, indigenous peoples, women's organizations, environmental groups, farmers' associations, and human rights organizations) resisting the ecological and human costs of export-led growth can achieve locally integrated economies and even potentially transform regional economies (Hart-Landsberg and Berkett 1998: 106–7). This is not the place to attempt to revise Thomas's framework for the contemporary period, except to add a few words in the case of Eritrea. The necessity of getting agriculture grounded around pro-poor policies cannot be overemphasized, since the sector itself is under severe stress due to ecological degradation and "deagrarianization" (e.g., long-term trends in peasant agriculture related to greater proportions of household incomes being based on nonfarm sources, intrahousehold specialization between the genders, and land ownership concentration), and hence will present further challenges to the developmental aspirations of the Eritrean state. There needs to be a shift away from EP, and to a well-integrated ISI approach in order to reverse agrarian dualism and industrial stagnation. These policy instruments could include, among others, a massive fiscal redirection of funds towards the rural areas as well as the promotion of state and cooperative units in areas such as food and procurement distribution channels. This would potentially reduce transaction costs and resolve institutional barriers to collective action dilemmas (Cypher and Dietz 1997: 413; Thomas 1974: 153–54). Backed by this kind of state support, trade unions and business enterprises should have the market autonomy to make rural-urban linkages.

Having said this, actual policies inside of Eritrea can only be charted as part of a political process that achieves maximum democratic participation. Popular sector control reasserted in areas such as autonomous village government and economic organs, the devolution of political power to regions and districts, and representative national associations of key constituencies in a new coalition could either pry open the monolithic state for greater corporate representation and accountability in economic policymaking, or peacefully supplant it through a popular movement. Only then will a democratically based developmental state be rooted in Eritrea that can harness the full promise of its peoples.

Notes

1. Singapore specialized in commercial and financial services before going to EP (Haggard 1999: 24).
2. Almost down to the last contributor in the book *Emergent Eritrea*, one finds American-educated Eritreans from either the US university system or the World Bank. Not surprisingly, they share strikingly similar worldviews on modernization in these articles as well as the ones on agriculture. Woldai Futur later became special advisor to the government before moving to the Ministry of National Development.
3. In another symbol of statehood, Eritrea acceded to the World Bank in a spirit of co-operation on 6 July 1994. "Eritrea and the Bank See Eye-to-Eye," *Eritrea Profile* 16 July 1994.
4. The aim being to create "a modern, technologically advanced, export-oriented economy, which will capitalize on its strategic, geographical position, natural resources, political stability, and hard-working people." "Eritrea: Open for Business," *Eritrean Profile* 27 August 1994.
5. During this period, agricultural growth was 5.4 percent and industry 18.3 percent (World Bank 2006).
6. This campaign was launched in 2002 with the purpose of employing the national army in economic development projects in various sectors, at suppressed wages.
7. The prevailing view on the origins of *diessa* is that the Italians formalized it through legal decrees but that it existed in some form in pre-Italian Eritrea. See Gebre-Medhin (1989: 43–44).
8. To "strike a Faustian bargain" is to be willing to sacrifice anything to satisfy a limitless desire for knowledge or power. Ethiopia's intervention against the Islamic Court Union (ICU), with tacit support from the US, would be a recent case in point. The EPRDF thus maintains its regional hegemony. The PFDJ's support of the authoritarian ICU, the logic apparently being "the enemy of my enemy is my friend," smacked of no more than hard-headed pragmatism, and which got Eritrea bumped into the US State Department's exclusive club of "the world's most systematic human rights violators," along

with Belarus, China, Cuba, Iran, Myanmar, North Korea, and Zimbabwe. It may soon join an even more exclusive club: the "State Sponsor of Terrorism" list comprising Iran, Syria, North Korea, Sudan, and Cuba.

9. The Chinese Communist Party (CCP) regime is a very different procapitalist entity from the one that welcomed the future Eritrean president to Nanjing military college in the 1960s.

10. The efforts since the WTO Cancun meeting by India, Brazil, and China, along with smaller groupings of like-minded Southern states, to demand access for their agriculture and textiles against Western protectionism remains a hopeful sign for export-centric strategies.

11. The potential effectiveness of African regional organizations relevant to the Horn, The Common Market for Eastern and Southern Africa (COMESA) and The Intergovernmental Authority on Development (IGAD), have not been tested due to regional instability.

12. An interesting comparative framework presents itself in relation to the South West People's Organization (SWAPO), which became independent in 1990 after the Cold War, like the EPLF. During their armed struggles both SWAPO and the EPLF espoused socialism, and both brutally dispatched intraparty left-wing challenges. After independence, both fronts quickly jettisoned socialism for a pragmatic nationalism. But in contrast to the EPLF/PFDJ, SWAPO's greater insertion into international diplomacy as well as competition from civil society and oppositional political forces, because of the total military supremacy of the apartheid South African army, meant that it had to forge compromises in its postindependence governance style rather than purely dominate it like in Eritrea. See Leys and Saul (1995).

13. FRELIMO's formative experience with the peasantry was in the liberated zones of Cabo Delgado, when armed struggle started in 1964. Socialist cooperatives were a key mobilization strategy during the liberation war, as it was with the EPLF. After independence, Mozambique's family and cooperative sectors were left to their own devices, bereft of marketing structures, inputs, incentives, and training. FRELIMO rapidly changed from a popular liberation front to an antipeasant one-party state (Bowen 2000: 49–50). The Ethiopian Derg and CCM Tanzania also imposed top-down villagization upon their peasantries.

14. Saleh AA Younis, 27 February 2007, www.awate.com.

15. "Totalitarian" has emotive connotations, and referral points to Nazi Germany and Stalinist USSR, both of which were extremely powerful states. I argue that the Southern state can rarely aspire to such power vis-à-vis either its own society and/or the wider global arena. For both of these reasons, "monolithic" is a better term.

16. This begs the question as to who represents "neo-Macedonia" and "neo-Rome." More to the point, an exhausted and eclipsed Sparta later became a backwater of the Roman Empire and a place of curiosity for its tourists.

CONCLUSION
Biopolitics and Dilemmas of Development in Eritrea and Elsewhere

e

Tricia Redeker Hepner and David O'Kane

The optimism with which independent Eritrea was once viewed both inside and outside the country all but disappeared at the turn of the twenty-first century. Certainly, a few traces still linger among trenchant supporters, propped up by the images and ideologies disseminated by the government via carefully orchestrated events and news media. But the ethnographic analysis of everyday Eritrean life, coupled with broader critical perspectives that mitigate against nationalist myths of exceptionalism, indicate otherwise.

Disappointing though they may be, Eritrea's lessons provide striking insights into the contemporary dilemmas of African (and other) societies in the contemporary era. In particular, they suggest that underpinning patterns of repression and violence is a principle common to the impetus for development in both advanced nations and those attempting to "catch up." The ethnographic analyses in this book have collectively pointed to the biopolitical strategies of one modernist, postrevolutionary state and the social impacts of its quest for political and economic sovereignty. In this concluding statement, we highlight once again the ways that these biopolitical strategies are historically and intimately linked to the pressures of capitalist development generally, whether expressed in the currently hegemonic discourse and policies of neoliberalism, or the contrasting language of revolutionary nationalism characteristic of many postcolonial African nations. Because they emerge from a common paradigmatic source, both neoliberal and revolutionary nationalist approaches to development depend upon interventions into human life that are at odds with their ideological justifications of securing individual or collective freedom and rights. Viewed this way, Eritrea's current crisis seems less rooted in the internal contradictions of that nation than in the way its political leadership has reshaped society as a deliberate response to the logic of the capitalist imperative, which itself may be described as at least partly "biopolitical" in nature.

Biopolitical Catastrophes

Rajeev Patel and Philip McMichael have argued (2004) that the dashing of hopes for true independence in postcolonial nations was rooted in their retention of assumptions and methods first introduced by the "modernizing" colonial regimes. By this they do not mean that the postcolonial order was simply the colonial order under new management; the new elite classes and political leaderships who installed themselves after independence did take their societies down new paths and along different routes of social change. But this "progress" was navigated, they argue, according to the paradigm inherited from the old colonial masters, who sought control through distinctly biopolitical strategies of reshaping bodies and minds according to the needs of capitalist development and the particular power configurations that enabled it. The implication is that postcolonial independence was not at all a radical emancipation from capitalism, despite the revolutionary rhetoric that has typically surrounded these struggles. To achieve freedom and independence, a more radical, and perhaps impossible, form of emancipation needed to take place.

Accordingly, when countries like Eritrea sought independence, this necessarily should have entailed freeing people not only from oppressive regimes but also from the paradigms and practices that breed oppression. In uncovering the links between militarism and development in Eritrea as biopolitical phenomena, and showing how these connections play out in everyday life, we have highlighted the processes by which the tyranny of colonialism and then neoliberalism is first subverted by nationalism and then substituted with authoritarianism. That is, in its efforts to resist neoliberal capitalist hegemony, the Eritrean regime has reproduced the very logic by which African countries were originally colonized, and brutalized, by the "modernizing" efforts of the capitalist North/West and the imposition of the nation-state form. This, then, is the utility of a concept like biopolitics: it exposes the singular foundation of both neoliberal and revolutionary nationalist approaches to development despite their contrasting rhetoric and often antagonistic relationship.

A similar biopolitical dynamic can be inferred based on analyses of the African political scene since the major wave of movements for multiparty democracy at the beginning of the 1990s, which (importantly) coincided with the acceleration of neoliberal structural adjustment policies. Linda Kirschke (2000), for example, has documented how democratization movements in several African countries in the 1990s precipitated "informal repression," or that which is carried out not by formal state structures but by private militias and other popular organizations. This type of response found perhaps its highest expression in the years of crisis that culminated in the Rwandan genocide of 1994. The militias and "special forces" that perpetrated the genocide emerged in Rwanda from 1990 onward, as the moderate Hutu regime's concessions to demands for multiparty democracy aroused the displeasure of Hutu extremists. Those extremists were then able to take advantage of Rwanda's highly efficient state structures to act out the most heinous biopolitical paradigm of social control on the basis of biologically grounded, racialized definitions of ethnic identities inherited from the Belgian colonial era (Hintjens 1999; De Heusch 1995).

While Rwanda is perhaps the best known of Africa's biopolitical catastrophes, Zimbabwe is another germane example. Unresolved problems of land distribution (which required some form of solution, if not that offered by Mugabe's violent demagoguery) were just one part of a larger turn towards open dictatorship, foretold by the mass killings in Matabeleland in the mid-1980s. The authoritarian exercise of power intensified as Zimbabwe became increasingly subject to the neoliberal policy prescriptions of the international financial institutions (IFIs). Alex de Waal (1997: 57) points out how, as Zimbabwe became more and more enmeshed in the strictures of the IFIs, the Mugabe government rapidly abandoned even the semblance of accountability to its citizens, with highly adverse consequences for human rights and economic development. To raise this point is not to exculpate Mugabe's criminal endeavors, nor those of genocidaires and other human rights abusers; rather, it is to point out how such violent regimes emerge out of particular constellations of power that are linked to development. Ong refers to these constellations explicitly in her definition of biopolitics as the "state organization of populations to secure ... control, welfare and productivity" (1990: 258). It might be observed that there is neither welfare nor productivity in today's Zimbabwe, but strong control is certainly exercised by Mugabe over the Zimbabwean people in the name of national sovereignty.

Thus, to reiterate the historical analysis offered in the introduction to this volume, biopolitical strategies are unique to neither neoliberal nor revolutionary strategies for social, political, or economic development. Rather, they form a common principle driving modernization processes in societies that share long mutual entanglements and gross inequities in power and the distribution of resources both within and between them. Rather than asking whether the disaster in places like Rwanda, Zimbabwe, and Eritrea are the direct result of colonialism, neoliberalism, or the resistance to these through ideologies like nationalism, we would suggest that they emerge from the drawing together of societies over time and across space through the common, if not equally achievable, drive for political-economic modernization and growth.

The distinct irony of modernist ideologies like neoliberalism and nationalism, and the biopolitical policies of governance and power related to them, is the way both tend in practice to work against the values they claim to embody. While neoliberalism emphasizes the liberty and the rights of the individual, and revolutionary nationalism emphasizes the liberation of the collective, both seem to fail repeatedly at safeguarding or achieving either. Thus, the first modern testing site for neoliberal policy prescriptions in the developing world was Chile after Pinochet's coup, wherein thousands of citizens subsequently disappeared, suffered torture, or were executed for suspected links to "terrorists" and opposition movements (Klein 2007: 77). The classical liberalism from which contemporary neoliberalism derives was always an elitist ideology that feared the power and intentions of the broad masses and therefore restricted the liberties and rights of some individuals, especially according to class status, in order to privilege others and the "free market." Similarly, the EPLF's efforts to liberate "the broad masses" from colonial oppression and occupation have resulted in neither the rights of the collective nor of the individuals who comprise it. When the state accrues to itself unmediated and unmitigated control over citizens' lives through compulsory and indefinite military service or forced labor, and when it fails to guarantee individual or community rights through the rejection of its own constitution, it empowers the elite political apparatus through the direct disempowerment of the people while claiming to prioritize development for all.

On one level, Eritrea's problem emerges from the deficiencies at the heart of the current configuration of power—its centralization, unaccountability, and exclusion of genuinely popular initiatives. For example, in his account of Eritrea's present crisis, veteran journalist and chronicler of the revolution since the 1970s, Dan Connell, has pointed out that while the postindependence Eritrean government may have implemented a number of policy measures intended to enhance the social status of women, these reforms were not actually led by women (2005: 72). Similarly, each of the contributors in this volume has shown in various ways how the deployment of state power throughout rural and urban regions of the country, and among diverse sectors and institutions of society, invariably reaches a point at which its chokehold then erodes the very foundations of communities and institutions themselves. If Connell is right to argue that the social reforms targeted at Eritrean women have not been woman led, it is the case mutatis mutandis that all social reforms targeted at Eritrean people as a whole have not been "people led." This again highlights the irony of revolutionary nationalist rhetoric, in which the EPLF, and then the PFDJ, has long claimed an isomorphic relationship between nation, party, and state.

On another level, Eritrea's current predicament, and indeed the very configuration of its power structure, is related to its embedding in a hazardous regional political environment and a global context dominated by neoliberalism. Like the revolutionary nationalism that responds to it, the latter also claims to be a singular mode for securing rights and resources. However, neither neoliberalism nor the apparent rejection of it in places like Eritrea can resolve the dilemmas that emerge from the common denominator of developmental demands. Hence, political independence and the establishment of a nation-state do not inevitably lead to freedom, prosperity, and rights, no matter how persuasive the ideological arguments may be. As Ferguson notes (2006: 22), "The most challenging current political demands go beyond the claims of political independence and instead involve demands for connection, and for relationship, even under conditions of inequality and dependence." That both neoliberalism and the challenges to it ultimately remain underpinned by biopolitical strategies intended to enable capitalist growth and development under conditions of worsening inequality suggests that, with the exception of isolated and ephemeral historical moments, nation-states will fall back repeatedly on patterns of coercion and violence to achieve this end.

Sovereign Claims

This book has asked, and sought to answer, questions that are at the heart of the Eritrean condition today. What sort of state is Eritrea within a global system of reshaped and reshaping nation-states, increasingly defined by the rigors of expanding capital, and diffuse and variegated modes of governance, power, citizenship, and political community? What are the Eritrean government's objectives, and what constraints and opportunities does it face? By what sociopolitical, cultural, and economic means, and through what kinds of disciplinary practices, does the state pursue its goals? Given the extent of internal repression in Eritrea at this moment in time, where are the spaces for resistance, and what meanings inhere in their modalities? What precisely does "resistance" mean for Eritrea as a nation-state, and for Eritrean people around the world? Most importantly, can the people of Eritrea find any respite from their present predicament, especially insofar as it appears foundationally linked to the inequities, and iniquities, of global capitalist development?

While each contributing author has addressed these questions and highlighted the interrelationship between biopolitics, militarism, and development in unique ways, another pattern emerges as profoundly important for Eritrea and many other nations today: the struggle for "sovereignty." The concept of sovereignty has recently received considerable attention in contemporary anthropological thinking about politics, the state, and strategies of governance and power, especially in postcolonial and postmodern settings. Building on the work of Foucault and Agamben in particular, scholars have sought to elucidate the tensions inherent in both legal and de facto manifestations of sovereignty (Hansen and Stepputat 2006). The former includes not only conceptualizations of the national, territorial polity and the legitimate and legal right to govern, but also the wars and security regimes that remain "the hard kernel of modern states" (Hansen and Stepputat 2006: 296). De facto sovereignty, meanwhile, refers to the ability of states and other powerful political actors to exercise power over human life itself. In its most extreme manifestations, de facto sovereignty includes the ability "to kill, punish, and discipline with impunity" (ibid).

In this formulation, sovereignty is understood as "a tentative and always emergent form of authority grounded in violence," performed and inscribed on the bodies of subjects in order to "generate loyalty, fear, and legitimacy from the neighbourhood to the summit of the state" (Hansen and Stepputat 2006: 297). As all states, and particularly postcolonial ones, pursue a modernist agenda in a postmodern world, it is de facto sovereign power that forms "the central, if unacknowledged, underside of modern and liberal forms of highly codified and regulated (self) government" (ibid).

The links between the developmental goals of the Eritrean state and the biopolitical strategies it pursues, expressed most powerfully in the intensifying militarization of society and in "disciplinary practices" such as prolonged detention and torture, must also be understood as a bid for sovereign power in both the legal and de facto sense. That is, the Eritrean state's simultaneous rejection of neoliberalism through reasserting revolutionary nationalism and deploying coercive and violent power over its own population is illuminated by what Kapferer (2004) refers to as the "founding paradox" of the nation-state itself. In his view, modern states are predicated at once on war and violence, and yet also provide the precondition for achieving peace, security, and—we would add—development. The contemporary Irish nation-state, for example, was born out of a bloody revolution that culminated in a civil war marked by atrocities such as the Ballyseedy massacre, in which rebel troops taken prisoner by forces loyal to the new Irish national government were tied to a landmine, which was subsequently exploded (Younger 1979: 501). The ensuing decades in which Ireland struggled for economic development were lived out in the bitter legacy of that civil war. Contemporary Eritrea has not yet escaped from the legacy of its own wars, and today militarism and development form the crucial biopolitical nexus through which independence (from both Ethiopia and neoliberal pressures) is now pursued by the logic and language of sovereignty and national security.

However, as we have also seen throughout these chapters, this project emerges from, and is most meaningful with respect to, the specificities of Eritrea's anticolonial nationalist past. Consideration of the specific trajectory along which Eritrean history has run raises the uncomfortable possibility that the nationalist revolution itself and the pursuit of independence are not only inherently ambiguous and inchoate, but that they are also inherently violent and exclusionary. Eritrea's search for sovereignty thus encapsulates not only the sublime dreams of peace, freedom, and dignity ostensibly realizable by the achievement of a nation-state, but also the nightmares of those within the political community who find themselves reduced to "bare life" in prison cells, refugee camps, foreign detention centers, and the hardships of compulsory military service. In the state's efforts to chart its own mode of sovereign inclusion in the regional and global networks of power and capital, it uses violence and force to both include, and exclude, its own national subjects both at home and abroad.

Practices of violent exclusion within nation-states and political communities (which clearly extend across territorial borders, and exist in nonterritories such as cyberspace) are thus also related to the dialectics of inclusion and exclusion experienced by whole societies historically. Political anthropologists analyzing the relationship between legacies of colonialism and the contemporary manifestations of empire (currently exemplified by the United States and the "War on Terror") again highlight the manner in which state formations and sovereignties are always already the product of globally entangled histories and political economies (Hansen and Stepputat 2006: 300; also Gledhill 1994; Wolf 1982). Certainly Eritrea's collective history has been marked and understood as one of both forced inclusion and violent exclusion vis-à-vis regional and global political-economic interests, which today structure the modes of inclusion and exclusion within the Eritrean territory and broader political community. First through colonization by Italy and subsequently via reabsorption into Ethiopia (itself a function of superpower geopolitics), and also expressed within the nationalist war of independence, Eritrea's past is marked at all turns by this tension. In recent decades, the inclusion-exclusion dynamic has been manifested largely in terms of the neoliberal global order into which Eritrea was born in 1991–1993 and to which it is now responding with such intensity.

Indeed, the optimism with which Eritrea was regarded in its initial seven years of independent statehood was part of a wider trend that characterized the 1990s as a whole. Conceptualized as the first decade after the so-called "end of history," it was assumed by many that a new world order would bring about the smooth incorporation of the world's nation-states into a seamless global market. Since the late 1990s, however, the world economy has been characterized more by instability and crisis than it has by the even and regular operations of a (benevolent?) invisible hand. This has been the context into which the Eritrean state has tried to insert itself as an independent entity, both during the interlude of peace in 1991–1998, and in the aftermath of the disastrous Ethio-Eritrean border war of 1998–2000. Thus, the blithe recommendations of Paul B. Henze (1990) that Eritrea could easily and unproblematically join the neoliberal utopia of free markets disregarded the reality in which Eritrea, like other postcolonial African countries, was embedded.

Henze was not the only one to disregard key aspects of Eritrean reality, however, and this was not by accident. Behind the trite and superficial descriptions that were once applied to Eritrea with such alacrity — "an African country that works," and "a leader in the African Renaissance" — lay the weight of previous failed development strategies in Africa and the desperate desire on the part of neoliberal imaginations to confirm the universal validity of their core assumptions and policies. These descriptions, and suspicion of the "real" motives of the North/West, were also the backdrop against which the Eritrean state maneuvered as it increasingly tightened its control over the activities and presence of nongovernmental organizations, foreign aid workers, researchers, journalists, students, religious bodies, refugees, soldiers, dissidents, and members of the government itself. In hindsight, it might be argued that those foreign observers who, in the first seven years after 1991, focused on the efficiency of the new Eritrean state did so in ways that legitimized the state's dark side. This legitimization was produced by the downplaying or ignoring of the authoritarian practices that were carried over without interruption from the time of the liberation war, and which should have been apparent even in the seven years of peace that followed independence. Again, this hardly seems accidental when we survey the empirical, historical evidence of how neoliberalism, like revolutionary nationalism, depends on violence and repression to achieve common developmental ends.

But as the studies in this book have also illustrated, the struggle for sovereignty in Eritrea, as in many other parts of the world, has been far more ambiguous, complex, fraught, and fragile than simple distinctions between legal and de facto sovereignty suggest. In addition to the close interrelationship between the Eritrean state's pursuit of legal sovereignty with the exercise of violence and coercion are its efforts to induce consent and compliance throughout everyday practices and institutions. The "bureaucratic logic" (Handelman 2004) of the sovereign state is present, not surprisingly, in virtually all policies and institutions that regulate and give shape and meaning to citizens' lives. The search for state sovereignty, and the efforts of Eritrean people to both assert autonomy against the state and to comply with its demands, can be found in virtually all areas of social life: classrooms and technical training centers (Müller and Riggan), food security and agricultural schemes in regions of refugee resettlement (Poole), urban bars and charismatic churches (Treiber), holiday celebrations (Tekle Woldemikael), the experiences of fleeing and seeking asylum abroad (Hepner), and the remaking of time, space, and place itself (Mahrt). In these more mundane experiences of negotiating the sovereign, citizen-subjects and the state encounter one another directly and constantly, routinizing national identity and the role of state as both the primary protector from violence and its primary regulator and perpetrator (see Handelman 2004). In its unwillingness to surrender legal sovereignty to external forces, from regional political disruptions to neoliberal institutions and free markets, the state intervenes ever more intensely into society, colonizing both the lifeworld and economy—as Cameron shows so clearly in this volume (cf. Habermas 1984).

Our collective analysis of the consequences of Eritrea's biopolitical strategies for defense, development, and sovereignty suggest that the benign and the malign practices of the regime are not easily separated from one another. Nor are they likely, in our opinion, to deliver their putative outcomes in terms of development and national security, both of which are ostensible aims of sovereignty. First and foremost, they represent forms of power over life that ultimately incite malaise and/or resistance among those subjected to them. This is evident in the ongoing flight of young urbanites in particular from Eritrea, as well as the proliferation of political opposition movements, pro-democratic platforms, and human rights-based organizations among Eritrean transnationals in Europe, North America, Australia, and South Africa (see Hepner 2008). Moreover, the policies and practices of the government invite further intervention into the domestic affairs of Eritrean society by foreign governments and nonstate entities as officials increasingly spurn most diplomatic dialogue involving Western powers, the United Nations, and the African Union, regarding its own human rights violations, the unresolved border issue with Ethiopia, and the regional crises in Somalia and the Darfur region of Sudan.

In 2007, for example, the Eritrean government withdrew the country (at least temporarily) from the seven-member Intergovernmental Authority on Development (IGAD), thus intensifying its alienation from neighboring Horn and East African governments. Well-founded allegations of Eritrean government support for the ousted Somali Islamic Courts Union against the US-backed Ethiopian intervention on behalf of the Transitional Federal Government, meanwhile, positions it on the "wrong side" of the so-called War on Terror. Regarding IGAD, the African Union, the UN, and nongovernmental rights organizations such as Amnesty International, Human Rights Watch, and Reporters without Borders as in league with foreign, and especially American, interests, the regime seeks to redefine regional peace and national security in ways that both radically challenge hegemonic discourses of democracy and rights as emblematic of neoliberal imperialism, while retrenching exclusivist nationalism in the service of sovereignty.

While there are objective reasons for voicing critical concern over Eritrea's role in the greater Horn of Africa, we must also keep in mind Kapferer's (2004) observation that the renewed struggle for sovereignty today is part of a global movement linked to post 9/11 shifts. For its part, the US has justified the War on Terror in terms not unlike those invoked by Eritrean authorities when defending policies and practices as essential to national security, while countries like China, North Korea, and large portions of the greater Arab world also articulate antipathy towards US hegemony and internal actors cooperating with US interests (often for purposes all their own). The meaning of modern sovereign statehood, in Eritrea and elsewhere, thus suggests more than the ability to defend national interests and territory against enemies both external and internal to the political community. It also entails the capacity to intervene into other struggles, other societies, and other lives for preemptive and myopically "patriotic" reasons, while isolating the nation and selectively sealing its borders from the real and potential dangers that lie beyond.

Dreams Deferred, Dreams Distorted

One of the objectives of this book has been to place Eritrea within a broad context in order to understand the relevance of its experience beyond the specificities of history and territory. Eritrea, clearly, is not the only country in the world where sovereign power bends human life to its will, nor is it the only country that represents in its policies of development and national security the dark side of modernity. Rather, the biopolitical strategies that characterize contemporary Eritrea, and the forms of power exercised over human life, are the product of the developmental goals defined by global capitalism, and those that the militaristic garrison state has set for itself. Far from utopian, these goals were decided by the poverty and underdevelopment produced by decades of colonial rule and war. Today, these are pursued not through guerrilla warfare, but through a complex and often contradictory engagement with global patterns of political economy and power.

The human rights abuses perpetrated in Eritrea since 2001 have not been the sole responsibility of one individual head of state, though certainly President Issayas Afeworki must be held accountable. Nor are they solely the result of the bitter war with Ethiopia. The fate of Eritrea since the outbreak of renewed war with Ethiopia is rooted, rather, in the ways in which the PFDJ regime, like the EPLF before it, has tried to reshape Eritrean society. The regime's search for the sovereign, its concomitant opposition to North/Western hegemony, and its resistance to other international liberal pressures like human rights norms, has increasingly led the Eritrean government to turn towards "alternatives" represented by countries like China. Ideologically, one might trace at least some aspects of the Eritrean state's dismissal of civil and political rights to both the historic and contemporary relationship between the EPLF/PFDJ leadership and post-Maoist China. Issayas Afeworki not only trained militarily in China in the 1960s, but also drew many political perspectives and organizational inclinations from Maoism even after EPLF nationalists had abandoned their original commitment to state socialism and turned increasingly towards state capitalism.

But even those "alternative" political and organizational principles emerged out of a wider modernist perspective that stressed both the ability and the right of technocratic elites to direct, manage, develop, and, where necessary, revolutionize their societies from the barrel of a gun. Today, as China cultivates its economic and political ties to many African countries, Eritrea included, development may proceed apace without the interference of the imperialist North/West and the (often cynical) demand for submission to hegemonic principles of democratization and rights. However, African countries that are forging links with China may well find in the near future that the effects of Chinese capitalist development in Africa will have more than a passing resemblance to those of Northern/Western imperialism. To recognize this fact is to recognize that Eritrea, like the rest of its continent, remains buffeted by a host of turbulent factors that are driving African societies towards an uncertain and unpredictable future. It is in response to the uncertainty of the future, and the harsh reality of present-day social crises that states such as Eritrea justify their assumption of the power to control, dominate, and oppress their populations.

The government's policies, tactics, and strategies will continue to evolve as Eritrea is buffeted by the storms of global economic and political turbulence. This is likely to introduce new twists and novel features to the ways in which Eritrea's government seeks to control, discipline, and remold the Eritrean people—and it will produce new forms of resistance also. In the case of a country such as Eritrea, research is never a scholastic activity conducted for its own sake. It is, and will continue to be for the foreseeable future, heavily determined by the political situation in the country—and by the Eritrean people's struggle and need for a better political and economic future. The one accurate prediction that can be made for Eritrea's long-term future is that the present crisis and present regime will not last forever—if for no other reason than that the revolutionary generation that occupies power at all levels in the state will have to pass away at some point. The certainty of change, however, does not mean the certainty of change for the better. One of Eritrea's fellow countries in the Horn of Africa, Somalia, provides an object lesson in the ways in which the fall of a repressive, dictatorial regime can lead not to the liberation of the people but to a new order of insecurity and strife between competing power blocs and armed groups, an order that devastates the rights and lives of the people as much as the old order of one-man, single-party rule did (Besteman 1996).

This, then, is why biopolitics as a concept appears useful for our task. It illuminates, and perhaps indicts, the very principles that underpin modernist drives for development—whether pursued as neoliberalism or as nationalism—in an evolving global capitalist economy. In recognizing these common principles, it may become possible to envision alternatives for Eritrea and for the rest of the world. For if global pressures for development and the desire for sovereignty inevitably require violence, repression, and the subversion of the rights and freedoms these are intended to guarantee, do we not share a collective, human responsibility to reconceptualize development and sovereignty altogether? Is it possible to imagine, for Eritrea and elsewhere, social, economic, and political changes that truly achieve the goals they articulate: peace, freedom, justice, and greater equality in the accessing of resources and rights? To imagine such a scenario, let alone to achieve it, requires a concerted global effort to prioritize humanity over profits, and people over power. At one time, not so long ago, this radical utopian notion was contained in the popular dream of the Eritrean struggle itself.

LIST OF CONTRIBUTORS

Greg Cameron is Assistant Professor of Political Science and Rural Community Studies at the Nova Scotia Agricultural College, Truro, Canada. He completed his Ph.D. at the University of London, School of Oriental and African Studies. He spent ten years working and researching in Tanzania prior to teaching political science at the University of Asmara, Eritrea. His research interests also include rural politics in Zanzibar and issues surrounding the postcolonial state and struggles for popular governance. His publications include articles in *Review of African Political Economy, Journal of Eritrean Studies,* and *Democratization* as well as chapters in edited volumes with Routledge, Africa World Press, Karthala, and Nordic Africa Institute.

Tricia Redeker Hepner is Assistant Professor of Anthropology at the University of Tennessee, Knoxville. She received her Ph.D. in anthropology from Michigan State University, where she was a Distinguished Doctoral Fellow. Her research on Eritrea was funded by the National Science Foundation, the Social Science Research Council, and the Wenner-Gren Foundation for Anthropological Research. Her published work includes a co-edited volume of the *Eritrean Studies Review* (4:2, 2005) and articles in *Ethnic and Racial Studies, Identities: Global Studies in Culture and Power,* and the *Africa Policy Journal.*

Michael Mahrt is a Programme Officer with Save the Children Denmark and a doctoral candidate in Anthropology at University College London. His research interests include war, land, and spatial perception, as well as political identity and population movements. He has conducted seven years of professional and academic fieldwork in Eritrea.

Tanja R. Müller is a Lecturer in Development Studies at the Institute for Development Policy and Management, University of Manchester, UK. She received her Ph.D. in Development Studies at the University of East

Anglia, Norwich, UK, in 2003. Over the past ten years she has worked as a university lecturer in Dublin and Asmara, a consultant for education in Japan, and as a journalist on development issues. She was assistant professor at Wageningen University from 2003–2005 with the program African Women Leaders in Agriculture and the Environment (AWLAE). She has published the book *The Making of Elite Women: Revolution and Nation Building in Eritrea* (2005), Boston and Leiden: Brill Publishers, and recent articles on developments in Eritrea appeared in *Development and Change, Progress in Development Studies, Conflict, Security and Development,* and *The Journal of Modern African Studies.*

David O'Kane received his doctorate in Social Anthropology from Queen's University Belfast, Northern Ireland, in 2005, and at the time of writing (August 2008) he is an independent scholar. His doctoral research was carried out on the topics of land reform and nationalism among a peasant community in a highland Eritrea. He has taught at the University of Asmara, Eritrea, at Queen's University Belfast, Northern Ireland, and at third-level institutions in the Republic of Ireland (Dublin Business School), the Russian Federation (Smolny College of Liberal Arts and Sciences, St. Petersburg), and the United Kingdom (Centre of West African Studies, University of Birmingham). In the February–July semester of 2008 he taught in the Department of Anthropology at the University of Auckland, New Zealand.

Amanda Poole is a doctoral candidate in the Environmental Anthropology program at the University of Washington. Her dissertation research, funded by the Social Science Research Council, focused on refugee resettlement and rural development in Eritrea. She has served as a Peace Corps Volunteer in Eritrea and Namibia, and her research explores displacement and resettled communities as sites of state-making and transnational governance through the frameworks of political ecology, critical gender and development studies, and refugee studies.

Jennifer Riggan is Assistant Professor of International Studies at Arcadia University in Glenside, Pennsylvania. She received her Ph.D. in the Education, Culture, and Society Program at the University of Pennsylvania. Her dissertation examined how teachers in Eritrea re-define the relationship between the nation and the state in times of political and educational change, and her research was funded by an International Dissertation Research Fellowship from the Social Science Research Council and a student research grant from Fulbright IIE. She first traveled to Eritrea as a Peace

Corps volunteer in 1995 and returned to Eritrea several times throughout the course of her graduate study.

Magnus Treiber completed his Ph.D. in Social Anthropology at the University of Munich. He has visited and conducted ethnographic field research in Eritrea from 2001 to 2005. He currently teaches at the universities of Munich and Bayreuth, Germany. His research interests include urban anthropology and milieu studies, political culture in the Horn of Africa, and migration from Africa to Europe.

Tekle M. Woldemikael is Chair of the Department of Sociology at Chapman University. He has published numerous articles on Eritrea and Eritreans in diaspora, including "Language, Education, and Public Policy in Eritrea," in *African Studies Review* (2003), "Eritrea's Identity as a Cultural Crossroads," in *Race and Nation: Ethnic Systems in the Modern World* (Routledge Press, 2005) and "Bridging the Divide: Muslim and Christian Eritreans in Orange County, California" in *Eritrean Studies Review* (2005).

BIBLIOGRAPHY

Ahmed Abdulrahaim . 2006. *Salamat Aya Isaias, Wasup?* 20 May. http://www.awate.com.

Admas. 2001. "Ab hospital k'ele ztsenhe tmaharay yuniversiti 'arifu." 20 August.

Afewerki Iyassu. 1999. "Pack my things." *Eritrea Profile.* 7 August.

Afflitto, Frank M. 2000. "The Homogenizing Effects of State Sponsored Terrorism: The Case of Guatemala." In *Death Squad: The Anthropology of State Terror,* ed. Jeffrey A. Sluka. Philadelphia: University of Pennsylvania Press.

Agamben, Giorgio. 1998. *Homo Sacer: Sovereign Power and Bare Life.* Stanford: Stanford University Press.

Agence France-Presse. 2004. "Eritrean authorities deny reports 20 died in prison 'incidents.'" 7 November.

———. 2005. "Eritrea's sole political party to open food shops." *Relief Web,* 18 March. www.reliefweb.int/rw/rwb.nsf/.

al-Ali, Nadje, Richard Black and Khalid Koser. 2001. "The Limits to 'Transnationalism': Bosnian and Eritrean Refugees in Europe as Emerging Transnational Communities." *Ethnic and Racial Studies* 24, no. 4 (July): 578–600.

Alberizzi, Massimo A. 2005. "Eritrea: Fotografie di morte." *Corriere della Sera.* 13 September. http://www.corriere.it/Primo_Piano/Esteri/2005/09_Settembre/11/speciale_eritrea.shtml.

Alemseged Abbay. 1998. *Identity Jilted or Re-Imagining Identity? The Divergent Paths of the Eritrean and Tigrayan Nationalist Struggles.* Lawrenceville, NJ: The Red Sea Press.

Alemseged Tesfai. 2003. "Land and Liberation in Eritrea: Reflecting on the Work of Lionel Cliffe." *Review of African Political Economy* 30, no. 96 (June): 249–54.

Alexander Naty. 2003. "Environment, Society, and the State in Western Eritrea." *Africa: Journal of the International African Institute* 72, no. 4: 569–97.

Alexander, Jocelyn, JoAnn McGregor, and Terence Ranger. 2000. *Violence and Memory: One Hundred Years in the Dark Forests of Matabeleland.* Oxford: James Currey.

Alter, Peter. 1994. *Nationalism,* 2nd edition. London: Edward Arnold.

Althusser, Louis. 1971. *Lenin and Philosophy and Other Essays.* New York and London: Monthly Review Press.

Ambaye Zekarias. 1966. *Land Tenure in Eritrea (Ethiopia).* Addis Ababa: n.pub.

Amnesty International. 2004. "ERITREA. 'You have no right to ask'—Government resists scrutiny on human rights." AFR 64/003/2004. May. http://www.amnesty.org.

———. 2005a. *Rundbrief Eritrea,* Herausgegeben von der ai-Äthiopien/Eritrea-Koordinationsgruppe. September.

———. 2005b. "ERITREA. Religious Persecution," AFR 64/013/2005, 7 December. http://web.amnesty.org/library/print /ENGAFR640132005.

Andall, Jacqueline. 2005. "Immigration and the Legacy of Colonialism: The Eritrean Diaspora in Italy." In *Italian Colonialism: Legacy and Memory,* eds. Jacqueline Andall and Derek Duncan. Oxford: Lang.

Anderson, Benedict. 1991. *Imagined Communities: Reflections on the Origin and Spread of Nationalism.* London: Verso (revised edition).

An-Na'im, Abdullahi Ahmed, ed. 2001. "Toward a Cross-Cultural Approach to Defining International Standards of Human Rights," in *Human Rights in Cross-Cultural Perspective.* Philadelphia: University of Pennsylvania Press.

Appadurai, Arjun. 1996. *Modernity at Large: Cultural Dimensions of Globalization.* Minneapolis: University of Minnesota Press.

Arato, Andrew and Jean Cohen. 1992. *Civil Society and Political Theory.* Cambridge, MA: MIT Press.

Arendt, Hannah. 1963. *On Revolution.* London: Penguin.

———. 1973. *The Origins of Totalitarianism,* 2nd edition. New York: Harcourt, Brace, Jovanovich.

Arnove, Robert F. 1994. *Education as Contested Terrain: Nicaragua, 1979–1993.* Boulder, CO: Westview Press.

asmarino.com. 2005. "Eritrea: Photographs of Death." 12 September. http://news9.asmarino.com/content/view/551/86/.

Assefaw Bariagaber. 2006a. *Conflict and the Refugee Experience: Flight, Exile, and Repatriation in the Horn of Africa.* Aldershot, UK: Ashgate.

———. 2006b. "Eritrea: Challenges and Crises of a New State." www.unhcr.org/home/RSDCOI/4538821e4.pdf (accessed 12 December 2006).

———. 2006c. "Explaining Fresh Refugee Movements Out of Eritrea." Paper presented at African Studies Association–UK annual meeting. London, 11–13 September.

Bakhtin, Mikhail. 1993 [1941] *Rabelais and His World.* Translated by Helene Iswolsky. Bloomington: Indiana University Press.

Bakonyi, Jutta. 2001. "Eritrea/Äthiopien." In *Das Kriegsgeschehen 2000. Daten und Tendenzen der Kriege und bewaffneten Konflikte,* eds. Thomas Rabehl and Wolfgang Schreiber. Opladen: Leske und Budrich.

Baro, Mamadou and Tara Deubel. 2006. "Persistent Hunger: Perspectives on Vulnerability, Famine, and Food Security in Sub-Saharan Africa." *Annual Review of Anthropology* 35: 521–38.

Basch, Linda Green, Nina Glick Schiller and Cristina Szanton Blanc. 1994. *Nations Unbound: Transnational Projects, Postcolonial Predicaments, and Deterritorialized Nation-States.* Luxembourg: Gordon and Breach.

Bascom, Johnathan. 1999. *Losing Place: Refugee Populations and Rural Transformations in East Africa.* New York: Berghahn Books.

Bauer, Dan Franz. 1985. *Household and Society in Ethiopia.* East Lansing: Michigan State University Press.

Bauman, Zygmunt. 1992. *Moderne und Ambivalenz. Das Ende der Eindeutigkeit.* Hamburg: Hamburger Institut für Sozialforschung.

BBC News. 2001. "Students die in Eritrea detention camp." 20 August. http://news.bbc.co.uk/1/hi/world/africa/1501092.stm. Accessed 30 August 2008.

———. 2002. "Student's daring jailbreak in Eritrea." 9 August. http://news.bbc.co.uk/1/low/world/africa/2182775.stm. Accessed 30 August 2008.

———. 2006. "Eritrea Incursion 'to Pick Crops.'" 17 Oct. http://news.bbc.co.uk/go/pr/fr/-/2/hi/Africa/6057352.stm. Accessed 29 August 2008.

Beck, Ulrich. 2002. "Individualisierung." In *Wörterbuch der Soziologie,* eds. Günter Endruweit and Gisela. Trommsdorff. 2nd edition. Stuttgart: Lucius und Lucius.

Ben-Eliezer, Uri. 1995. "A Nation-In-Arms: State, Nation and Militarism in Israel's First Years." *Comparative Studies in Society and History* 37, no. 2: 264–85.

Berhe Habte-Giorgis. 1993. "The Direction of the Eritrean Economy: Some Thoughts About Strategy." In *Emergent Eritrea Challenges of Economic Development,* ed. Gebre Hiwet Tesfagiorgis. Lawrenceville, NJ: Red Sea Press.

Berman, Edward. 1992. "Donor Agencies and Third World Educational Development, 1945–1985." In *Emergent Issues in Education: Comparative Perspectives*, eds. Robert Arnove, Phillip Altbach, and Gail Kelly. New York: SUNY.

Bernal, Victoria. 2004. "Eritrea Goes Global: Reflections on Nationalism in a Transnational Era." *Cultural Anthropology* 19, no. 1 (February): 3–25.

———. 2006. "Diaspora, Cyberspace and Political Imagination: The Eritrean Diaspora Online." *Global Networks* 6, no. 2 (April): 161–79.

Besteman, Catherine. 1996. "Violent Politics and the Politics of Violence: The Dissolution of the Somali Nation-state." *American Ethnologist* 23, no. 3 (August): 579–96.

Biles, Peter. 2003. "Celebration Hides Discontent in Eritrea." BBC News, http://news.bbc.co.uk/1/hi/world/africa/2935752.stm. Accessed August 29th 2008.

Billig, Michael. 1995. *Banal Nationalism*. London: Sage Publishers.

Boerma, Pauline. 1999. "Seeing the Wood for the Trees: Deforestation in the Central Highlands of Eritrea Since 1890." PhD dissertation. Oxford: University of Oxford Press.

Bosswick, Wolfgang. 2000. "Development of Asylum Policy in Germany." *Journal of Refugee Studies* 13, no. 1 (March): 43–60.

Bourdieu, Pierre. 1977. *Outline of A Theory of Practice*. Cambridge: Cambridge University Press.

———. 1982. *Die feinen Unterschiede. Kritik der gesellschaftlichen Urteilskraft*. Frankfurt: Suhrkamp.

———. 1989. "Antworten auf einige Einwände." In *Klassenlage, Lebensstil und kulturelle Praxis. Beiträge zur Auseinandersetzung mit Pierre Bourdieus Klassentheorie*, ed. Klaus Eder. Frankfurt: Suhrkamp.

———. 1993. *Sozialer Sinn, Kritik der theoretischen Vernunft*. Frankfurt: Suhrkamp.

———. 1997. "Ortseffekte." In *Das Elend der Welt Zeugnisse und Diagnosen alltäglichen Leidens an der Gesellschaft*, eds. Pierre Bourdieu et al. Konstanz: UVK.

———. 2005. "Taste of Luxury, Taste of Necessity." In *The Taste Culture Reader: Experiencing Food and Drink*, ed. Carolyn Korsmeyer. Oxford: Berg.

Bourdieu, Pierre and Jean-Claude Passeron. 1977. *Reproduction in Education, Society and Culture*. London: Sage Publications.

Bowen, Merle. 2000. *The State against the Peasantry: Rural Struggles in Colonial and Postcolonial Mozambique*. Charlottesville: University Press of Virginia.

Bräutigam, Deborah A. 1994. "What Can Africa Learn from Taiwan? Political Economy, Industrial Policy, and Adjustment." *Journal of Modern African Studies* 32, no. 1 (March): 111–38.

Brubaker, Rogers. 1996. *Nationalism Reframed: Nationhood and the National Questioning the New Europe*. Cambridge: Cambridge University Press.

Buchert, Lene, ed. 1998. *Education Reform in the South in the 1990s*. Paris: UNESCO.

Buck-Morss, Susan. 2000. *Dreamworld and Catastrophe: The Passing of Mass Utopia in East and West*. Cambridge, MA: MIT Press.

Bundegaard, Christian. 2004. "The Battalion State: Securitization and Nationbuilding in Eritrea." Geneva: Programme for Strategic and International Security Studies (PSIS).

Calhoun, Craig. 1998. *Nationalism*. Minneapolis: University of Minnesota Press.

Carney, Judith and Michael Watts. 1990. "Manufacturing Dissent: Work, Gender, and the Politics of Meaning in a Peasant Society." *Africa* 60, no. 2: 207–41.

———. 1991. "Disciplining Women? Rice, Mechanization, and the Evolution of Gender Relations in Senegambia." *Signs* 16, no. 4 (Summer): 651–81.

Carnoy, Martin. 1995. "Structural Adjustment and the Changing Face of Education." *International Labour Review*, 134 no. 6: 653–73.

Carroll, Peter N., and David W. Noble. 1988 (1977). *The Free and the Unfree: A New History of the United States*. Harmondsworth, UK: Penguin Books.

Castells, Manuel. 1992. "Four Asian Tigers With a Dragon Head: A Comparative Analysis of the State, Economy and Society in the Asian Pacific Rim." In *States and Development in the Asian Pacific Rim,* eds. Richard P. Appelbaum and Jeffrey Henderson. London: Sage Publications.

Cederlof, Gunnel and K. Sivaramakrishnan. 2006. *Ecological Nationalisms: Nature, Livelihoods and Identities in South Asia.* Seattle: University of Washington Press.

Chabal, Patrick and Jean-Pascal Daloz. 1999. *Africa Works: Disorder as Political Instrument.* Oxford: James Currey.

Chatterjee, Partha. 1993. *The Nation and Its Fragments: Colonial and Postcolonial Histories.* Princeton, NJ: Princeton University Press.

Clark, Cal and Steve Chan. 1994. "The Developmental Roles of the State: Moving Beyond the Developmental State in Conceptualizing Asian Political Economies." *Governance: An International Journal of Policy and Administration* 7, no. 4 (October): 332–59.

Cliffe, Lionel. 1989. "Forging a Nation: The Eritrean Experience." *Third World Quarterly* 11, no. 4 (October): 131–47.

Coleman, James S. 1994. "The Idea of the Developmental University." In *Nationalism and Development in Africa. Selected Essays,* ed. Richard L. Sklar. Berkeley: University of California Press.

Collins, Sheila. 1987. "Education in Nicaragua: What Difference Can A Revolution Make?" *Social Policy* (Fall): 47–53.

Connell, Dan. 1997. *Against All Odds: A Chronicle of the Eritrean Revolution.* Lawrenceville, NJ: Red Sea Press.

———. 2001. "Inside the EPLF: The Origins of the 'People's Party' and its Role in the Liberation of Eritrea." *Review of African Political Economy* 28, no. 89 (September): 345–64.

———. 2004. "Enough! A Critique of Eritrea's Post-Liberation Politics." *All Africa,* 2 March 2004. http://allafrica.com.

———. 2005. "Redeeming the Failed Promise of Democratization in Eritrea." *Race & Class* 48, no. 4 (April): 68–79.

Conrad, Bettina. 2005. "'We are the prisoners of our dreams': Exit, Voice and Loyalty in the Eritrean Diaspora in Germany." *Eritrean Studies Review* 4, no. 2: 211–61.

———. 2006. "'We are the Warsay of Eritrea in Diaspora': Contested Identities and Social Divisions in Cyberspace." In *Diasporas Within and Without Africa: Dynamism, Heterogeneity, Variation,* eds. Leif Manger and Munzoul A.M. Assal. Uppsala, Sweden: Nordiska Afrikainstitutet.

Corrigan, Phillip and Derek Sayer. 1985. *The Great Arch: English State Formation as Cultural Revolution.* Oxford: Basil Blackwell.

Cowan, Laning G., James O'Connell, and David G. Scanlon, eds. 1965. *Education and Nation-Building in Africa.* New York: Frederick Praeger.

Crummey, Donald. 2000. *Land and Society in the Christian Kingdom of Ethiopia: From the Thirteenth to the Twentieth Century.* Chicago: University of Illinois Press.

Cypher, James M. and James L. Dietz. 1997. *The Process of Economic Development.* London: Routledge.

Daniel Mebrahtu. 1994. "National Service—the facts." *Eritrea Profile.* 4 June.

Daniel Mekonnen and Samuel Abraha. 2004. "The Plight of Eritrean Students in South Africa." Unpublished paper.

Das, Veena and Deborah Poole, eds. 2004. *Anthropology in the Margins of the State.* Santa Fe, NM: School of American Research Press.

Dashwood, Hevina. 2000. *Zimbabwe: The Political Economy of Transition.* Toronto: University of Toronto Press.

De Heusch, Luc. 1995. "Rwanda: Responsiblities for a Genocide." *Anthropology Today* 11, no. 4 (August): 3–7.

de Waal, Alex. 1997. *Famine Crimes: Politics and the Disaster Relief Industry in Africa.* Oxford: James Currey.

Deleuze, Gilles and Felix Guattari. 1986. *Nomadology: The War Machine*. Cambridge, MA: Semiotext(e) [MIT Press].

Denison, Edward, Guang-Yen Ren and Naigzy Gebremedhin. 2003a. *Asmara: Africa's Secret Modernist City*. London, New York: Merrell.

———. 2003b. *Asmara: A Guide to the Built Environment*. Asmara: CARP.

Desta Asayehgn. 1979. *The Role of Women in Tanzania: Their Access to Higher Education and Participation in the Labor Force*. IIEP Research Report 33. Paris: UNESCO, International Institute for Educational Planning.

Dickinson, Edward Ross. 2004. "Biopolitics, Fascism, Democracy: Some Reflections on our Discourse About 'Modernity.'" *Central European History* 37, no. 1 (March): 1–48.

Donham, Donald L. 1992. "Revolution and Modernity in Maale, Ethiopia, 1974–1987." *Comparative Studies in Society and History* 34, no. 1 (January): 28–57.

———. 1999. *Marxist Modern: An Ethnographic History of the Ethiopian Revolution*. Berkeley: University of California Press.

Douglas, Mary. 1969. *Purity and Danger: An Analysis of Concepts of Pollution and Taboo*. London: Routledge.

———. 1981. *Ritual, Tabu und Körpersymbolik, Sozialanthropologische Studien in Industriegesellschaft und Stammeskultur*. Frankfurt: Suhrkamp.

Durkheim, Emile. 1998 (1912). "The Cultural Logic of Collective Representations." In *Social Theory: The Multicultural and Classic Readings*, ed. Charles C. Lemert. Boulder, CO: Westview Press. Excerpted from *The Elementary Forms of Religious Life*.

EAI/C.e.V. 2004, 2005. "Eritrea: Conscientious Objection and Desertion. A Documentation by Connection e.V., Germany; War Resisters International; and the Eritrean Anti-Militarism Initiative." [English and German versions].

Eberstadt, Nicholas. 2000. "Disparities in Socio-Economic Development in Divided Korea." *Asian Survey* 40, no. 6. (November–December): 867–93.

Edelman, Marc. 2005. "Bringing the Moral Economy back in…to the Study of 21st-Century Transnational Peasant Movements." *American Anthropologist* 107, no. 3 (September): 331–45.

Engel, Ulf. 2004. "Simbabwe." In *Das Afrika-Lexikon. Ein Kontinent in 1000 Stichwörtern*, ed. Jacob Mabe. Wuppertal: Peter-Hammer-Verlag. 554–56

Englund, Harri. 1999. "The Self in Self-Interest: Land, Labour and Temporalities in Malawi's Agrarian Change." *Africa* 69, no. 1: 139–59.

Enloe, Cynthia. 1988. *Does Khaki Become You? Militarization of Women's Lives*. London: Pandora.

———. 2000. *Maneuvers: The International Politics of Militarizing Women's Lives*. Berkeley: University of California Press.

Erdheim, Mario. 1991. "Revolution, Totem und Tabu. Vom Verenden der Revolution im Wiederholungszwang." In *Ethnopsychoanalyse 2: Herrschaft, Anpassung, Widerstand*, ed. Eva Maria Blum et al. Frankfurt: Brandes & Apsel.

"Eritrea." 1998. *Time*, 30 March, 41.

Eritrea Profile. 1994. "Eritrea and the Bank See Eye-to-Eye." 16 July.

———. 2001. "University Students Return to Capital, New School Year to Start October 8." 29 September.

———. 2005a. "Work: Main Cornerstone for Success of Economic Emancipation."10 September.

———. 2005b. "Community Development and Food Security in Eritrea: A Focus on Zoba Debub." 14 Sept.

———. 2005c. "Activating Self Capabilities, Prologue to Economic Emancipation." 17 Sept.

———. 2005d. "Work: Law of Survival and Sustainability." 29 Oct.

———. 2005e. "Rural Development: Strong and Secure Foundation for Economic Development." *Eritrea Profile*, 27 Nov.

Eritrean People's Liberation Front. 1982. "The Eritrean Revolution and the World Revolution." *Vanguard,* January 1973, 30–35, and "Banality of Soviet Propaganda," *Eritrea Now,* October 1979, 162–68. In *Selected Articles From EPLF Publications (1973–1980).* Rome: Eritrean People's Liberation Front.

Erlich, Haggai. 1996. *Ras Alula and the Scramble for Africa, A Political Biography, Ethiopia and Eritrea, 1875–1897.* Lawrenceville, NJ: The Red Sea Press.

Escobar, Arturo. 1995. *The Making and Unmaking of the Third World.* Princeton, NJ: Princeton University Press.

Evans, Peter. 1995. *Embedded Autonomy: States and Industrial Transformation.* Princeton, NJ: Princeton University Press.

Fanon, Frantz. 1963. *The Wretched of the Earth.* New York: Grove Press.

Farquhar, Judith and Qicheng Zhang. 2005. "Biopolitical Beijing: Pleasure, Sovereignty, and Self-Cultivation in China's Capital." *Cultural Anthropology* 20, no. 3 (August): 303–27.

Fengler, Wolfgang. 2001. *Politische Reformhemmnisse und ökonomische Blockierung in Afrika. Die Zentralafrikanische Republik und Eritrea im Vergleich.* Baden-Baden: Nomos.

Ferguson, James. 2006. *Global Shadows: Africa in the Neoliberal World Order.* Durham, NC: Duke University Press.

Fisher, J. 2003. "A ride in the clouds of Eritrea." *BBC News,* 9 July.

Fouad Makki. 1996. "Nationalism, State Formation and the Public Sphere: Eritrea 1991–96." *Review of African Political Economy* 23, no. 70 (December): 475–97.

Food and Agriculture Organization FAO/WFP. 2005. Special Report: Crop and Food Supply Assessment Mission to Eritrea. http://www.fao.org/giews/.

Forrest, Joshua. 1988. "The Quest for State 'Hardness' in Africa." *Comparative Politics* 20, no. 4 (July): 423–42.

Foucault, Michel. 1976. *Überwachen und Strafen. Die Geburt des Gefängnisses.* Frankfurt: Suhrkamp.

———. 1978. *The History of Sexuality.* Volume One: *An Introduction.* Translated by Robert Hurley. New York: Pantheon Books.

———. 1979. *Discipline and Punish: The Birth of the Prison.* New York: Random House.

Frelick, Bill. 2005. "US Detention of Asylum Seekers and Human Rights." Migration Policy Institute. http://www.migrationinformation.org/USfocus/display.cfm?ID=296.

Friedman, Jonathan. 1994. *Cultural Identity and Global Process.* London: Sage.

Fuest, Veronika. 1996. *"A job, a shop, and a loving business": Lebensweisen gebildeter Frauen in Liberia.* Münster: LIT-Verlag.

Fukuyama, Francis. 1992. *The End of History and the Last Man.* New York: The Free Press.

Gaim Kibreab. 1985. *African Refugees: Reflections on the African Refugee Problem.* Lawrenceville, NJ: The Red Sea Press.

———. 2005. "Eritrean Refugees in Sudan: Yearning for Home or the Diaspora?" *Eritrean Studies Review* 4, no. 2: 115–141.

———. 2006. "Eritrea: The National Service and Warsai-Yikeaalo Campaign as Forced Labour." Paper presented at African Studies Association–UK annual meeting, 11–13 September.

Gedab News. 2004. "21 Wounded At Adi Abeito Die At Halibet," 17 November. http://www.awate.com.

Gettleman, Jeffrey. 2007. "Eritrea Defiant on US Diplomatic Pressure." *International Herald Tribune,* 18 September. http://www.iht.com/articles/2007/09/18/africa/eritrea.php.

Gibney, Matthew J. 2004. *The Ethics and Politics of Asylum: Liberal Democracy and the Response to Refugees.* Cambridge: Cambridge University Press.

Giddens, Anthony. 1991. *Modernity and Self-Identity. Self and Society in the Late Modern Age.* Cambridge: Polity Press.

Gilkes, Patrick. 1991. "Eritrea: Historiography and Mythology." *African Affairs* 90, no. 361 (October): 623–28.

Gilkes, Patrick, and Martin Plaut. 1999. *War in the Horn: The Conflict between Eritrea and Ethiopia*. London: Royal Institute of International Affairs.

Girtler, Roland. 1995 *Randkulturen, Theorie der Unanständigkeit*. Wien: Böhlau.

———. 2004. *Der Strich, Soziologie eines Milieus*, 5th Edition. Wien: LIT-Verlag.

Glick Schiller, Nina and Georges Eugene Fouron. 2001. *Georges Woke Up Laughing: Long-Distance Nationalism and the Search for Home*. Durham, NC: Duke University Press.

Goffman, Erving. 1961. *Asylums: Essays on the Social Situation of Mental Patients and Other Inmates*. New York: Doubleday.

———. 1969. *Wir alle spielen Theater, Die Selbstdarstellung im Alltag*. Munich: Piper.

Goldsmith, Arthur. 2004. "Predatory versus Developmental Rule in Africa." *Democratization* 11, no. 3 (June): 88–110.

Gottesman, Les. 1998. *To Fight and Learn. The Praxis and Promise of Literacy in Eritrea's Independence War*. Lawrenceville, NJ and Asmara: The Red Sea Press.

Government of Eritrea. 2003. "Eritrea Food Security Strategy Draft." Asmara: GoE.

Gramsci, Antonio. 1971. *The Modern Prince: Selections from the Prison Notebooks*. Translated by Quintin Hoare. New York: International Publishers.

Green, Andy. 1997. *Education, Globalization and the Nation State*. London: MacMillan.

Green, Linda. 1995. "Living in a State of Fear." In *Fieldwork under Fire: Contemporary Studies of Violence and Survival*, eds. Carolyn Nordstrom and Antonius C.G.M. Robben. Berkeley: University of California Press.

Grohs, Gerhard. 2004. "Eliten." In *Das Afrika-Lexikon*, ed. Jacob Mabe. Wuppertal, Germany: Peter-Hammer-Verlag.

Haggard, Stephen. 1999. *Pathways from the Periphery: The Politics of Growth in the Newly Industrializing Countries*. Ithaca, NY: Cornell University Press.

Hall, Stuart. 1989. "Ethnicity: Identity and Difference." *Radical America*. 23, 4:9–20.

———. 1996. "The Problem of Ideology: Marxism Without Guarantees." In *Stuart Hall: Critical Dialogues in Cultural Studies*, eds. David Morley, and Kuan-Hsing Chen. London: Routledge.

Hammer, Joshua. 1996. "Eritrea: Back From the Ruins." *Newsweek*, 26 February, 40

Handelman, Don. 2004. *Nationalism and the Israeli State: Bureaucratic Logic in Public Events*. Oxford: Berg Publishers.

Handmaker, Jeff. 2001. "No Easy Walk: Advancing Refugee Protection in South Africa." *Africa Today: Special Issue: Evaluating South African Immigration Policy After Apartheid* 48, no. 3: 91–113.

Hann, Chris. 2006. *"Not the Horse We Wanted!": Postsocialism, Neoliberalism, and Eurasia*. Munster: Lit Verlag.

Hannerz, Ulf. 1974. "Ethnicity and Opportunity in Urban America." In *Urban Ethnicity*, ed. A. Cohen. London, New York: Tavistock.

Hansen, Randall and Matthew J. Gibney. 2003. "Asylum Policy in the West: Past Trends, Future Possibilities." United Nations University, World Institute for Development Economics Research, Discussion Paper No. 2003/68.

Hansen, Thomas Blum and Finn Stepputat, eds. 2005. *Sovereign Bodies: Citizens, Migrants and States in the Postcolonial World*. Princeton, NJ: Princeton University Press.

———. 2006. "Sovereignty Revisited." *Annual Review of Anthropology* 35: 295–315.

Harrington, John A. 2005. "Citizenship and the Biopolitics of Post-Nationalist Ireland," *Journal of Law and Society* 32, no. 3 (September): 424–29.

Harris, Ed. 2006. "Self Reliance Could Cost Eritrea Dear." *BBC News*, 5 July 2006. http://news.bbc.co.uk/2/hi/business/5121212.stm.

Harris, Nigel. 1987. *The End of The Third World: Newly Industrialising Countries and the Decline of an Ideology*. Harmondsworth, UK: Penguin Books.

Hart-Landsberg, Martin and Paul Berkett. 1998. "Contradictions of Capitalist Industrialization in East Asia: A Critique of 'Flying Geese' Theories of Development." *Economic Geography* 74, no. 2 (April): 87–110.

Hartmann, Peter H. 2002. "Lebensstilgruppe und Milieu." In *Wörterbuch der Soziologie* 2nd Edition, eds. Günter Endruweit, and Gisela Trommsdorff. Stuttgart: Lucius und Lucius.

Harvey, David. 2003. "The City as a Body Politic." In *Wounded Cities. Destruction and Reconstruction in a Globalized World*, eds. Jane Schneider and Ida Susser. Oxford: Berg.

Hawthorn, Geoffrey. 1994. "The Crises of Southern States." *Political Studies* 42, no. 1 (August): 130–45.

Hayman, Rachel. 2003. *Reconciling Ownership of Development and External Assistance: Aid and Nationbuilding in Eritrea*. Edinburgh: University of Edinburgh, Centre of African Studies.

Hebrew Immigrant Aid Society (HIAS). 2005. "Concerns about Current Asylum Policy and Practices." http://www.hias.org/advocacy/Docs/ConcernAsylum_05_2005.php (accessed 2 November 2007).

Heinlein, Peter. 2007. "Uncertainty haunts refugees as Ethiopia-Eritrea border tensions rise." *Voice of America*, 31 October 2007.

Hendrie, Barbara. 1997. "'Now the people are like a lord': local effects of revolutionary reform in a Tigray village, northern Ethiopia." Unpublished Phd. Thesis. University of London.

Hennig, Rainer Chr. 2005. "Donors shy away Eritrea despite famine." *Afrol News*, 16 June 2005. www.afrol.com/printable_article/16601.

Henze, Paul B. 1990. "Eritrea: The Economic Challenge." unpublished manuscript.

Hepner, Tricia Redeker. 2003. "Religion, Nationalism and Transnational Civil Society in the Eritrean Diaspora." *Identities: Global Studies in Culture and Power* 10: 269–93.

———. 2005. "Transnational Tegadelti: Eritreans for Liberation in North America and the Eritrean Peoples Liberation Front." *Eritrean Studies Review* 4, no. 2: 37–83.

———. 2007. "Transnational Political and Legal Dimensions of Emergent Eritrean Human Rights Initiatives." *Forced Migration Studies Programme Working Papers Series 36*. Johannesburg: University of the Witwatersrand.

———. 2008. "Transnational Governance and the Centralization of State Power in Eritrea and Exile." *Ethnic and Racial Studies* 31, no. 3 (March): 476–502.

———. 2009. *Soldiers, Martyrs, Traitors and Exiles: Political Conflict in Eritrea and the Diaspora*. Philadelphia: University of Pennsylvania Press.

Hepner, Tricia Redeker and Bettina Conrad. 2005. "Eritrea Abroad: An Introduction." *Eritrea Abroad: Critical Reflections on the Global Diaspora*. Special Edition of the *Eritrean Studies Review* 4, no. 2: v–xvii.

Hepner, Tricia Redeker and Lynn Fredriksson. 2007. "Regional Politics, Human Rights, and U.S. Policy in the Horn of Africa." *Africa Policy Journal of the John F. Kennedy School of Government, Harvard University* 3 (Spring).

Hepner, Tricia Redeker and Randal L. Hepner. "Arresting Faith: Religion and State Repression in Contemporary Eritrea." In *New Religiosity and Intergenerational Conflict in Northeast Africa*, ed. D. Dea, C. Falge, and G. Schlee, forthcoming.

Herbst, Jeffrey. 1990. "Migration, the Politics of Protest, and State Consolidation in Africa." *African Affairs* 89, no. 355 (April): 183–203.

Herzfeld, Michael. 1997. *Cultural Intimacy: Social Poetics in the Nation-State*. New York and London: Routledge.

Hildenbrand, Bruno, Hermann Müller, Barbara Beyer, and Daniela Klein. 1984. "Biographiestudien im Rahmen von Milieustudien." In *Biographie und soziale Wirklichkeit*, eds. Martin Kohli and Günther Robert. Stuttgart: Metzler.

Hintjens, Helen M. 1999. "Explaining the 1994 Genocide in Rwanda." *The Journal of Modern African Studies* 37, no. 2 (June): 241–86.

Hirt, Nicole. 2000. *Eritrea zwischen Krieg und Frieden. Die Entwicklung seit der Unabhängigkeit*. Hamburg: Institut für Afrikakunde.

Hoben, Allan. 1982. "Anthropologists and Development." *Annual Review of Anthropology*. 11: 349–75.

Hobsbawm, Eric. 1969 [2000]. *Bandits*. London: Abacus Books.

————. 1990. *Nations and Nationalism since 1780: Programme, Myth, Reality.* Cambridge: Cambridge University Press.

————. 1995. *Age of Extremes: The Short Twentieth Century 1914–1991.* New York: Pantheon Books.

Hoogvelt, Ankie. 1997. *Globalization and the Postcolonial World. The New Political Economy of Development.* London: MacMillan.

Husserl, Edmund. 1986. *Phänomenologie der Lebenswelt.* Stuttgart: Reclam.

Hutchinson, John. 2005. *Nations as Zones of Conflict.* London: Sage.

International Monetary Fund. 2005. "IMF Executive Board Concludes Article IV Consultation with Eritrea." http://www.imf.org/external/np/sec/pn/2005/pn0518.htm.

————. 2006. The State of Eritrea, Staff Report for the 2005 Article IV Consultation, February 2006 (Draft).

IRIN. 2005. "Eritrea: Fears of Widespread Malnutrition as Food Shortages Worsen." *Irin News,* 2 March 2005. www.irinnews.org.

Issayas Afeworki. 1998. "Democracy in Africa: An African View." *Eritrean Studies Review* 2, no. 2: 133–41.

Jahoda, Marie, Paul Lazarsfeld, and Hans Zeisel. 1975. *Die Arbeitslosen von Marienthal. Ein soziographischer Versuch über die Wirkungen langandauernder Arbeitslosigkeit.* (Leipzig 1933). Frankfurt: Suhrkamp.

Joireman, Sandra. F. 2000. *Property Rights and Political Development in Ethiopia and Eritrea.* Oxford: James Currey.

Jordan Gebre-Medhin.1989. *Peasants and Nationalism in Eritrea.* Lawrenceville, NJ: Red Sea Press.

Kapferer, Bruce, ed. 2004. *State, Sovereignty, War: Civil Violence in Emerging Global Realities.* New York and Oxford: Berghahn Books.

Kea, Pamela. 2004. "Maintaining Difference and Managing Change: Female Agrarian Clientelist Relations in a Gambian Community." *Africa* 74, no. 3: 361–82.

Kellner, Douglas. 1995. "The Obsolescence of Marxism?" In *Whither Marxism?,* eds. Bernd Magnus and Stephen Cullenberg. London: Routledge Press.

Kiflai Gebremedhin and Afeworki Asghedom Measho. 1998. "Strategies for Technology Transfer: Lessons for Eritrea." *Eritrean Studies Review* 2, no. 2 (November): 111–131.

Killion, Tom. 1997. "Eritrean Workers' Organization and Early Nationalist Mobilization. 1948–1958." *Eritrean Studies Review* 2, no. 1: 1–58

————. 1998. *Historical Dictionary of Eritrea.* African Historical Dictionaries, vol. 75. London: Scarecrow Press.

Kipnis, Andrew. 2003. "The Anthropology of Power and Maoism." *American Anthropologist* 105, no. 2 (June): 278–88.

Kirschke, Linda. 2000. "Informal Repression, Zero-sum Politics, and Late Third Wave Transitions." *The Journal of Modern African Studies* 38, no. 3 (September): 383–405.

Klaaren, Jonathan and Jaya Ramji. 2001. "Inside Illegality: Migration Policing in South Africa after Apartheid." *Africa Today: Special Issue: Evaluating South African Immigration Policy After Apartheid* 48, no. 3: 35–47.

Klein, Naomi. 2007. *The Shock Doctrine: The Rise of Disaster Capitalism.* London: Allen Lane Press.

Koehn, Peter. 1991. *Refugees from Revolution: U.S. Policy and Third-World Migration.* Boulder, CO: Westview Press.

Kolonialwissenschaftliche Neuigkeiten. 1937. "Eine Seilbahn für Eritrea." In *Koloniale Rundschau.* Leipzig: C. Troll, 443–44.

Kong, Tat Yan. 2004. "Corruption and the Effect of Regime Change Type: The Case of Taiwan." *New Political Economy* 9, no. 3 (September): 341–64.

Koo, Hagen. 1987. "The Interplay of State, Social Class, and World System in East Asian Development: The Cases of South Korea and Taiwan." In *The Political Economy of the New Asian Industrialism,* ed. Frederic C. Deyo. Ithaca, NY: Cornell University Press.

Kwesiga, Joy C. 2002. *Women's Access to Higher Education in Africa: Uganda's Experience.* Kampala: Fountain Publishers.

Landau, Loren. 2004. "The Laws of (In)Hospitality: Black Africans in South Africa." *Forced Migration Working Paper Series 7.* Johannesburg: University of the Witwatersrand.

Leach, Michael and Fethi Mansouri. 2004. *Lives in Limbo: Voices of Refugees Under Temporary Protection.* Sydney: University of New South Wales Press.

Levinson, Bradley. 2001. *We Are All Equal: Student Culture and Identity at a Mexican Secondary School.* Durham, NC: Duke University Press.

Leys, Colin and John S. Saul. 1995. *Namibia's Liberation Struggle: The Two-Edged Sword.* London: James Currey.

Locatelli, Francesca. 2003. "Colonial History of Asmära." In *Encyclopedia Aethiopica*, Volume 1, ed. Siegbert Uhlig. Wiesbaden: Harrassowitz.

Luckham, Robin. 1994. "The Military, Militarization and Democratization in Africa: A Survey of Literature and Issues." *African Studies Review* 37, no. 2: 13–75.

———. 2002. "Radical Soldiers, New Model Armies and the Nation-State in Ethiopia and Eritrea." In *Political Armies. The Military and Nation Building in the Age of Democracy*, eds. Kees Koonings, and Dirk Kruijt. London: Zed Books.

Lutz, Catherine. 2002. *Homefront: A Military City and the American Twentieth Century.* Boston: Beacon Press.

Luykx, Aurolyn. 1999. *The Citizen Factory: Schooling and Cultural Production in Bolivia.* Albany: SUNY Press.

Mahmood, Cynthia. 1992. "Asylum, Violence, and the Limits of Advocacy," *Human Organization* 55, no. 4: 493–98.

Malkki, Liisa. 1995a. *Purity and Exile: Violence, Memory, and National Cosmology.* Chicago: University of Chicago Press.

———. 1995b. "Refugees and Exile: From 'Refugee Studies' to the National Order of Things. *Annual Review of Anthropology* 24: 495–523.

Malone, Barry. 2007. "War fears swell refugee Camp near Eritrea border." *Reuters*, 1 November 2007. http://africa.reuters.com/country/ET/news/usnL01227423.html (accessed 1 November 2007).

Mannheim, Karl. 1978. "Das Problem der Generationen." (1928). In *Soziologie des Lebenslaufs*, ed. Martin Kohli. Darmstadt: Luchterhand.

Mao, Tse-Tung. 1967. *Selected Works of Mao Tse-Tung*, vol. II. Peking: Foreign Languages Press.

Marcus, Harold G. 1983. *Ethiopia, Great Britain and the United States, 1941–1974: The Politics of Empire.* Berkeley: University of California Press.

Marinetti, Filippo Tommaso. [1909] 1989. "Manifest des Futurismus." In *Handbuch literarischer Fachbegriffe*, Frankfurt/M.: Otto F. Best, 167–68.

Markakis, John. 1974. *Ethiopia: Anatomy of a Traditional Polity.* Oxford: Oxford University Press.

Mbabazi, Pamela K., and Ian Taylor. 2005. *The Potentiality of 'Developmental States' in Africa: Botswana and Uganda Compared.* Dakar: CODESRIA.

Mbembe, Achille. 1992. "The Banality of Power and Aesthetics of Vulgarity in the Post Colony." *Public Culture* 4, no. 2 (Spring): 1–30.

———. 2001. *On the Postcolony.* Berkeley: University of California Press.

McClure, Jason. 2007. "Waiting for War." *Newsweek International, US.* 30 October.

McCrone, David. 1998. *The Sociology of Nationalism.* London: Routledge.

McDonogh, Gary Wray. 2003. "Myth, Space, and Virtue: Bars, Gender, and Change in Barcelona's Barrio Chino." In *The Anthropology of Space and Place: Locating Culture*, eds. Setha M. Low and Denise Lawrence-Zúniga. Oxford: Blackwell.

McFaul, Michael, 2002, "The Fourth Wave of Democracy and Dictatorship: Noncooperative Transitions in the Postcommunist World," *World Politics* 54, no. 2 (January): 212–44.

McKinley, Jr., James C. 1996. "Eritrea: African Success Story Being Written." *New York Times*, 30 April.

McSpadden, Lucia Ann. 2000. *Negotiating Return: Conflict and Control in the Repatriation of Eritrean Refugees*. Uppsala, Sweden: Life and Peace Institute.

Mebrahtu Abraham. 2003. "Early History of Asmara." In *Asmara: A Guide to the Built Environment*, eds. Edward Denison, Guang-Yu Ren, Mebrahtu Abraham, and Naigzy Gebremedhin. Asmara: CARP.

Melber, Henning. 2003. *Limits to Liberation in Southern Africa: The Unfinished Business of Democratic Consolidation*. Cape Town: HSCR Press.

Meron Abraha. 2005. "Independence Day Carnival." *Sheiba*, 23 May 2005. http://www.sheiba .org/artman/publish/printer_3752.html.

Merry, Sally Engle. 2006. "Transnational Human Rights and Local Activism: Mapping the Middle." *American Anthropologist* 108, no. 1 (March): 38–51.

Mesfin Araya. 1997. "Issues of Hegemony in Post-independent Eritrea." In *Ethiopia in Broader Perspective. Papers of the XIIIth International Conference of Ethiopian Studies*, vol. 2, eds. Katsuyoshi Fukui, Eisei Kurimoto, and Masayoshi Shigeta. Kyoto: Shokado.

Meyer, Thomas. 1997. *Identitäts-Wahn. Die Politisierung des kulturellen Unterschieds*. Berlin: Aufbau.

Ministry of Education (MoE). 1999. *Education for All in Eritrea: Policies, Strategies and Prospects*. Asmara: MoE.

———. 2002. Concept Paper for a Rapid Transformation of the Eritrean Education System. Unpublished paper.

Mitchell, Timothy. 1991. "The Limits of the State: Beyond Statist Approaches and Their Critics." *American Political Science Review* 85, no. 1 (March): 77–96.

Mkandawire, Thandika. 2001. "Thinking about Developmental States in Africa." *Cambridge Journal of Economics* 25, no. 3: 289–313.

Mongalvy, Sophie. 2007. "Exile at all costs for many young Eritreans." *Agence France-Presse*, 30 August 2007.

Moore Jr., Barrington. 1966. *Social Origins of Dictatorship and Democracy: Lord and Peasant in the Making of the Modern World*. Boston: Beacon Press.

Moore, Donald. 2005. *Suffering for Territory: Race, Place, and Power in Zimbabwe*. Durham, NC: Duke University Press.

Morrow, Raymond Allen and Carlos Alberto Torres. 2000. "The State, Globalization, and Educational Policy." In *Globalization and Education: Critical Perspectives*, eds. Nicholas Burbules and Carlos Alberto Torres. New York: Routledge Press.

Müller, Tanja R. 1998. "Out of Ethiopia's Shadow." *Times Educational Supplement*, 10 April: 19.

———. 2004. "'Now I am Free' — Education and Human Resource Development in Eritrea: Contradictions in the Lives of Eritrean Women in Higher Education." *COMPARE* 34, no. 2 (June): 215–29.

———. 2005. *The Making of Elite Women: Revolution and Nation Building in Eritrea*. Boston and Leiden: Brill Publishers.

———. 2006a. "Education for Social Change: Girls' Secondary Schooling in Eritrea." *Development and Change* 37, no. 2: 353–73.

———. 2006b. "State Making in the Horn of Africa: Notes on Eritrea and Prospects for the End of Violent Conflict in the Horn." *Conflict, Security and Development* 6, no. 4 (December): 503–30.

———. 2008. "Bare Life and the Developmental State: Implications of the Militarization of Higher Education in Eritrea." *The Journal of Modern African Studies* 46, no. 1: 111–31.

Murtaza, Niaz. 1998. *The Pillage of Sustainability in Eritrea, 1600s–1990s: Rural Communities and the Creeping Shadows of Hegemony*. Westport, CT: Greenwood Press.

Mussie T. Tessema and Joseph L. Soeters. 2006. "Challenges and Prospects of HRM in Developing Countries: Testing the HRM-Performance Link in the Eritrean Civil Service." International Journal of Human Resource Management 17, no. 1: 86–105.

Nadel, Siegfried Frederick. 1946. "Land Tenure on the Eritrean Plateau." *Africa* 16, no. 1 (January): 1–22, and no. 2 (April): 99–108.

Nageeb, Salma Ahmed. 2004. *New Spaces and Old Frontiers. Women, Social Space, and Islamization in Sudan.* Lanham, MD: Lexington Press.

Nairn, Tom. 1977. "The Modern Janus." *New Left Review* (old series) 94 (November–December): 3–29.

———. 1997 (1981). *The Break-Up of Britain.* London: Verso Press.

Nazarea, Virginia. 2006. "Local Knowledge and Memory in Biodiversity Conservation." *Annual Review of Anthropology* 35: 317–35.

Neuman, Roderick. 2002. *Imposing Wilderness: Struggles over Livelihood and Nature Preservation in Africa.* Los Angeles: University of California Press.

News24. 2007. "Eritrea Exodus Gathers Speed." 30 August. http://www.news24.com/News24/Africa/News/0,,2-11-1447_2174545,00.html. Accessed 30 August 2007.

Norris, Andrew. 2000. "Giorgio Agamben and the Politics of the Living Dead." *Diacritics* 30, no. 4 (Winter): 38–58.

Nyamnjoh, Francis B. 2006. *Insiders and Outsiders: Citizenship and Xenophobia in Contemporary Southern Africa.* London: Zed Books.

O'Kane, David. 2004. "Peasant Nationalism in Embaderho: Land and National Identities in an Eritrean Village." Unpublished Ph.D. Thesis. Queen's University Belfast.

Okbazghi Yohannes. 1991. *Eritrea: A Pawn in World Politics.* Gainesville: University of Florida Press.

Olwig, Karen Fog, and Sorenson, Ninna Nyberg. 2001. *Work and Migration, Life and Livelihoods in a Globalizing World,* Routledge, London.

Ong, Aihwa. 1988. "The Production of Possession: Spirits and the Multinational Corporation in Malaysia." *American Ethnologist* 15, no. 1 (February): 28–42.

———. 1990. "State Versus Islam: Malay Families, Women's Bodies, and the Body Politic in Malaysia." *American Ethnologist* 17, no. 2 (May): 258–76.

———. 1991. "The Gender and Labor Politics of Postmodernity." *Annual Review of Anthropology* 20: 279–309.

Oppenheimer, Martin. 1971. *Stadt-Guerilla.* Frankfurt: Ullstein.

Ortiz, Sister Dianna. 2001. "The Survivor's Perspective: Voices from the Center." In *The Mental Health Consequences of Torture,* eds. Ellen T. Gerrity, Terence Martin Keane, and Farris Tuma. New York: Kluwer Academic/Plenum Publishers.

Ottaway, Marina. 1999. *Africa's New Leaders: Democracy or State Reconstruction?* Washington, DC: Carnegie Endowment for International Peace.

Panayiotopoulos, Prodromos I. 1995. "Cyprus: The Developmental State in Crisis." *Capital and Class* 57: 13–53.

Papstein, Robert. 1992. *Eritrea: Revolution at Dusk.* Lawrenceville, NJ: The Red Sea Press.

Patel, Rajeev, and Philip McMichael. 2004. "Third Worldism and the Lineages of Global Fascism: The Regrouping of the Global South in the Neoliberal Era." *Third World Quarterly* 25, no. 1: 231–54.

Pateman, Roy. 1990. "Liberté, Egalité, Fraternité: Aspects of the Eritrean Revolution." *The Journal of Modern African Studies* 28, no.3 (September): 457–72.

———. 1998 (1990). *Eritrea: Even the Stones are Burning.* Lawrenceville, NJ: The Red Sea Press.

Pempel, T. J. 1999. "The Development Regime in a Changing World Economy." In *The Developmental State,* ed. Meredith Woo-Cumings. Ithaca, NY: Cornell University Press.

PFDJ. 1994. *National Charter: Adopted by the 3rd Congress of the EPLF/PFDJ.* Nakfa, Eritrea. www.alenalki.com; or www.shaebia.org-new-archives.html (accessed 16 February 1994).

Pham Minh Hac 1998. *Vietnam's Education: The Current Position and Future Prospects.* Hanoi: Thê Giói Publishers.

Plaut, Martin. 2007. "Eritreans Risk Death in the Sahara." *BBC News,* 25 March 2007.

Pool, David. 1993. "Eritrean Independence." *African Affairs* 92, no. 368: 389–402.

————. 1995. "The Eritrean People's Liberation Front." In *African Guerrillas*, ed. Christopher Clapham. Oxford: James Currey.

————. 2001. *From Guerrillas to Government: The Eritrean People's Liberation Front*. Oxford: James Currey.

Pottier, Johan. 1999. *Anthropology of Food: The Social Dynamics of Food Security*. Cambridge: Polity Press.

Psacharopoulos, George. 1993. *Why Educational Policies Can Fail: An Overview of Selected African Experiences*. Washington, DC: World Bank.

Reid, Richard. 2003. "Old Problems in New Conflicts. Some Observations on Eritrea and Its Relations with Tigray. From Liberation Struggle to Inter-state War." *Africa* 73, no. 3: 369–401.

————. 2005. "Caught in the Headlights of History: Eritrea, the EPLF and the Post-war Nation-state." *Journal of Modern African Studies* 43, no. 3: 467–88.

Reischer, Erica and Kathryn S. Koo. 2004. "The Body Beautiful. Symbolism and Agency in the Social World." *Annual Review of Anthropology* 33: 297–317.

Richman, Michele. 1992. "On the Power of the Banal: (Un)Common Categories in Recent Social Thought" *Public Culture* 5, no. 1: 113–22.

Rigi, Jakob. 2003. "The Conditions of Post-Soviet Dispossessed Youth and Work in Almaty, Kazakhstan." *Critique of Anthropology* 23, no. 1: 35–49.

Rokkan, Stein. 1975. "Dimensions of State Formation and Nation Building: A Possible Paradigm for Research on Variations Within Europe." In *The Formation of National States in Western Europe*, ed. Charles Tilly. Princeton, NJ: Princeton University Press.

Rozenwurcel, Guillermo. 2006. "Why have all development strategies failed in Latin America?" Tokyo: United Nations University, World Institute for Development Economics Research.

Ruth Iyob. 1995. *The Eritrean Struggle for Independence: Domination, Resistance, Nationalism 1941–1993*. Cambridge: Cambridge University Press.

————. 1997. "The Eritrean Experiment: A Cautious Pragmatism?" *The Journal of Modern African Studies* 35, no. 4 (December): 647–73.

————. 2000. "The Ethiopian-Eritrean conflict, diasporic vs. hegemonic states in the Horn of Africa, 1991-2000." *The Journal of Modern African Studies,* 38, no. 4, pp. 659-682.

Saini, Ravinder Singh. 2005. "Consolidated Report on the Information Gathering Workshops Conducted in Sub-Zoba Hagaz." Asmara: The State of Eritrea Ministry of Agriculture.

Saleh AA.Younis. 2007. "Opposition Norming." www.awate.com. 27 February. Accessed 2 March 2007

Samoff, Joel. 1999. "Institutionalizing International Influence." In *Comparative Education: the Dialectic of the Global and the Local*, eds. Robert Arnove and Carlos Alberto Torres. Lanham, MD: Rowman Littlefield.

Sanford, Victoria. 2003. *Buried Secrets: Truth and Human Rights in Guatemala*. New York: Palgrave MacMillan.

Schamanek, C. 1998. *Frauen Emanzipation in revolutionären und militärischen Kontexten. Aspekte der Geschlechteverhältnisse am Beispiel eritreische-EPLF-Kämpferinnen (1988- 1992)*. Wien. Institut für Afrikanistik.

Scheper-Hughes, Nancy and Phillippe Bourgois, eds. 2004. *Violence in War and Peace: An Anthology*. London: Blackwell Publishing.

Scheuer, Georg. 1996. *Mussolinis langer Schatten. Marsch auf Rom im Nadelstreif*. Köln: ISP.

Schmidinger, Thomas. 2004. *ArbeiterInnenbewegung im Sudan*. Frankfurt: Lang.

Schroeder, Richard. 1999. *Shady Practices: Agroforestry and Gender Politics in the Gambia*. Berkeley: University of California Press.

Schulze, Gerhard. 2000. *Die Erlebnisgesellschaft. Kultursoziologie der Gegenwart*. 8th Edition. New York: Campus Books.

Schütz, Alfred and Thomas Luckmann. 1975. *Strukturen der Lebenswelt*. Neuwied: Luchterhand.

Scott, James. 1990. *Domination and the Art of Resistance: Hidden Transcripts.* New Haven, CT: Yale University Press
———. 1998. *Seeing Like a State: How Certain Schemes to Improve the Human Condition Have Failed.* New Haven, CT: Yale University Press.
Selahadin Abdela and Magnus Treiber. 2007. "Naqfa." In *Encyclopedia Aethiopica.* Siegbert Uhlig and Verena Böll, eds. vol. 3. Wiesbaden: Harrassowitz.
Shabait.com. 2005. "Eritrea; President Isaias Afwerki's Interview With the Local Media—Part I." *Africa News,* 23 November.
———. 2006. "The Eritrean Defence Force—Soldiers of Development and Security." December. http://allafrica.com/stories/200612131015.html. Accessed 21 April 2007.
Shaebia.org. 2005. "New Tractors to Boost Agricultural Production," 21 May.
———. 2007. "Practical Action: The Only Way to Eradicate Poverty." 21 February. Accessed 26 February, 2007.
Siltanyesus Tsigeyohannes. 2005. "Soil and Water Conservation Vital Efforts for Development." 14 September.
Simmel, Georg. 2001. *Die Philosophie des Geldes.* Gesamtausgabe, vol. 6. (Leipzig 1900) Frankfurt: Suhrkamp.
Skjelsbaek, Kjell. 1979. "Militarism, Its Dimensions and Corollaries: An Attempt at Conceptual Clarification." *Journal of Peace Research* 16, no. 3: 213–29.
Sluka, Jeffrey, ed. 2000. *Death Squad: The Anthropology of State Terror.* Philadelphia: University of Pennsylvania Press.
Smidt, Wolbert. 2003. "Asmära after 1952." In *Encyclopaedia Aethiopica,* vol. 1, ed. Siegbert Uhlig. Wiesbaden: Harrassowitz.
Smith, Ron. 1983. "Aspects of Militarism." *Capital and Class* 19.
Soeters, Joseph L. and Mussie T. Tessema. 2004. "Public Management in Developing Countries: Some Notes on Eritrea." *International Review of Administrative Sciences* 70, no. 4: 623–35.
Sorensen, Christian. 2000. "Alebu: Eritrean Refugees Return and Restore their Livelihoods." In *Risks and Reconstruction: Experiences of Resettlers and Refugees,* ed. Michael Cernea. Washington, DC: The World Bank.
Sperling, Valerie. 2003. "The Last Refuge of a Scoundrel: Patriotism, Militarism and the Russian National Idea." *Nations and Nationalism* 9, no. 2 (April): 235–53.
Stepputat, Finn. 2001. "The Rise and Fall of the Internally Displaced People in the Central Peruvian Andes." *Development and Change* 32, no. 4 (September): 769–91.
Taylor, Ian. 2003. "Globalization and Regionalization in Africa: Reactions to Attempts at Neoliberal Regionalism." *Review of International Political Economy* 10, no. 2 (May): 310–30.
Tekeste Fekadu. 2002. *Journey From Nakfa to Nakfa: Back to Square One 1976–1979.* Asmara: Sabur Printing Press.
Tekeste Negash. 1987. *Italian Colonialism in Eritrea 1882–1941: Policies, Praxis, and Impact.* Uppsala, Sweden: University of Uppsala.
———. 1997. *Eritrea and Ethiopia: The Federal Experience.* New Brunswick, NJ: Transaction Publishers.
Tekeste Negash and Kjetil Tronvoll. 2000. *Brothers at War: Making Sense of the Eritrean-Ethiopian War.* Oxford: James Currey.
Tekie Fessehatzion. 2005. "Eritrea's Remittance-Based Economy: Conjectures and Musings." *Eritrean Studies Review* 4, no 2 (Fall): 165–83.
Tekle Woldemikael. 1993. "The Cultural Construction of Eritrean Nationalist Movements." In *The Rising Tide of Cultural Pluralism: The Nation-State at Bay?* ed. Crawford Young. Madison: University of Wisconsin Press.
———. 1998. "Eritrean and Ethiopian Refugees in the United States." *Eritrean Studies Review* 2, no. 2: 89–109.
———. 2005a. "Bridging the Divide: Eritrean Muslims and Christians in Orange County, California." *Eritrean Studies Review* 4, no. 2: 143–64.

———. 2005b. "Eritrea's Identity as a Cultural Crossroads." In *Race and Nation*, ed. Paul Spickard. New York: Routledge Press.

Tesfai G. Gebremedhin. 1996. *Beyond Survival; The Economic Challenges of Agriculture and Development in Post-Independence Eritrea*, Red Sea Press, New Jersey.

Teshale Tibebu. 1995. *The Making of Modern Ethiopia 1896–1974*. Lawrenceville, NJ: The Red Sea Press.

Thieman-Dino, Angela and James A. Schechter. 2004. "Refugee Voices: The Missing Piece in Refugee Policies and Practices." In *Human Rights: The Scholar as Activist*, eds. Carole Nagengast and Carlos M. Vélez-Ibáñez. Oklahoma City: Society for Applied Anthropology.

Thomas, Clive. 1974. *Dependence and Transformation: The Economics of the Transition to Socialism*. New York: Monthly Review Press.

Thompson, Kenneth W. and Barbara R. Fogel. 1976. *Higher Education and Social Change: Promising Experiences in Developing Countries*. New York: Praeger Publishers.

Townshend, Charles. 1983. *Political Violence in Ireland: Government and Resistance since 1848*. Oxford: Clarendon Press.

Tranberg Hansen, Karen. 2004. "The World in Dress: Anthropological Perspectives on Clothing, Fashion, and Culture." *Annual Review of Anthropology* 33: 369–92.

Treiber, Magnus. 2005. *Der Traum vom guten Leben, Die eritreische warsay-Generation im Asmara der zweiten Nachkriegszeit*. Spektrum 92. Berliner Reihe zu Gesellschaft, Wirtschaft und Politik in Entwicklungsländern. Münster: LIT-Verlag.

———. 2007a. "Nara," in *Encyclopaedia Aethiopica*, vol 3, ed. Seigbert. Uhlig. Wiesbaden: Harrassowitz.

———. 2007b. "Dreaming of a Good Life–Young Urban Refugees from Eritrea between Refusal of Politics and Political Asylum." In *Cultures of Migration. African Perspectives*, eds. Hans Peter Hahn and Georg Klute. Berlin: LIT-Verlag.

Tronvoll, Kjetil. 1998. *Mai Weini; A Highland Village in Eritrea*. Lawrenceville, NJ: The Red Sea Press.

Trouillot, Michel-Rolph. 2001. "The Anthropology of the State in the Age of Globalization: Close Encounters of the Deceptive Kind." *Current Anthropology* 42, no. 1 (February): 125–38.

Tuan, Yi-Fu. 1977. *Space and Place: The Perspective of Experience*. Minneapolis: University of Minnesota Press.

Turner, Bryan S. 2004. *The Body and Society: Explorations in Social Theory*. London: Sage.

Turner, Simon. 2005. "Suspended Spaces—Contesting Sovereignties in a Refugee Camp." In *Sovereign Bodies: Citizens, Migrants, and States in the Postcolonial World*, eds. Thomas Hansen and Finn Stepputat. Princeton, NJ: Princeton University Press.

Turshen, Meredeth. 2004. "Militarism and Islamism in Algeria." *Journal of Asian and African Studies* 39, no. 1–2 (January): 119–32.

UK Home Office. 2004. *Immigration and Nationality Directorate: Fact finding Missions: Eritrea*. http://www.ind.homeoffice.gov.uk/ind/en/home/0/country_information/fact_finding_missions/eritrea/military_service.html.

Wade, Robert. 1990. *Governing the Market. Economic Theory and the Role of Government in East Asian Industrialization*. Princeton, NJ: Princeton University Press.

Weber, Max. 1947. "Die protestantische Ethik und der Geist des Kapitalismus." In *Gesammelte Aufsätze zur Religionssoziologie*, 4th Edition, ed. M. Weber. Tübingen: Mohr.

Wedi Asmara. 2004. "I was there." 6 November. www.news.asmarino.com.

Weiss, Meira. 1997. "War Bodies: Hedonist Bodies: Dialectics of the Collective and the Individual in Israeli Society." *American Ethnologist* 24, no. 4: 813–32.

Welch, Anthony R. 2001. "Globalisation, Post-modernity and the State: Comparative Education Facing the Third Millennium." *Comparative Education* 37 no. 4: 475–92.

Werthmann, Katja. 1997. *Nachbarinnen. Die Alltagswelt muslimischer Frauen in einer nigerianischen Großstadt*. Frankfurt: Brandes und Apsel.

Wilson, Fiona. 2001. "In the Name of the State? Schools and Teachers in an Andean Province." In *States of Imagination: Ethnographic Exploration of the Postcolonial State,* eds. Thomas Blom Hansen and Finn Stepputat. Durham, NC: Duke University Press.

Wimmer, Andreas and Nina Glick Schiller. 2002. "Methodological Nationalism and Beyond: Nation-state Building, Migration, and the Social Sciences." *Global Networks* 2, no. 4: 301–34

Woldai Futur. 1993. "Importance of Trade and Industrial Policy for Socioeconomic Development: Reflections on the Eritrean Economy." In *Emergent Eritrea: Challenges of Economic Development,* ed. Gebre Hiwet Tesfagiorgis. Lawrenceville, NJ: Red Sea Press.

Wong, Ting-Hong and Michael Apple. 2002. "Rethinking the Education/State Formation Connection: Pedagogic Reform in Singapore, 1945–1965." *Comparative Education Review* 46, no. 2 (May): 182–210.

World Bank. 2003. *Eritrea Education Sector Improvement Project: Project Information Document.* World Bank. 17 April. http://www.worldbank.org/infoshop (accessed 2 May 2006).

———. 2006. "Africa Development Indicators 2006." Washington, DC.

Wrong, Michela. 2005. *I Didn't Do It for You: How the World Betrayed a Small African Nation.* London: Harper Perennial.

Yemane Mesghenna. 1989. *Italian Colonialism. A Case Study of Eritrea, 1869–1934. Motive, Praxis and Result.* Maryland: International Graphics.

Yonas Mehari. 2007. "Eritrean Prisoners of Conscience, Refugees and Asylum Seekers Worldwide." Presentation at *Human Rights in the Horn of Africa: A Panel Discussion on Eritrea,* University of Tennessee, 12 April.

Young, Crawford. 1994. "Zaire: The Shattered Illusion of the Integral State." The *Journal of Modern African Studies* 32, no. 2 (June): 347–63.

Young, John. 1996. "The Tigray and Eritrean Peoples Liberation Fronts: A History of Tensions and Pragmatism." *Journal of Modern African Studies* 34, no. 1 (March): 105–20.

Younger, Calton. 1979. *Ireland's Civil War.* London: Fontana Books.

INDEX